LIBRARY OF INTERNATIONAL RELATIONS

The Age of Terrorism and the International Political System

ADRIAN GUELKE

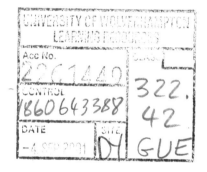
I.B.Tauris Publishers

LONDON · NEW YORK

Paperback edition published in 1998 by I.B.Tauris & Co Ltd
Victoria House, Bloomsbury Square, London WC1B 4DZ
175 Fifth Avenue, New York NY 10010

First published in 1995 by Tauris Academic Studies

In the United States and Canada distributed by St. Martin's Press
175 Fifth Avenue, New York NY 10010

In the United States of America and in Canada distributed by
St Martin's Press, 175 Fifth Avenue, New York NY 10010

A full CIP record for this book is available from the British
Library

A full CIP record for this book is available from the Library of
Congress

ISBN 1 86064 338 8

Set in Monotype Ehrhardt by Ewan Smith, London

Printed and bound in Great Britain by WBC Ltd, Bridgend,
Mid Glamorgan

Contents

List of tables

Preface

An Air France plane was hijacked at Algiers airport. The presidential candidate of Sri Lanka's United National Party, Gamini Dissaneyake, was assassinated. A British tourist was shot dead during a trip to the ancient temple of Luxor in Egypt. Three Westerners were taken hostage and then murdered in Cambodia. A bomb destroyed a commuter plane in Panama, killing 21 passengers. This incident was linked to an attack the previous day on a Jewish community centre in Buenos Aires, Argentina, which killed 96 people. These examples, all taken from the second half of 1994, suggest that it would be extremely foolhardy to suggest that an end to the age of terrorism was in prospect. Yet other events of 1994 suggested a world that had moved on. Nelson Mandela was inaugurated as president of a democratic, non-racial South Africa, with scarcely a murmur from white supremacists. Yasser Arafat received the Nobel Peace Prize. There were cease-fires by Republican and Loyalist paramilitaries in Northern Ireland. Carlos the Jackal was arrested in Sudan and then extradited to France. At the same time, the genocide in Rwanda, the civil war in Angola, and the conflicts in the former Yugoslavia and the former Soviet Union were not the mark of a world at peace. However, by and large, the term 'terrorism' was not applied to these horrors.

The notion that we live in an age of terrorism which began in the late 1960s became prevalent during the 1970s. This book examines the basis of that perception. It also contends that the notion of an age of terrorism is fading, partly because of changing meanings and applications of the term 'terrorism' and partly because of changes of policy by governments in their handling of clandestine violence by small groups. The starting point of the book is an analysis of the concept of terrorism itself. One reason why so much of the literature on terrorism is held in such contempt is precisely that it takes the issue for granted, despite the fact that it is evident, on very little reflection, just how slippery the concept is. Where a definition of the term is given, it all too frequently bears little relationship to the nature of the violence discussed. In particular, a literal definition, that the purpose of terrorism is to induce fear, is often used and then applied to the clandestine violence of small groups, a form of violence plainly less terrifying than overt violence on a mass scale.

Chapter 1 examines the difficulties in the way of understanding the concept of terrorism in the light of the emotive force of the term. Chapter 2 analyses the attempts by academics to distinguish terrorism from other forms of violence. Chapter 3 examines critically the generalizations that have been made about terrorism in the vast literature that has grown up about the subject. Chapter 4 explores the different strands of political violence in the late 1960s and early 1970s that gave rise to modern usage of the term. Chapter 5 analyses the background to the legitimization of violence by small groups at the onset of the age of terrorism. Chapter 6 examines the case of terrorism in West Germany, while Chapter 7 tackles the very different case of Northern Ireland. Chapter 8 considers the application of the concept of terrorism to conflicts in the Third World. Chapter 9 looks at why an international dimension is so central to terrorism, while Chapter 10 examines the stopping of terrorism, discussing the evolution of international law and employing case studies to analyse factors that have influenced the ending of campaigns of violence. In conclusion, Chapter 11 explores the relationship between the age of terrorism and the nature of the international political system.

I first started work on this book eight years ago. On the recommendation of Professor Adam Roberts of the University of Oxford, a publisher's agent, Jim Reynolds, asked me to write what he described as a different book on terrorism. Finding a publisher did not prove easy. In particular, the established experts on terrorism that publishers invariably consulted thoroughly disliked my synopsis, though I continued to be sustained by encouragement from Adam Roberts. Eventually Jim Reynolds did find a publisher. Unfortunately, that publisher was taken over as I was about to submit the manuscript, and the new owners did not find the idea of a contentious book on terrorism attractive. When Jim Reynolds died, that seemed the end of the project. The idea of turning my manuscript into a thesis occurred to me when I accompanied Professor James Mayall of LSE on a trip to Namibia in 1990. I was very conscious of weaknesses in my existing manuscript, and subjecting it to the rigorous scrutiny entailed in producing a thesis seemed the right remedy. I am most grateful to James Mayall for taking me on. I eventually completed the thesis in December 1993 and was awarded the Ph.D. in July 1994. I was now ready to turn the thesis back into a book.

In the process of writing both thesis and book, I have incurred many debts. My thanks are due to the staff at the following libraries for their assistance in helping me to track down the very diverse material that I have needed: Queen's University, Belfast; the British Library of Economics and Political Science; Jan Smuts House Library; United States Information Service library in Johannesburg; and Linenhall Library, Belfast. I am also most grateful to the United States Consulate in Belfast for help in getting hold of copies of the State Department publication *Patterns of Global Terrorism*. Colleagues at both Queen's and Wits have influenced my ideas in informal discussions. Of these, special mention needs to be made of Frank Wright, Professor of Peace Studies at the University of Limerick when he died of cancer in February 1993. For 17 years he and I were colleagues in the Department of Politics at Queen's. He had a profound influence on my thinking about violence in deeply divided societies. His insights into why people resorted to political violence complemented his own personal commitment to peace. Of colleagues at other universities who have helped me to clarify my ideas, I would like to mention Didier Bigo, Conor Gearty, Peter Merkl, Edward Moxon-Browne, Adam Roberts, Klaus Wasmund, and Leonard Weinberg.

I am also most grateful to the following for helpful comments on earlier drafts: my LSE supervisor, James Mayall, the two examiners of my thesis, Jack Spence and Christopher Coker, Lester Crook of I.B.Tauris, and Charles Townshend, who acted as the publisher's external assessor. My thanks to all the above are subject to the disclaimer that I accept full responsibility for the final product, with all its limitations.

Adrian Guelke, Johannesburg
January 1995

Introduction: barriers to understanding terrorism

By the 1990s, the concept of terrorism had become so elastic that there seemed to be virtually no limit to what could be described as terrorism. For example, among titles of books published in 1989 and 1991 were the following: *Narcoterrorism*; *Western State Terrorism*; *Apartheid Terrorism: The Destabilization Report*; and *Pornography: The New Terrorism*.[1] An attempt by criminals to extort money from manufacturers by lacing jars of baby foods on supermarket shelves with broken glass, tacks, and other harmful objects was quickly labelled 'consumer terrorism' by much of the media.[2] In the United States the long-established phenomenon of anonymous obscene phone-calls was given the new description 'telephone terrorism'.[3] An academic text analysed rape as 'a terrorist institution'.[4] On the eve of the Argentinian presidential election in 1989, the country's finance minister described speculation against its currency as 'economic terrorism',[5] while the Iraqi ambassador to the United States used the same term in outlining allegations in October 1990 that Kuwait had sought to sabotage his country's economy.[6] These examples should be distinguished from the metaphorical use of the terms 'terrorism' and 'terrorist' by the media, such as the description in a British newspaper of a breed of dog involved in a series of attacks on children as 'a terrorist on four legs'.[7]

The stretching of the term to cover a wider and wider field of activity is in part a response to constant reference in the media to terrorism as a pervasive reality of the modern world. It has become almost impossible to pick up a newspaper or to listen to a news bulletin without coming across a reference to terrorism or terrorists. Twenty years ago, Brian Jenkins, one of the leading specialists in the field, made a revealing comment. 'At some point in this expanding use of the term,' he declared, 'terrorism can mean just what those who use the term (not the terrorists) want it to mean – almost any violent act by any opponent.'[8] Jenkins did not anticipate that the application of the term would eventually extend beyond even the notion of violence against an opponent.

The fact that the term has lost its automatic association with the political realm is in part attributable to the way that terrorism has been analysed, opening the way to the term's application to phenomena lacking any political resonance. While the diverse range of phenomena to which the term has come to be applied threatens the concept's coherence, it is possible to identify some common, if very general, themes in current usage of the term, as a brief examination of the examples given in the first paragraph will show. One theme common to each of the examples is the connotation of harm. The theme of violence is present in most, as is that of coercion. The generation of fear or intimidation is another element to be found in a number of the cases, but it is not as pervasive an element as might be expected. Another feature of the examples is the fact that an international dimension is present in the majority of the cases. Finally, in a majority of the examples, the actions described as terrorism were or are covert in character.

Of course, it must be emphasized that the examples in the first paragraph are far from typical of current usage of the term. They represent the outer limits of its application and consequently form a poor sample for drawing any conclusions about elements common to terrorism. It is not because of pornography, obscene phone-calls, or currency speculation that the present era has been identified as an age of terrorism. The notion that an age of terrorism began in the late 1960s is one of the most common propositions in the literature on terrorism.[9] Some writers have even identified the beginning of the era with particular events in this period. For example, in *Ten Years of Terrorism*, published in 1979, Tony Geraghty identifies the student revolutionaries of Paris in May 1968 as 'the precursors of terrorism'.[10] (It is fair to say that this retrospective judgement owes more to the shift in the ideological climate that took place in the West in the 1970s than it does to any empirical evidence linking the generation of 1968 with political violence.)

Other events of the late 1960s that have more reasonably been identified as key points in the development of terrorism were the Six-Day War in the Middle East in June 1967 and the death of Che Guevara in Bolivia in October 1967. The latter was retrospectively seen as marking the failure of rural guerrilla warfare in Latin America, opening the way to urban terrorism as an alternative strategy. The former had greater influence at the time on the use of the term. The virtually universal sympathy for the cause of Israel in the West following the Six-Day War was a significant factor in loosening the media's inhibitions over the use of the term, and this was reflected in the coverage of violent action by Palestinians in response to Israel's military victories.[11] Academic studies followed in the wake of media usage. It is therefore not surprising that the overwhelming majority of books and articles with the term 'terrorism' in their title should date from the 1970s and 1980s; Norman Provizer has noted that in two major bibliographies on terrorism, over 99 per cent of the general works cited had been published from 1968 on.[12]

History of usage

Yet the term itself was not by any manner of means an invention of the late 1960s. According to the *Oxford English Dictionary* (*OED*), the terms 'terrorism' and 'terrorists' were first used in the English language in 1795, in response to the reign of terror in post-revolutionary France. The *OED* quotes the conservative Edmund Burke on the unleashing on the people of 'hell-hounds called terrorists'.[13] In the nineteenth century, the terms were applied to the violence of the agrarian agitation against landlords and their agents in Ireland. Later in the century, the description 'terrorist' became specifically linked to the strategy of political assassination employed by Narodnaya Volya (People's Will) against the Tsarist regime, particularly the 'blow at the centre', that is to say, the assassination of Tsar Alexander II in March 1881.[14] By the turn of this century, the bomb-throwing an-archist espousing the notion of 'propaganda by the deed' came to be seen as the archetypal terrorist,[15] establishing a link between anarchism and terrorism that remains important to the interpretation of terrorism as ideology.

The terms were next applied to a now largely forgotten wave of assassinations in the 1930s, culminating in Marseilles in 1934 with the killing of the King of Yugoslavia and the foreign minister of France. The Marseilles assassinations were carried out by Croatian nationalists, and the international dimension of the killings prompted a response from the League of Nations. A committee of experts was set up to study the problem. The results of its labours were proposals for two international conventions, one for the prevention and punish-ment of terrorism and another to set up an international criminal court. They were both adopted in 1937. However, neither came into force. Understandably, few states gave the issue a priority. Both the conventions and the problem they addressed were overtaken by the outbreak of the Second World War.[16]

In the late 1940s and the 1950s, 'terrorism' was largely associated with colonial conflicts, particularly those in Palestine, Malaya, Cyprus, Algeria, and Kenya. However, partly because there was a question-mark over the legitimacy of colonial rule itself, terms other than 'terrorist' were often used even by the authorities to describe those fighting colonial rule. For example, the insurgents in Malaya were more usually referred to as bandits than as CTs or Communist Terror-ists, and this was reflected in the establishment by the authorities of a Director of Anti-Bandit Operations.[17] Another factor that dis-couraged use of the term was doubt as to whether it was appropriate to apply it to campaigns targeted on the security forces. That remains a contentious issue, and some writers continue to insist that, properly speaking, the term should be applied only to violence directed against non-combatants.[18]

It is notable that apart from its identification with actions by the state during the French Revolution, the term has usually been applied to violence from below directed against the *status quo*, though counter-examples from other periods can be found, such as reference to the Nazi participants in *Kristallnacht* as terrorists in a contemporary news report of those events.[19] The use of the term to apply to the violent activities of socially conservative groups such as the Ku Klux Klan in the United States provides another counter-example. However, such usage appears to be relatively uncommon. In this respect, the record of the usage of the term is one of continuity. For all its elasticity, current usage likewise revolves largely around violence from below. The 1989 edition of the *OED* identifies two meanings of terrorism. The first relates specifically to government by intimidation during the reign of terror in post-revolutionary France. The second defines terrorism as 'a policy intended to strike with terror those against whom it is adopted; the employment of methods of intimidation; the fact of terrorizing or condition of being terrorized'.[20] Significantly, all the examples the *OED* gives of this definition, with perhaps the arguable exception of a reference to OAS terrorism in Algeria in the early 1960s, are of violence directed at the overthrow of the existing political authority. The most startling aspect of the definition and its examples, contemporary as well as historical, is the discrepancy between the words used in the definition and the situations in the main to which the term is applied. To put the point starkly, the term 'terrorism' evidently does not mean quite what it says it does. In other words, actual usage departs somewhat from the word's etymo-logical roots. Some illustration will help to elucidate this issue.

Firstly, let us reflect for a moment on 'the employment of methods of intimidation'. As an example one might think of the prevalence in much of the Third World of the intimidation of peasants by powerful

landowners. Alternatively, one might take the case of the deployment
of the army in a show of force by an authoritarian state wishing to
demonstrate to its citizenry its possession of a monopoly of force. In
both these cases the instrumental value of intimidation to the user is
self-evident. However, in neither of these cases would one expect the
term 'terrorism' to be employed, even in extreme instances where
such intimidation was accompanied by high levels of overt violence. It
may be objected that in the case of the intimidation of peasants, this
is because the intimidation has a social rather than a political context.
However, the way that the concept of terrorism has come to cover
violence for social as well as political purposes makes this argument
unpersuasive. In any event, the objection does not address the case of
intimidation by an authoritarian regime. While governments are sometimes accused of practising state terrorism, usage of this term *in a
domestic context* tends to be restricted to genocidal regimes such as
existed in Uganda under Idi Amin or Cambodia under Pol Pot.

The Lockerbie example

To the problem that in a wide variety of situations 'the employment
of methods of intimidation' tends not to be seen as terrorism, one
may add the problem that in some of the most notorious instances of
terrorism, causing terror has not loomed large in the objectives of the
perpetrators, in so far as these are known (the qualification is necessary
because in practice it is virtually impossible to uncover the whole
truth about any atrocity). Let us take the case of the Pan Am jet
brought down in Lockerbie, Scotland, by a bomb in December 1988,
resulting in the deaths of 270 people. How does this act fit in with the
OED definition? One cannot reasonably argue that it was designed to
strike the passengers and crew with terror. From the circumstances, it
is quite evident that the objective was to kill them, not to frighten
them.

Initially, there was speculation that the atrocity was conceived as
an act of revenge for the shooting down by the *USS Vincennes* of an
Iranian airliner during the Iran–Iraq conflict.[21] However, the criminal
investigation conducted by the Scottish authorities eventually led to
the charging of two Libyans, though suggestions of both Syrian and
Iranian involvement have persisted. The most plausible explanation of
Libyan involvement in the atrocity was that it was intended as an act
of revenge or retaliation for the bombing of Libya by the United
States in April 1986. That American action in turn was a response to
the United States government's belief that Libya had been a party to
attacks on American citizens. If revenge does turn out to be the motive

for the bombing of Pan Am Flight 103, it would not be surprising; it is a very common motive for violence in human affairs. In many parts of the world, chains of revenge and retaliation are an important factor in the perpetuation of political violence. If it is accepted that the motive for the Lockerbie bomb was primarily revenge, which is certainly quite possible, then the only basis that is left in the dictionary definition for calling the Lockerbie bomb an act of terrorism is that fear was generated among the public as an unintended consequence of the bomb. Certainly, it is plausible to argue that the bomb increased the anxieties of air passengers. However, there is no reason for supposing that this effect played an important part in the public's perception of the deed as an act of terrorism. The deaths caused by the bomb provide a much simpler and more direct explanation of the public outrage at the bomb and of public perception of the deed as an act of terrorism. Furthermore, the emphasis that the dictionary definition places on intimidation as a motive or consequence of terrorism in no way helps us to distinguish terrorism from other acts of violence. Practically any act of violence has an intimidatory effect of some kind. For that matter, accidents that cause fatalities also generate fear. What needs to be underlined at this stage in the argument is the mismatch between the scope of the dictionary definition of terrorism and the ground that is covered by the term in practice. This is very far from being merely a semantic quibble.

The dictionary definition is not simply a quirky piece of etymology. Both academic and official definitions follow much the same lines, as we shall see when we examine them in the next chapter. For the moment, it is sufficient that the reader should be aware that the obvious implication that terrorism causes fear may often be a barrier to understanding particular acts of terrorism and, indeed, terrorism as a whole. It is a cliché in the literature that terrorists kill small numbers of people in order to frighten many more.[22] That may sometimes be true but, in practice, spreading fear among a civilian population by the indiscriminate killing of a few rarely advances any political or social cause, while violence that is explicitly and clearly targeted at a particular set of people cannot be expected to induce extreme anxiety in those outside that group.

The terrorism paradox

Part of the explanation for the emphasis that much of the literature places on the psychological impact of terrorism beyond its immediate victims is to be found in what has perhaps been the most striking paradox of the age of terrorism. This is the fact that the number of people that have been killed in acts of terrorism world-wide appears to have been extremely small. However, this statement needs to be carefully qualified. Most statistical estimates of the numbers killed in acts of terrorism confine themselves to international or transnational terrorism. On this basis, the number of people killed since the late 1960s is in the low thousands.[23] Estimates that include those killed in domestic as well as international terrorism are much harder to come by, but Laqueur's estimate for a single decade suggests a figure in the low tens of thousands for the period since the 1960s.[24] By comparison, in the various conflicts in the countries of Central America, the fatalities from political violence over the same period run into the hundreds of thousands. At first sight, their exclusion from statistics on terrorism seems inexplicable. The overwhelming majority of those who have died have been civilians and the fact that the civilian population has been terrorized in the process is very evident from this description of the situation prevailing in El Salvador in 1985:

> Salvadorean society, affected by terror and panic, a result of the persistent violation of basic human rights, shows the following traits: collective intimidation and generalised fear, on the one hand, and on the other the internalised acceptance of the terror because of the daily and frequent use of violent means. In general, society accepts the frequent appearance of tortured bodies, because basic rights, the right to life, has absolutely no overriding value for society.[25]

Why then has there been a reluctance to apply the term to these conflicts? What accounts for the concentration in the literature on situations in which political violence kills very few people?

To answer these questions, the most obvious problem in applying the term to any situation needs to be faced. This is the fact that the word 'terrorism' cannot possibly be treated as if it were a neutral, technical term for a particular category of violence. The term carries a massive emotive punch. Indeed, it is probably one of the most powerfully condemnatory words in the English language. However, its utility would be limited, were it simply seen as an emotive term for any type of violence, even any type of political violence. In fact, the very emotive power of the word has helped to shape the more specific application of the term. In particular, its judgemental character has strongly influenced the political context in which it is applied, because that judgement carries the implication that the violence in question lacks any legitimacy.

Illegitimate violence

Indeed, 'the illegitimate use of violence for some social or political purpose' might reasonably be put forward as a loose definition of current usage of the term (though such a definition would not cover all the examples of its current usage given at the beginning of this chapter). In this context we need to distinguish between two different senses of 'illegitimate', a subjective meaning and one derived from the existence of a consensus in society on the issue. The subjective perspective is summed up in the dictum that one man's terrorist is another man's freedom fighter, perhaps the most frequently quoted aphorism about terrorism to be found in the literature. But the term 'terrorism' is also often used on the assumption that there is a broad consensus in the society in question that the violence being described is generally perceived as illegitimate. From this perspective, not merely can the word be used more or less objectively but its features can be determined by examining the terms of society's consensus on the issue.

It is easiest to establish in what context violence is generally perceived as illegitimate by considering how violence is normally justified. It is rare for violence to be glorified as an end in itself. The usual justification of its use is that it constitutes an effective means to a legitimate end. Often further qualifications are added that the means employed must be proportionate to the end being sought and that other means must not be available to achieve the same end. In Western societies, it is generally argued that there can be no justification for the use of political violence within an effectively functioning liberal-democracy, because other means are available to influence public policy and, periodically, the composition of the government. Further, given the existence of such democratic processes, there would seem to be little likelihood in practice that violence for a social or political purpose would attract significant support in a stable democracy. Such considerations explain why in the West organized violence of a life-threatening character which has the aim of coercing the government of an established liberal-democracy is almost invariably labelled terrorism and why the perpetrators of such deeds are almost as consistently labelled terrorists. It should be noted that spontaneous forms of violence, such as rioting, are normally not regarded as a species of terrorism, even though in extreme cases they may lead to loss of life. Attitudes towards violence directed against property vary among liberal-democracies, though much depends on whether the act in question is seen as part of a larger campaign that does threaten life.[26]

However, outside of stable liberal-democracies, a category of states that tends to overlap with the industrialized countries of the First World, the use of the terms 'terrorism' and 'terrorist' is seen as far more problematic for a number of reasons. Firstly, the legitimacy of forms of government other than the liberal-democratic tends to be regarded as questionable in the West, a perception that has been reinforced by the frequency of their collapse. A consequence of such doubts is a reluctance to apply the term 'terrorism' to acts of violence directed at the overthrow of such systems. Secondly, any doubts about the regime's legitimacy naturally tend to be reinforced by signs of political instability, including violence. Indeed, the higher the level of violence in any conflict, the more reluctance there is likely to be in the Western media to apply the term 'terrorism' to the situation. Thirdly, there is less pressure on the Western media to condemn political violence in countries not seen as part of the West. As a result, there is less likelihood that the term 'terrorism' will be used simply for the purpose of condemnation. In these circumstances, a narrow view of the applicability of the term is likely to be taken.

Application in the Third World

For all of these reasons, the terms 'terrorism' and 'terrorist' tend to be used much less consistently outside the specific context of stable liberal-democracies. A few examples will illustrate the point. Shortly after the bloody expulsion of pro-democracy demonstrators from Tiananmen Square, Beijing, in June 1989, an explosion on a Shanghai train killed eight passengers. There was widespread speculation in the Western media that the explosion was caused by a bomb in response to the killings in Beijing, but it was noticeable that reporters avoided using the term 'terrorism' in connection with this speculation.[27] A similar reluctance to use the term was evident in the reporting of car-bombs in Kabul, Afghanistan, during the 1980s that caused large numbers of civilian casualties. It would be fair to interpret these inhibitions as the desire to avoid legitimizing either the regime in question or its methods for dealing with political opponents. By contrast, the media have had no hesitation in describing as terrorism some events that have taken place in the Third World, such as the explosion of a bomb that brought down a South Korean jet off the coast of Burma in November 1987 or the taking and imprisonment of Western hostages in Lebanon.

One can identify a third category of cases where the Western media have been divided over whether to use the terms. An example is the 'armed struggle' that the African National Congress (ANC) conducted against the South African government up to the suspension of the campaign in August 1990. The comparatively rare instances in which bomb attacks in the urban areas killed civilians in the course of the campaign generally were labelled acts of terrorism. The much more contentious issue was the appropriateness of labelling the ANC itself a terrorist organization. But how the ANC was described, in practice, reflected political attitudes towards the African nationalist cause more than judgements about the ANC's involvement in particular acts of violence. Thus, when the British prime minister, Margaret Thatcher, branded the ANC 'a terrorist organization'[28] in October 1987, her statement was widely interpreted as an expression of her attitude towards the political aspirations of the ANC and was welcomed or criticized on that assumption. This was also apparent in respect of the American State Department publication *Patterns of Global Terrorism*, which listed the ANC in its 'worldwide overview of organizations that engage in terrorism'.(29) By contrast, while the liberal press in South Africa remained extremely critical of the ANC's strategy of armed struggle, it by and large shrunk from using the term 'terrorist' to describe either the campaign itself or individual members of Umkhonto we Sizwe, the ANC's military wing.[30]

The political importance attached to the use of the term 'terrorism' and its interpretation is even more clearly illustrated in the case of the Palestinians. In December 1988 the leader of the Palestine Liberation Organization (PLO), Yasser Arafat, made clear his acceptance of the right of Israel to exist, which is embodied in UN Security Council Resolution 242. He also renounced all forms of terrorism. The American government responded by declaring that Arafat's statements had met its conditions for establishing a dialogue with the PLO. This was disputed by the Israeli government which claimed that Arafat's support for the continuation of the Palestinian uprising in the occupied territories, the *intifada*, constituted backing for a form of terrorism. It was a theme that Israel continually harped on. For example, in July 1989 the Israeli government expressed disappointment when the American State Department declined to call an incident in which a Palestinian caused a number of deaths by grabbing the steering wheel of a bus and propelling the vehicle into a ravine an act of terrorism.[31]

Israel was unsuccessful in persuading the West of its view of the *intifada* for three main reasons. Firstly, the prime concern of the West was the ending of Palestinian involvement in *international* terrorism. Violence within greater Israel was a lesser concern. Secondly, the stone-throwing and other spontaneous acts of political violence that appeared to embody the *intifada* did not fit Western conceptions of the nature of terrorism. Thirdly, the actions taken by the Israeli army to quell the *intifada* cast the Palestinians in the role of the principal victims of violence. In the event, the dialogue between the American government and the PLO was suspended as a result of the failure of the PLO to condemn an attack on Israel across international frontiers in May 1990. For the United States, the international dimension of the episode was crucial. The difficulty for the PLO at the time lay in repudiating an attack on Israel as opposed to one on a third party.

International dimension

Given that there has been a tendency to apply the term 'terrorism' by and large to political violence in Western liberal-democracies or directed against such states internationally, the enormous disjunction that exists between the numbers killed in acts of terrorism and the global figure for those who die in all forms of political violence becomes explicable. Western liberal-democracies predominate among stable polities, and stable polities, virtually by definition, face far less political violence than their less stable counterparts. It is therefore not at all surprising that the numbers killed in terrorism appear to be very small in relation to those killed in all forms of political violence. It could hardly be otherwise. The consequence is that it is inevitably the citizenry of the industrialized democracies that appears to be most at risk from terrorism. This impression is compounded by the concentration of the statistical research into terrorism on *international* terrorism, interpreted in the first instance as situations in which the nationality of the victim and that of the perpetrator differ. Unsurprisingly, the highly mobile peoples of the First World tend to be disproportionately represented in such situations. Consequently the figures on international terrorism simply provide further evidence for what is a logical but ultimately somewhat absurd implication of current usage of the term. This is that it is the affluent and secure citizens of the West who are most threatened by terrorism, and not the truly terrorized peoples in countries afflicted by civil war, whether in the Third World or in formerly communist states.

Earlier, some of the reasons for the reluctance in the Western media to apply the term 'terrorism' to conflicts in the Third World were explored. An important aspect of that reluctance, which is particularly salient to the conflicts in Central America, remains to be discussed. This is the issue of the role of the state in political violence. In most serious civil conflicts, actions by the armed forces of the state account for a large majority of the deaths. This is partly because the lethal capacity of the state is almost invariably greater than that of its opponents. It is also because there are few restraints on the behaviour of the forces of the state in situations of the breakdown of political authority. In extreme cases of the massacre of large numbers of civilians, the action of the security forces would be likely to attract international criticism as a human rights violation. However, such cases are not generally described as acts of terrorism. The charge of state complicity in terrorism usually refers to its involvement in covert action undertaken outside the boundaries of the state in question. For example, during the 1980s the American State Department's *Patterns of Global Terrorism* limited its accusations against the Afghan government of involvement in terrorism to activities undertaken outside Afghanistan itself.[32] Reluctance to use the term 'terrorism' in relation to the actions of the state stems from an important principle that underlies the political organization of the modern world. This is the principle that the state possesses a monopoly of legitimate violence in any society.

As the overarching authority within domestic society, the state is responsible for the maintenance of law and order within its own boundaries. In the absence of an overarching authority within the society of states, it is also solely responsible for the defence of the realm against external attack. These two roles have reinforced the privileged position of the state in relation to the use of violence or force, as the action of the state to maintain order or for self-defence is more commonly called. In general, a presumption of legitimacy attaches to the action of the state in this field. This even applies to situations where doubts exist as to the regime's legitimacy, on the assumption that public interest in the maintenance of order or the defence of the country transcends the issue of the political colour of the regime in power. Where a regime's hold on power is threatened by violent conflict, this assumption is less likely to be made. In such circumstances, as we saw earlier, the violent opponents of the state are unlikely to be called terrorists by outside opinion. But the readiness to deny legitimacy to regimes challenged by popular forces does not generally extend to applying the term 'terrorist' either to the actions of state forces under their control or to the regimes themselves. Some writers in the field of terrorism use the concept of state terrorism in this context,[33] but there is little likelihood of such usage gaining general acceptance because of the absolutist judgement involved in the use of the term 'terrorism'. The corollary of accusing a regime of state terrorism would be that it lacked any legitimacy. In many circumstances, such a judgement would seem dangerously unbalanced.

That leaves the special case of the 'terrorist state', the designation developed by the Reagan administration to apply specifically to states engaged in, or giving support to, clandestine violence outside their own boundaries. Clearly, if it were interpreted literally it would apply to the United States itself, though that implication would be rejected by most Americans. In practice, the term is used for propaganda purposes to pillory states in conflict with the United States. Which states to pillory has inevitably become an issue in American domestic politics. For example, the question of whether South Africa should be included among the designated terrorist states was a minor issue in the 1988 American presidential election. Iraq was reinstated on the list after the invasion of Kuwait. The obvious difficulty with the whole notion of a 'terrorist state' is that it implies that an illegitimate regime (or one so regarded by the United States) has no right to take action in its own defence beyond its own borders. In a world in which the self-help principle applies to the defence of states, this is a difficult proposition to sustain.

However, in general, there is less difficulty in labelling the state's use of clandestine violence beyond its borders as terrorism than there is in calling states that authorize such acts terrorist states. Thus, *outside of France*, the sinking of the *Rainbow Warrior* by French agents in 1985 was widely characterized as an act of terrorism.[34] However, very few would suggest that this episode would justify calling the French government a terrorist regime, with all the overtones of political illegitimacy that such a description would imply. That is not to say that describing a state's use of clandestine violence beyond its borders as terrorism is generally unproblematic. Context matters. A state under attack from forces beyond its borders would argue that it was justified in using such methods to defend itself. Whether its actions were described by others as terrrorism would partly hinge on international perceptions of that regime's legitimacy and partly on the clarity of the link between the state's actions and its defence.

Ideological dimension

The American government's use of the term 'terrorism' is clearly related to its own particular ideological perspective. But it would be wrong to suppose that the term's ideological dimension simply resides in the rather superficial bias that governments demonstrate when applying the term. It is deeply embedded in the judgemental character of the term itself. The invariable implication of condemnation positively requires the application of ideological principles to determine when it is legitimate to use the term. Given the origins of the term in Western political discourse, it is inevitable that it should be the liberal principles which underpin government in the West that have shaped the ideological boundaries of the term in practice. Indeed, it is evident that it is easier to understand current usage of the term by applying liberal principles to the question of the legitimacy of political violence than by examining the etymology of the word itself. It should be noted that the word 'liberal' in this context refers to the principles of the rule of law and of competitive elections on which there is a broad consensus in the West. It should not be confused with the narrower use of the term 'liberal' to refer to left-of-centre opinion in the United States.

Admittedly, the stretching of the term 'terrorism' to apply to acts with a criminal rather than a social or political purpose has muddied the waters somewhat. In such cases, the question of the legitimacy of political violence is no longer relevant. However, that does not alter the fact that in its primary application to political violence, the term has an ideological dimension that clearly needs to be recognized in any discussion of the meaning of terrorism. In fact, the failure of much of the literature on terrorism to acknowledge this ideological dimension constitutes one of the most significant barriers to understanding terrorism. Without paying due regard to the term's ideological dimension, much about how and why it is used is likely to be missed. For example, it is because the term is rooted in a specifically Western political perspective of the world that it has proved so useful to those in the West who wish to assert the superiority of Western values and who do not wish to accommodate other values or perspectives.

Understanding

So far the barriers to the understanding of terrorism that have been identified in this introduction have concerned the term 'terrorism' itself. They can usefully be summarized under five headings: firstly, the widening scope of the term; secondly, the fact that the term does not quite mean what it says it does; thirdly, the related point that causing fear is not a distinguishing feature of terrorism; fourthly, the exceptionally strong emotive overtones of the term; and fifthly, its ideological dimension. What remains to be discussed is the issue of understanding itself. How to approach the subject of terrorism with a view to developing an understanding of it is much more problematic than it might appear at first sight.

The difficulty is best elucidated through an example. On 21 November 1974, 21 people were killed and 162 injured by bombs placed in two public houses in the centre of Birmingham. An inadequate telephone warning minutes before the explosions identified the bombings as the work of the Provisional IRA (Irish Republican Army). There was a strong reaction to the bombings throughout

British society. *The Guardian* described them in an editorial as 'an outrage beyond endurance'.[35] Anti-Irish demonstrations across the English Midlands provided an indication of the public mood. The fear that the backlash against the Irish might lead to public disorder was one factor in the government's response to the bombings, the introduction of the Prevention of Terrorism Act, which was described by the Home Secretary of the time, Roy Jenkins, as a 'draconian measure'.[36] In justifying the measure, Jenkins declared that he had given up trying to *understand* the motives of people responsible for outrages such as the pub bombings. His words encapsulated the mood of the moment.

Their resonance derived from the double meaning of the word 'understand'. While its primary sense is to comprehend the sources and causes of the object of explanation, the word has a secondary connotation in human affairs of empathy with the actions being examined. Jenkins clearly had the latter connotation in mind. In the context of British policy towards Northern Ireland, Jenkins's words signalled an end to the rationalistic assumption that British governments had made hitherto. This was that an end to the violence could be achieved through tackling the legitimate political grievances of people in Northern Ireland. A contributory factor to the government's pessimism in this respect had been the failure earlier in 1974 of the power-sharing executive in Northern Ireland, which had been established with the support of the British government. In terms of wider public opinion, the Birmingham pub bombings represented a watershed in attitudes towards violence emanating from the conflict in Northern Ireland.[37]

In particular, there was a marked hardening of opinion which was most clearly reflected in the disappearance of any equivocation in applying the term 'terrorism' to political violence taking place in Northern Ireland or emanating from the province. The change in the atmosphere produced a marked shift in public discourse away from attempts to understand the causes of the violence in Northern Ireland. Against the background of the Birmingham bombs, they smacked too much of attempting to provide rationalizations for what was totally unacceptable. One consequence was that British opinion on the UK mainland became blinded to the state of opinion in Northern Ireland. The result was that when Sinn Fein, the political wing of the Provisional IRA, achieved a relatively modest measure of electoral success in the 1980s, the British public was both deeply shocked and surprised. The public's lack of empathy for the Northern Ireland problem had led to a diminution of its understanding in the broader sense.

Understanding terrorism in general presents the problem that the term 'terrorism' entails an absolutist judgement that seems quite incompatible with the retention of any element of empathy for its perpetrators or the situation that spawned them. As a matter of fact, absence of empathy is a very evident feature of the literature on terrorism. It is most clearly reflected in a relative lack of interest in the explanations those identified as terrorists have to offer for their actions. It is not difficult to suggest why. In the first place, no writer seeking to establish his or her credentials in the field of terrorism would wish to provide, or even appear to provide, any rationalizations for acts of terrorism. That is clearly a risk in any exploration of the motivations of the terrorist from the terrorist's point of view. A much safer procedure is to attribute bad motives to terrorists on the basis that they intended the very worst consequences of their actions. In the second place, there is the problem of fitting the explanations that terrorists give into the framework provided by the concept of terrorism. The 'ism' of terrorism clearly implies the existence of an underlying philosophy of violence or mentality that all terrorists share whatever their differences of political ideology. The difficulty is that the explanations of terrorists, as will be seen, provide scant empirical evidence of such a coherent basis for terrorism.

The approach that will be taken in this book is that analysing how people labelled as terrorists justify their actions is necessary to an understanding of the violence that the term 'terrorism' encompasses. Such an approach entails a number of difficulties. The most important as well as the most obvious is that it is difficult to get to grips with the motivations of terrorists in the sense not just of appreciating the political objectives of their actions but of understanding how they view the moral content of the means employed. The literature on terrorism is littered with plausible explanations of terrorist actions that make no reference to the terrorists' view of how the world works or their expectations of the consequences of their actions. The weakness of such external explanations is that in the absence of information about the perceptions of the terrorists themselves, they tend to present a picture of terrorists either as calculating robot-like machines or as mentally deranged. Both pictures have contributed to the existence of an inordinate fear of terrorism that may ironically have contributed to its utility as an instrument of political action. More healthily, the fear has also contributed to a hunger for explanations of terrorism so as to enable society to come to terms with the phenomenon. Of course, that begs the question whether terrorism can be regarded as a coherent phenomenon, a question that will be addressed in the next chapter.

Some readers may feel that the discussion in this chapter has already exposed so many difficulties in the application of the term 'terrorism' to contemporary political violence as to cast doubt on the value of the whole concept. (How the academic literature on terrorism has defined the term is examined in greater depth in the next chapter.) They may also feel that the small numbers of people killed in acts of terrorism, as the term is used in the Western media, does not justify the attention lavished on the subject. It is notable, for example, that in no single year since the late 1960s, when statistics on the subject first came to be collected, has the number of deaths from international terrorism, as measured by a number of different research groups and official agencies, reached even a thousand. Ironically, it is almost certainly the case that proportionately fewer people have died in Western societies as a result of political violence in the present 'age of terrorism' than in any other period in these societies' history.

However, there is no getting away from the influence that the concept of terrorism exerts on contemporary political life, especially in the West. Ignoring the concept because of its misleading connotations does nothing to reduce that influence. Indeed, it simply leaves the field open to others. If the concept has done damage in deeply divided societies by encouraging self-righteousness on the part of the different communities, that needs to be explained, not neglected. These are some of the reasons why the influence of terrorism on the modern world is worth examining, not in spite of, but in the light of, the barriers that exist to understanding the term. Furthermore, an elucidation of the issue of terrorism has a wider relevance to an understanding of both the nature of the world and of the age in which we live.

2

Distinguishing terrorism from other forms of violence

The question considered in this chapter is whether terrorism can be distinguished from other forms of violence and, if so, in what way. It is crucial to the intellectual credibility of terrorism as a concept that it should be possible to do so on grounds other than simply one's own subjective disapproval of particular actions. That terrorism is a special form of violence is an assumption that runs through virtually all of the literature on the subject. A useful starting point for a discussion of the distinguishing features of terrorism is the scholarship of Alex Schmid. In his monumental work of reference, *Political Terrorism*,[1] Alex Schmid analysed the content of 109 definitions of terrorism. He identified 22 elements in these definitions and calculated the frequency of their occurrence. His results are set out in Table 2.1.

At the end of a lengthy consideration of criticisms of an earlier attempt to define the term, Schmid offers his own definition of terrorism, drawing on 16 of the 22 elements identified in Table 2.1. It is worth quoting in full as probably the most rigorous effort there has been to define terrorism.

Terrorism is an anxiety-inspiring method of repeated violent action, employed by (semi-)clandestine individual, group, or state actors, for idiosyncratic, criminal, or political reasons, whereby – in contrast to assassination – the direct targets of violence are not the main targets. The immediate human victims of violence are generally chosen randomly (targets of opportunity) or selectively (representative or symbolic targets) from a target population, and serve as message generators. Threat- and violence-based communication processes between terrorist (organization), (imperiled) victims, and main targets are used to manipulate the main target (audience(s)), turning it into a target of terror, a target of demands, or a target of attention, depending on whether intimidation, coercion, or propaganda is primarily sought.[2]

18

Table 2.1 Frequency of definitional elements in 109 definitions

Element	Frequency (%)
1. Violence, force	83.5
2. Political	65
3. Fear, terror emphasized	51
4. Threat	47
5. (Psych.) effects and (anticipated) reactions	41.5
6. Victim-target differentiation	37.5
7. Purposive, planned, systematic, organized action	32
8. Method of combat, strategy, tactic	30.5
9. Extranormality, in breach of accepted rules, without humanitarian constraints	30
10. Coercion, extortion, induction of compliance	28
11. Publicity aspect	21.5
12. Arbitrariness; impersonal, random character; indiscrimination	21
13. Civilians, non-combatants, neutrals, outsiders as victims	17.5
14. Intimidation	17
15. Innocence of victims emphasized	15.5
16. Group, movement, organization as perpetrator	14
17. Symbolic aspect, demonstration to others	13.5
18. Incalculability, unpredictability, unexpectedness of occurrence of violence	9
19. Clandestine, covert nature	9
20. Repetitiveness; serial or campaign character of violence	7
21. Criminal	6
22. Demands made on third parties	4

Source: Alex P. Schmid (and Albert J. Jongman), *Political Terrorism: A New Guide to Actors, Authors, Concepts, Data Bases, Theories and Literature*, North-Holland Publishing Company, Amsterdam 1988, p. 5.

Schmid leaves it to the reader to infer which six elements he has left out. It is easy enough to identify one cluster of elements that has been excluded. These are the normative elements, numbers 9, 13, and 15 in the table. They emphasize that terrorism strikes at innocent or non-combatant victims in breach of norms governing the humanitarian conduct of conflicts. Their exclusion can be explained by Schmid's desire to provide an objective and, as he sees it, scientific definition of 'terrorism'.

What Schmid fails to recognize is that his use of the term 'violence' gives his own definition a normative dimension, as 'violence' is far from being a value-free word. Its emotive overtone is only slightly less powerful than that of 'terrorism' itself. Indeed, the concept of violence is sufficiently important in the context of understanding terrorism to warrant consideration at some length before other aspects of Schmid's definition are analysed.

Defining violence

If the essence of violence is, as Gerald Priestland argues, 'that physical power is deliberately employed with the ultimate sanction of physical pain and little choice but surrender or physical resistance',[3] characterization of an action as violent also usually entails disapproval and implies that it is illegitimate. Legitimate violence, if not quite an oxymoron, is usually described by another word, such as 'force'. This applies most obviously to actions of the agents of the state such as the police in upholding law and order, but it also applies to the private individual in circumstances such as self-defence. Thus, to describe the actions of a householder in relation to a burglar as violent would imply that the householder's reaction had gone beyond what was reasonable in the circumstances. Similarly, in a sporting context violent play is action beyond the limits of the game, such as a low blow in a boxing contest. In short, a presumption of illegitimacy attaches to the use of the word 'violence'. What that means in relation to terrorism is that any definition of the concept that employs the term 'violence', as most do, also carries that normative presumption with it. In his listing of the frequency of definitional elements, Schmid treats the term 'force' as a synonym for violence, but in fact the normative connotations of the two words are quite different. Of course, the same action is often described as an act of violence and as an act of force by individuals with different perspectives on the event in question.

Judgement of whether a particular action is violent or not is likely to vary, according to the perceptions of those making it. This point was nicely demonstrated by a survey carried out by the Institute of Social Research at the University of Michigan in the late 1960s. The Institute asked a sample of 1,374 American males to characterize a series of acts as violent or not. Of the sample, 57 per cent replied that shooting a looter was not a violent act, while almost a third of the sample even considered beating students not to be violent. On the other hand, 58 per cent characterized the burning of draft cards, at that time a widespread form of protest against American involvement in the war in Vietnam, as an act of violence.[4] These results illustrate the impact of conflict on perceptions of what constitutes violence. At times of crisis there may be little disposition to accept a view of violence that accords with liberal principles, even in a relatively stable liberal-democracy. However, it would be wrong to draw the conclusion that the use of the term should therefore be regarded as simply subjective, a way of saying 'I disapprove of this'.

In the first place, in most societies there is a widespread measure of agreement on what the notion of violence broadly encompasses. For example, most societies share the same notion of what constitutes an act of murder. Further, in some societies there is sufficient agreement on what is or is not violent to allow one clearly to identify the existence of a consensus on where the line is to be drawn between violence and force. In the second place, while use of the term 'violence' carries a presumption of illegitimacy, it does not automatically imply condemnation in the way that the term 'terrorism' does. This is because people recognize that in certain special circumstances actions which they would normally characterize as violent may be justified in order to achieve a legitimate end. For example, the legitimacy of tyrannicide has long been recognized in many parts of the world. Most contemporary political philosophies envisage circumstances in which the violent overthrow of the existing political system or revolution is justified. At a slightly more mundane level, the riot has gained a measure of acceptability as a means of expressing a community's grievances, especially in circumstances where that community has little access to other forms of political expression. However, the semi-legitimacy of the riot depends on its being seen as a spontaneous expression of discontent. Governments consequently tend to play up the role of outside agitators as a way of discrediting rioters.

In stable liberal-democracies in the West, the riot is one of the few forms of violence about which there is any measure of equivocation. Action against criminals by vigilantes is another, though the degree of equivocation varies from country to country. In countries with effective criminal justice systems, sympathy for the vigilante is likely to be minimal. In fact, for the most part, there is a consensus in such societies that criminalizes the use of violence, clearly distinguishing violence from the force used by the police to uphold law and order. The distinction is underpinned by the placing of legal limits on what agents of the state may do in the name of force.

Criminalization

The purpose of criminalization is to isolate the perpetrator of acts of violence from the rest of society and to deny him or her the defence that his or her actions had a social or political justification. Its effectiveness depends on the existence of a legal system that can be relied upon to punish individuals guilty of such acts regardless of the motivation behind them, except where it constitutes a mitigating circumstance. The most obvious test of such a system is how it treats cases in which individuals take the law into their own hands, such as a man seeking revenge for a wrong done to his sister. In an ethnically divided society, the test may be even starker, simply whether the system is capable of punishing a member of a dominant or majority community appropriately for an act of violence against a member of a subordinate or minority community.[5]

In a society where there is a large measure of consensus in relation to the peaceful conduct of political affairs, criminalization may make possible a simple equation between acts of political violence and terrorism. Thus, the British Prevention of Terrorism Act of 1984 defines terrorism in the first instance simply as 'the use of violence for political ends'.[6] Alternatively, the term 'terrorism' may be applied to forms of violence that present a real or perceived threat to the lives of members of the general public, regardless of their motivation. Thus, the British Prevention of Terrorism Act defines terrorism in the second instance as including 'any use of violence for the purpose of putting the public or any section of the public in fear'.[7] In either case, such criminalization of violence depends on its perpetrators being perceived as a tiny, anti-social minority. Criminalization as a strategy for isolating those resorting to violence for political ends is by no means confined to liberal-democracies. It is also an attractive option for authoritarian states. However, criminalization in an authoritarian state will often be different from that in a liberal-democracy in a number of respects.

Firstly, much greater latitude will generally be allowed to the agents of the state under the rubric of force. Secondly, the state will often seek to criminalize a much larger range of political acts under the heading of violence or terrorism than would a liberal-democracy. An example is the very extensive definition of terrorism in South Africa's 1967 Terrorism Act. This defined terrorism as any activity likely to 'endanger the maintenance of law and order'. The Act included activities with any of 12 listed results within this category. These included, among others, the promotion of 'general dislocation, disturbance or disorder', 'prejudice' to 'any industry or undertaking', causing 'hostility between the White and other inhabitants of the Republic', 'obstruction' to the 'free movement of any traffic on land, at sea or in the air', and even 'embarrassment' to 'the administration of the affairs of the state'.[8] Furthermore, the Act placed the onus on those accused under its provisions to prove that they did not intend their actions to have any of the listed results.

Using 'terrorism' as a blanket term for virtually any form of extra-parliamentary opposition serves a number of purposes. Firstly, it is designed to establish the illegitimacy of such opposition in the eyes of the dominant community, if not the general public. Secondly, it provides a justification for the severe punishment of dissent by associating such dissent with acts of violence such as murder. Thirdly, it is aimed at persuading the outside world of the marginal nature of political opposition to the *status quo*. Such labelling is most likely to be successful where violent or other acts of protest against the regime are perceived as isolated incidents without political resonance among the population at large. At the other end of the spectrum, in a society engulfed by political violence, such labelling rapidly loses any external credibility. When it is apparent that the state has lost the capacity to criminalize acts of violence directed at its rule, its own legitimacy is likely to be in question. This is especially true of the authoritarian state, which is often lacking in credible sources of legitimacy other than its capacity to maintain law and order and the outward appearance of political stability. Consequently, the suppression of violent opposition inevitably constitutes a high priority for such states.

Representative violence

However, political violence may not be directed against the state *per se*. Indeed, one of the most common situations of political violence is inter-community conflict. It is a context in which it is very difficult either to sustain a cross-community consensus on the dividing line between force and violence or to criminalize individual acts of violence. What is more, political violence may no longer be perceived as solely the actions of individuals but as representative of the community from which it emanates, so that it seems reasonable to make members of that community accountable for it. In such circumstances, attitudes towards violence inevitably become coloured by whose violence one feels threatened by. When representative violence[9] has taken hold in a situation of inter-community conflict, it becomes common to justify violence in the strategic terms that states use in an external context.

Thus, violence against the other community may be presented as a form of deterrence or as a pre-emptive attack, when the justifications of community self-defence or of reprisal are not available. In this way, cycles of violence may become established that prove almost impossible to control. In many societies, the danger of accidentally triggering such cycles constitutes a powerful influence on political behaviour, reflected by an insistence on the observance of formalities which may seem excessive to the outsider from a politically stable society. An example is the taboo in Northern Ireland on discussing politics or religion with members of the other community.[10] The existence of social mechanisms to restrain violence is often reflected in societies like Northern Ireland by a very low level of violent crime. In contrast, the very success of stable liberal-democracies in criminalizing violence has reduced the need to retain such social mechanisms, because incidents of violence are no longer so threatening to the society at large. A theme that runs through much of the literature on terrorism is that terrorism itself is in part the product of a weakening of restraints on violence,[11] thus projecting the conditions within stable societies that suffer very little political violence on to other societies where quite different conditions prevail.

Defence of one's community provides one of the most basic justifications of political violence, analogous to the defence of one's country against external attack. Indeed, where the action taken appears intrinsically defensive, it is unlikely that it will even be called violent, since such action requires no justification. Calling an act violent is tantamount to an acknowledgement that it does require justification. This is because no society or community approves of violence as an end in itself. Its justification rests on its being reasonably seen as the only effective means to a legitimate end. The implications of this aspect of usage of the term 'violence' have been most lucidly expounded by Hannah Arendt.

> Violence, being instrumental by nature, is rational to the extent that it is effective in reaching the end that must justify it. And since when we act we never know with any certainty the eventual consequences of what we are doing, violence can remain rational only if it pursues short-term goals. Violence does not promote causes, neither history nor revolution, neither progress nor reaction; but it can serve to dramatize grievances and bring them to public attention. As Conor Cruise O'Brien (in a debate on the legitimacy of violence in the Theatre of Ideas) once remarked, quoting William O'Brien, the nineteenth-century Irish agrarian and nationalist agitator: sometimes 'violence is the only way of ensuring a hearing for moderation'. To ask the impossible in order to obtain the possible is not always counter-productive. And indeed, violence, contrary to what its prophets try to tell us, is more the weapon of reform than of revolution.[12]

But while acknowledging that violence may serve reformist ends, Arendt points out that 'the danger of violence, even if it moves consciously within a non-extremist framework of short-term goals, will always be that the means overwhelm the end'.[13] Of course, reform is already a step beyond the use of violence for ends perceived as defensive, though it is not uncommon for defensive ends to be mixed in with more ambitious political goals.

Judging violence

A fundamental implication of the instrumental character of violence is that violence can only be judged in relation to the ends for which it is being used. Thus, it is easy to produce a reaction of horror to an act of violence, simply by ensuring that the presentation of the violence is detached from its instrumental justification. A writer may wish to evoke such a reaction in order to cast particular events in an unfavourable light or to make a more general comment on the darker aspects of human nature. At the other end of the spectrum apparently gratuitous acts of violence may be rationalized by placing a favourable construction on the motivation of their perpetrators. An obvious difficulty is that no outside observer can fully know what is in the mind of the perpetrator of an act of violence. Judging violence inevitably involves interpretation, and differences of interpretation may be as important in accounting for conflicting reactions to particular episodes of violence as differences in basic norms about what is right or wrong.

The same story told differently may evoke quite different reactions. The various ways in which the violence in Shakespeare's plays has been interpreted at different times provides an illustration of this point. For example, the Royal Shakespeare Company's production of the *Henry VI* trilogy in the 1960s, which condensed it and put it together with *Richard III* under the title *The War of the Roses*, treated the violent events it encompassed as an integral part of the political power struggle and subordinate in importance to the objective of office. By contrast, when the same company performed the full trilogy in the mid-1970s, the violence was portrayed in terms of wanton and arbitrary cruelty rather than instrumental necessity. Power was presented as simply the means to satisfy lust for bloodletting. The change in interpretation mirrored the hardening of attitudes towards political violence in Britain, which was perhaps mainly due to the impact on British society of the Northern Ireland conflict. Both productions were acclaimed in their time.[14]

Another more recent example was provided by the debate on the French Revolution generated by the celebrations of the bicentenary of the storming of the Bastille in 1789. In both Britain and the United States, a negative view of the revolution tended to prevail, matching the dominantly conservative mood of the two societies. It was most clearly reflected in the success of Simon Schama's book *Citizens*.[15] Schama urged his readers not to avert their eyes from the violence that accompanied the revolution in its various stages, with the implication that apologists for the revolution had glossed over its gorier aspects. In reality, there was little danger of that in either America or Britain, where the guillotine and the reign of terror formed the principal images people had of the French Revolution, images reinforced by the thrust of current historical interpretation of its events, which cast doubt both on the progressive intent of the revolutionaries and on the reactionary nature of the *ancien régime*.

In fact, there would appear to be a much greater danger of an exaggeration of the centrality to the revolution of the loss of life in the reign of terror. Thus, in comparison with the vast numbers that have been killed in the revolutions of the twentieth century, the victims of the French terror were relatively few, both absolutely and proportionately to population: some 14,000 in the period between 1792 and 1794.[16] Perhaps even more strikingly, far more people were killed in the reprisals taken by the British authorities following the defeat of the 1798 rebellion in Ireland,[17] a rebellion which the French Revolution had inspired, than in the French reign of terror. Admittedly, these killings were themselves outstripped by those that occurred in the Vendée region of France following the revolution.[18]

In spite of such comparisons, there is no denying the effectiveness of the use of the reign of terror to evoke horror, reflected in its contribution to the establishment of the term 'terrorism'.[19] Indeed, it probably also accounts for the fact that one of the meanings that became attached to the word 'terrorist' during the nineteenth century was that of alarmist or scaremonger. The *Oxford English Dictionary* gives the following example of this usage: 'the terrorists of this country are so extremely alarmed at the power of Bonaparte',[20] quoting the liberal cleric Canon Sydney Smith. This usage appears to have died out towards the end of the nineteenth century, and despite the alarmist nature of much of the contemporary debate on terrorism (especially in relation to the possibility of a terrorist organization making use of a crude nuclear device), it has not been revived. Whether a particular act of violence or type of violence evokes horror is very much dependent on the perspective from which it is viewed. It is worth recalling that the guillotine itself was introduced to provide a swifter and more humane form of execution with the intention that the privilege of execution by decapitation should no longer be confined to the nobility.[21]

If such a view of the guillotine seems scarcely credible today, it simply reflects the fundamental truth that there is no nice way to execute anyone, whether by lethal injection, the electric chair, or any other method. Indeed, one can go further. There is no nice way to kill anyone. However, while many countries have abolished capital punishment, even most pacifists would accept that there are circumstances when killing a human being is justified. The most obvious of these is where it appears to be the only way to prevent someone from killing other people. Furthermore, in this context, the means used would be regarded as wholly subordinate to the end being achieved. In the face of an unambiguous threat, the use of virtually any means whatsoever would appear justified, provided of course that it did not itself endanger the lives of others.

In practice, the justification of violence is rarely about acts as straightforwardly protective of human life as that. It generally turns on two elements, the issue of what is in the mind of the perpetrator and its actual consequences. Since the latter is usually somewhat easier to establish than the former, consequences tend to loom larger than motives in the judgement of violence. In particular, where a campaign of violence is successful in achieving its political objectives, perceptions of the campaign will tend to hinge on the legitimacy of the objectives rather than the means employed. Typically, the winners will label the campaign a war, a liberation struggle, or a revolution, as they think appropriate, but will dwell more on the outcome than on the process itself. Those who died on the winning side will usually be commemorated, but a veil tends to be drawn over the loss of life on the other side and its circumstances. But if such an attitude on the part of the winners seems hypocritical, the alternative to such selective memories may be the honest justification of atrocities rather than the acknowledgement of wrong-doing. This is because such acknowledgement may seem to detract from the legitimacy of one's cause. Thus, Benny Morris's research into the truth behind the creation of the Palestinian refugee problem prompted accusations that the effect of his work was to delegitimize Zionism.[22]

One may compare the Palestinian case with the selective memories that opinion in the Republic of Ireland retained of its War of Independence. This became evident after the onset of the troubles in Northern Ireland in the late 1960s, and more particularly, the emergence in the 1970s of the Provisional Irish Republican Army (IRA), claiming lineal descent from the Irish Republican Army that had fought the British during the Irish War of Independence. There was relatively little sympathy for the Provisional IRA in the Republic, which had evolved into a stable liberal-democracy, in marked contrast to the political situation in Northern Ireland. Many people in the South, particularly those of the older generation, who still regarded the achievement of independence from Britain as providing the basis of the legitimacy of the country's political institutions, insisted that the activities of the Provisional IRA had nothing in common with the IRA of the past, often referred to in this context as the good old IRA. While a distinction could clearly be drawn between the political context of the Provisional campaign and the War of Independence, many genuinely believed that the actual methods of violence employed by the IRA in the past had been different from what they saw as the terrorist methods of the Provisional IRA. This eventually prompted Sinn Fein, the political wing of the Provisional IRA, to bring out a pamphlet under the title of *The Good Old IRA*.[23] It simply reproduced contemporary newspaper accounts of IRA activities in the years 1919, 1920, and 1921.

The irresistible and shocking implication was that there were no grounds for distinguishing between the old IRA and the new in terms of methods. What the pamphlet brought out very persuasively was the striking similarity in detail of atrocities in the two campaigns. While this similarity has discouraged further reference to the good old IRA by the Provisionals' critics, it has not helped to rehabilitate the Provisionals' image in the eyes of Southern opinion. This is partly because the present conflict in Northern Ireland has itself been a stimulus to a historical revisionism in the Republic that has permitted a de-romanticization of the nationalist heroes of the past.[24] Such revisionism has become possible because the South's political institutions have in practice achieved a legitimacy that is independent of the historical foundations of the state.

Ends and means

As a generalization one can say that acts of violence will appear more legitimate if the ends are emphasized and less legitimate if the means form the focus of attention. This is evidently true of words describing different forms and types of violence. Categories of ends, such as revolution, coup d'état, and counter-insurgency, are far less emotive or derogatory than categories of means, such as assassination, bombings, and torture, despite the evident interdependence of means and ends. Terrorism, while not as specific a description of method as bombing or assassination, clearly belongs with them, among the means. Like torture, terrorism *per se* has few defenders. But to distinguish terrorism from other forms of violence, more needs to be established than simply that it is an indefensible means, assuming that the judgement of means can ever be separated from the issue of ends. However, precisely because the term obviously does carry an implication of condemnation, there is a good case to be made for an explicitly normative definition of terrorism. Such an approach would require the restriction of the term to methods of violence seen as absolutely illegitimate in all circumstances or, more realistically, very clear definitions of the circumstances in which such methods were wholly illegitimate. Its weakness is the absence of a clear consensus among states or world opinion at large as to the content of such a norm, compounded by the problem of trying to judge means without reference to ends.

A striking aspect of Schmid's definition of terrorism quoted at the beginning of this chapter is its general exclusion of assassination. Schmid argues that 'while assassination aims at having the victim dead, terrorism does not care about the victim itself'.[25] This is an attempt by Schmid to meet the point that there is often no reasonable basis for inferring an intent to cause terror to others in the case of an assassination. In particular, the political purpose behind an assassination may be achieved directly by the death of the targeted individual. Where that is the case, it may not seem appropriate to label the act one of terrorism. None the less, that has not prevented assassination along with bombings from being seen by the media and the public as typical of terrorism. However, from Schmid's reservations about including assassination in a definition of terrorism, a more general implication about the characteristics of terrorism may be inferred.

This is that terrorism tends to be seen as a method of violence where the connection between means and ends is indirect rather than direct. This makes it possible to generalize about the purposes of terrorism through reference to aims such as coercion, intimidation, and propaganda that are themselves simply means to the ultimate political objectives of a campaign of terrorism. Furthermore, since coercion, intimidation, and propaganda are not in themselves legitimate ends, such generalization reinforces the assumption that terrorism is absolutely illegitimate as a method of violence. Thus, in practice, the term 'terrorism' tends to be applied to acts of violence where the distance between means and ends seems particularly large.

One obvious circumstance in which the distance between means and ends will appear large is in the case of failure. It follows from the instrumental character of violence that if it does not work, it cannot easily be justified. Of course, no one embarking on a campaign of violence can possibly know for certain what the outcome will be. But clearly the longer the odds against success the more difficult it will be to justify resort to violence. Further, the larger the disproportion between the means available and the ends being sought, the less credible a campaign of violence is likely to appear and the more likely it is to be labelled one of terrorism. The most obvious example would be the attempt to achieve a revolution in an outwardly stable and prosperous society like that of, say, Japan through small-scale violence. The other side of the coin is that where a campaign of violence is successful in achieving its aims or is on a scale that makes success appear a possibility, there is likely to be a reluctance to apply the label 'terrorism' to it.

Of course, judgements of the morality of campaigns of violence are not simply based on judgements of the likelihood of success, but on judgements of the legitimacy of the ends as well. But the very existence of large-scale conflict is likely to make a judgement of the legitimacy of the end more difficult, especially if the wishes of the people affected are considered important in reaching such a judgement. Admittedly, the attitudes, beliefs, and desires of peoples in the Third World are often difficult to discern in situations of conflict, and their perceptions tend to be neglected when judgements are made about the legitimacy of violence in such situations. However, there is usually sufficient sensitivity to this issue to undermine any consensus on the use of the term 'terrorism' in the context of extensive conflict.

Guerrillas and terrorists

The association of terrorism by and large with small-scale violence is reflected in a cluster of elements in Schmid's analysis of definitions of terrorism, in particular, numbers 11, 17, 19, and 21 in Table 2.1. Symbolic violence carried out covertly but with a view to publicity is characteristic of low-level conflicts. Clearly, too, the issue of criminality arises only in circumstances where political authority is sufficiently secure to make such a judgement possible. This perspective fits in well with the stereotype of the terrorist as someone engaged in a clandestinely conducted campaign of violence as part of a small group on the extreme fringe of the political spectrum. The obvious contrast is with the stereotype of the guerrilla as someone who is part of a large, and often uniformed, army, openly carrying arms. However, while these stereotypes play a part in how the words are used, 'guerrilla' and 'terrorist' are also used interchangeably with respect to context to indicate disapproval (in the case of 'terrorist') and a more neutral attitude (in the case of 'guerrilla'). Such usage tends to cut across the much more substantive distinction between the two in terms of scale.

The application of the term 'terrorism' to the lowest level of conflict seems somewhat paradoxical in view of the massive emotive punch that the word carries. In short, why should the lowest level of violence evoke the most horror? One can construct a partial answer to this question by drawing a distinction between violence in the context of peace and violence in the context of war, and by arguing that terrorism is political violence in the context of peace and shocking for that reason. Providing a measure of support for this perspective is the practice in libraries of classifying books on terrorism under crime and those on guerrillas under war. However, one factor that has tended to cut across the use of the term 'terrorism' to apply to the lowest level of conflict is the tendency in the West to treat any violent challenge to a liberal-democracy or even to any polity that meets the formal requirements of a liberal-democracy, as illegitimate and hence an example of terrorism, even if the violence escalates to a level that points to a fundamental breakdown of political authority. An example is the use of the term 'terrorist' to apply to the various protagonists in the conflict in Sri Lanka.[26] It is also a factor in the tendency to classify the Sendero Luminoso in Peru as terrorists rather than guerrillas, notwithstanding their mode of operation.[27]

So far we have identified two ways of distinguishing terrorism from other forms of violence. One is normative, identifying terrorism with action that violates basic notions of what is acceptable on humanitarian grounds in the conduct of conflicts. The other identifies terrorism with a particular level of conflict, in effect treating the word as a technical term for political violence within the confines of basically stable polities. One can relate the two together in so far as what is perceived as acceptable on humanitarian grounds tends to vary according to the level of conflict. However, neither approach suggests what, in concrete terms, acts of terrorism encompass. In fact, definitions in general are unhelpful in this respect; but a concrete picture of what acts the term is applied to can be constructed through examining common usage over a period of time, providing us with a third way of distinguishing terrorism from other forms of violence.

Testing usage

To do this I have analysed the chronology of terror in Dobson and Payne's study, *The Never-Ending War*.[28] Their chronology covers events between July 1968 and October 1988. It fits in well therefore with the notion that the late 1960s were the beginning of an age of terrorism that continues to afflict the planet. The authors do not claim that their chronology is comprehensive, merely that it highlights the main trends in terrorism. Altogether, there are 286 items in the chronology, some of them referring to more than one actual incident. At the same time, some of the items refer to political declarations, extradition cases, arrests, the interception of weapons, and the outcome of trials that clearly are not themselves acts of terrorism.

The following types of violence are included in the chronology: hijackings, kidnapping and hostage-taking (including one incident in which the victim was a horse), bombings of various kinds (fire, letter, car, lorry, among other forms of bombs, and including bombing for the purpose of sabotage), assassinations, attacks on diplomats, attacks on civil airliners, missile and rocket attacks, product contamination, and some incidents of shootings that do not fall into the category of assassination. The American bombing of Libya in April 1986 is included in the chronology, but the authors' comments make it absolutely clear that they do not regard it as itself an act of terrorism. That also applies to some other acts taken by security forces that they list. Excluding these cases, the frequency of different types of violence is, to take the leading categories, as follows. Bombings and attempted bombings of various kinds account for 39 per cent of the total. Assassinations and attempted assassinations constitute 24 per cent of the total, while kidnapping and hostage-taking account for 14 per cent. Finally, hijackings feature in 8 per cent of the items. If one looks at frequencies from another angle, attacks on diplomats of all kinds feature in 9 per cent of the items and attacks on airliners in 17 per cent. Over two-thirds of the items in the chronology are cases of international or transnational terrorism. Most of the cases of purely domestic terrorism are drawn from four countries: the United Kingdon (in respect of Northern Ireland), West Germany, Italy, and Spain. Not a single incident in the chronology is located in Central America.

While a more comprehensive chronology of the last twenty years of terrorism would certainly show a wider geographical spread of incidents and would probably encompass a rather wider range of types of violence than that devised by Dobson and Payne, their chronology does accurately reflect the priorities and general orientation of the Western media in relation to terrorism. In particular, any chronology relying on the major daily papers of the United States or Britain would cover much the same ground as theirs does and provide much the same picture of terrorism. Specifically, what many of the items in Dobson and Payne's chronology have in common is that they refer to acts of violence that frighten or affront citizens of politically stable countries in the First World. Thus, the average citizen is frightened by bombs, since they pose a threat to him or her as a bystander. The bombs may come in various forms, though they do not include aerial bombing or artillery bombardment, since these are not risks that citizens of the developed world face, and one would not expect to find either in a chronology of terrorism, however terrifying such action may be to those on the receiving end. Hijackings do pose a threat to the ordinary citizen of the West in an age of mass transit by air, as does any other form of attack on a civil airliner. While assassination is not generally perceived as a threat to the ordinary citizen, it is an affront, especially where the target is a politician or diplomat whose role is to represent the citizen.

Of course, the likelihood of the ordinary citizen being affected directly by these types of violence is extremely small and very, very much smaller than that of his or her being a victim of ordinary crime. However, the indirect influence of terrorism on the ordinary citizen is considerable in terms of the security precautions which it has necessitated. Furthermore, the ordinary citizen is often conscious of being the target of the political message that the violence is seeking to convey, the communication function referred to by Schmid in his definition of terrorism. In practice, this generally compounds the citizen's sense of outrage, since it carries the implication that his or her political response is open to such manipulation. It also points to the obvious limitation of this approach to distinguishing terrorism from other forms of violence. This is that it describes a phenomenon principally of concern to the First World and leaves out the truly terrifying violence that people in much of the Third World face.

To summarize, in this chapter we have identified three ways of distinguishing terrorism from other forms of violence: firstly, normatively; secondly, as an indicator of the level of violence; thirdly, as a description of the types of violence of a generally political or social character that threaten Western citizens. Each approach has its advantages. For example, whatever its other drawbacks, the last does conform with common usage, which is an important consideration if confusion is to be avoided in discussing any issue. In fact, none of these approaches can reasonably be discarded. Clearly, a consensus on a single approach to defining the concept would help to assist its intellectual credibility, and the existence of a number of possible approaches leaves a question-mark over that issue. As necessary in subsequent chapters, the reader will be reminded of which approach is the most salient in the context of what is being discussed.

It also needs to be borne in mind that common to all three approaches is that terrorism is a form of violence and what follows from that. This is that it is virtually impossible to judge any act of violence simply as a means without reference to the end that provides the motivation for the deed. Because the ends matter so much, we should not expect method alone to provide us with the basis for reaching a judgement about any act of violence. In the case of terrorism this issue tends to be obscured, because the term tends to be applied to campaigns of violence where the distance between means and ends appears particularly large. Indeed, the concept of terrorism carries the implication that absolute judgements about methods of violence are possible without reference to ultimate purposes or basic motivation. This has encouraged the belief that a general theory of the causes of terrorism is, in principle, possible. This is the issue we examine next.

3

The poverty of general explanations

The inadequacy of theories of the causes of terrorism is a frequent complaint in the literature on the subject.[1] None the less, the usefulness of generalizing about the causes of terrorism as if it could be treated as a single phenomenon tends rarely to be questioned, except perhaps for the acknowledgement that overt state terror requires rather different treatment from small-scale clandestine violence, the principal focus of the theorists of terrorism. While typologies of terrorism are common as a way of handling the different circumstances in which 'terrorism' is employed, the very use of the term generally indicates a commitment to the proposition that terrorism constitutes a clearly distinct form of violence. Not surprisingly, the most powerful and influential theories are those that build on the assumption of terrorism's singularity. The best-known of these are the conspiracy theories that seek to explain terrorism in its primary manifestations with reference to a common hidden hand manipulating events from afar.[2]

The most famous of these is Claire Sterling's *The Terror Network*.[2] In her view, the hidden hand behind much international terrorism in the 1970s was the Soviet Union, with Cuba and Libya cast in the role of junior accomplices.[3] While the Soviet Union has been the favourite target of most of the conspiracy theorists, alternative conspiracy theories centring on Washington and the American Central Intelligence Agency also exist,[4] though some of these have been constructed more in reaction to the Soviet-conspiracy school than as complete world-views in themselves. But what virtually all conspiracy theories have in common, regardless of their particular target, is that they portray terrorism as part of a strategy aimed at establishing world domination and unrestrained by moral considerations.

In this respect, they have quite a lot in common with approaches to terrorism that locate the phenomenon in the casting off of all moral restraint, what might be called the demonic view of terrorism.

35

For example, Paul Wilkinson, the most prominent British analyst of terrorism, identifies the following as some of the key characteristics of political terrorism: 'indiscriminateness, unpredictability, arbitrariness, ruthless destructiveness, and the implicitly amoral and antinomian nature of a terrorist's challenge'.[5] Such a perspective clearly begs the further question of why such an abandonment of moral restraint should occur. The answers given to this question vary considerably. Some theorists attribute lack of moral restraint to psychological failings of the terrorists. Other writers have emphasized the role of the permissive society in creating the basis for such lack of restraint, a view that provides a convenient explanation of why the age of terrorism began in the late 1960s. Still others have insisted that moral breakdown has to be understood in its own terms as the product of moral choice.[6] But because each of these answers shares an underlying assumption that terrorism is absolutely evil, whichever approach is taken in the end projects the same, extremely gloomy view of human nature.

Causes of terrorism

In practice, few writers apart from the crudest conspiracy theorists opt for entirely monocausal explanations of terrorism. For example, Martha Crenshaw's widely quoted article 'The Causes of Terrorism' identifies a broad range of preconditions, 'factors that set the stage for terrorism over the long run', and precipitants, 'specific events that immediately precede the occurrence of terrorism'.[7] She further divides preconditions into 'enabling or permissive factors, which provide opportunities for terrorism to happen, and situations that directly inspire and motivate terrorist campaigns'.[8] Thus, she argues that modernization has produced a number of factors that have been a significant permissive cause of terrorism, in particular, through the creation of networks of transport and communication. She gives as one example that 'the Popular Front for the Liberation of Palestine could not indulge in hijacking without the jet aircraft'.[9] Less tritely, she identifies Nobel's invention of dynamite in 1867 as an example of a technological discovery that opened the way to bombing as a terrorist tactic in the late nineteenth century.[10] These two examples underscore the association of terrorism with specific methods such as bombings and hijacking.

At the same time, Crenshaw's emphasis on modernization as an enabling factor begs the question of whether what distinguishes terrorism from violence of the past is simply a question of methods and the availability of new means. On this basis, one might plausibly argue that the age of terrorism really began in the 1870s with the first anarchist bombings and has continued ever since, though interrupted by the twentieth century's two world wars. From this perspective, the late 1960s did not mark the beginning of a new form of violence but the resumption of the use of methods that went back, in the case of bombings, nearly a hundred years. Taking this argument further, one might contend that what needs explaining is less present-day terrorism than the state of relative political quiescence in the liberal-democracies of the West in the two decades that followed the Second World War.

Other enabling factors identified by Crenshaw – and by many other writers, for that matter[11] – are urbanization, the existence of a tradition of the use of violence for political ends, and the government's inability or unwillingness to prevent terrorism. Political factors loom much larger in Crenshaw's discussion of the direct causes of terrorism. She sensibly emphasizes the role that the terrorist organization's perception and interpretation of the situation plays as a causal factor. Given the wide diversity of political circumstances in different parts of the world, the corollary of this observation would seem to be that useful generalization about terrorism on a global basis is likely to be limited. However, this is not a line of argument that Crenshaw follows. Despite taking a very wide view of what terrorism encompasses, she seems reluctant to abandon the quest for psychological explanations capable of cutting across the political differences in context. Further, nowhere does Crenshaw question the coherence of the concept of terrorism itself.

Generalizations about terrorism

Set out below are a number of the more significant generalizations that have been made in the literature about the nature and causes of terrorism. They include propositions derived from the theories touched on above and a few others, as well as some of the commoner building blocks used in theorizing about the subject.

1. Terrorism is a form of surrogate warfare directed against the West.
2. Terrorism is a concomitant of a modern industrial or post-industrial society.
3. Terrorism is a pathological phenomenon.
4. Liberal-democracies are by nature more vulnerable to terrorism than are other forms of government.
5. Terrorism is a product of the democratization of violence.
6. Terrorism is a weapon of the weak.

7. Terrorism kills relatively few people.
8. Terrorism is a reaction to violence by the state.
9. Terrorism is a response to the failure of mass political movements.
10. An age of terrorism began in the late 1960s.

Much of the rest of this chapter will be devoted to assessing these propositions in relation to the three meanings of terrorism identified in the last chapter. None of the propositions is satisfactory by itself as an explanation of terrorism, which is hardly surprising given the conflicting strands of meaning to be found in the notion of terrorism itself. However, there is something to be learned from examining each of them.

The first proposition, that terrorism is in effect a form of indirect aggression, of covert warfare in an era of ostensible peace, is a central contention of those who see terrorism as a conspiracy directed against the West, usually from Moscow. Claire Sterling is the most obvious representative of this viewpoint. In *The Terror Network* she identified 1968 as the year when the Kremlin's terrorist offensive was launched, but with the preparations for its launch going back earlier. Thus, she attached particular importance to the Tricontinental Conference held in Havana in 1966, which was attended by some five hundred delegates representing organizations in different parts of the Third World.[12] The openly stated purpose of the conference was to give support to groups in a variety of contexts through expressions of international solidarity with their struggle against imperialism, conceived as their common enemy. Little more than that can be gleaned from the public record of the proceedings.

Sterling is by no means the first person to place importance on an open gathering as the origin of a conspiracy. For example, during the 1960s, Brian Crozier's theory that Moscow had handed out the orders for revolution in South-East Asia at an Asian Youth Conference in Calcutta in February 1948 enjoyed a measure of influence. The theory has not stood the test of time.[13]

The gist of Sterling's argument was that Moscow was linked directly or indirectly to a variety of Palestinian groups, the Baader-Meinhof group in West Germany, the Red Brigades (Brigate Rosse) in Italy, ETA (Euzkadi ta Askatasuna – Basque Homeland and Liberty) in Spain, and the Provisional IRA in Northern Ireland, and others. The implication of her work was not merely that the Soviet Union was behind much of this terrorism but that it was a result of a Soviet Master Plan directed against the West. The weakness of the thesis was most evident on a case-by-case basis. In particular, none of the detailed studies of Baader-Meinhof, the Red Brigades, ETA, or the

Provisional IRA gave any weight to links with the Soviet Union.[14] This was perhaps least surprising of all in the case of the Provisional IRA, since one of the reasons for its founding was hostility to communist influence in the Official Republican movement.[15]

What is true is that international links of all kinds have assumed some importance at an operational, as opposed to a causal, level in the case of many, if not most, terrorist organizations. However, this reflects the growth of international interdependence more than it does a plot on the part of any particular country or group of countries. One consequence of interdependence is that there has been more than sufficient material available to connect not just America and the Soviet Union but even smaller countries such as Israel, Iran, and South Africa in one way or another with many of the world's conflicts.[16] But the existence of such connections usually has little or nothing to do with the reasons for violence in these situations. Furthermore, the establishment of external links frequently took place at the initiative of the local parties and therefore cannot reasonably be attributed to any global design on the part of the outside power or powers involved. It is notable that the conspiracy theories of international terrorism have exercised very little influence on academic studies of any state's foreign policy.[17]

The credence given to Sterling's thesis owes much to the fact that the Western liberal-democracies are often seen as the primary victims of terrorism, in part because of the particular methods that tend to be associated with terrorism and in part because of the disproportionate attention that events in these countries receive in the Western media. Given the intensity of hostility between West and East that existed at various times after 1945, it is hardly surprising that the Soviet Union should have been lighted on as a scapegoat for such events. Another attraction of the thesis was that it was an explanation that suggested to a Western audience that the violence in question was utterly without legitimacy and nicely underscored the justification for condemning it as terrorism. The disadvantage of less exotic explanations was their tendency to highlight issues that threw an unfavourable light on the country in question, even if they fell short of justifying resort to violence. That accounts for the readiness of police chiefs and other public officials faced by episodes such as bombings to give credence to notions of external manipulation. Not surprisingly, Sterling made considerable use of such statements to buttress her argument.[18]

The credibility of conspiracy theories of terrorism derives from a further factor. This is simply the fact that the clandestine use of violence tends naturally to involve a hidden conspiracy. In fact, it is often extremely difficult to establish the full truth about particular clandestine acts of violence. Who carried out an act and why is frequently the subject of controversy and may be quite impossible to establish beyond doubt. For example, it seems unlikely that there will ever be fully satisfactory explanations of such mysteries as the assassination of President Kennedy or the attempted assassination of Pope John Paul II. Such uncertainty, whose existence in fact signifies nothing in particular, provides grist for the conspiracy theorist's mill. At the same time, the long history of the involvement of state intelligence agencies in acts of violence such as bombings, attempted bombings, assassinations, and attempted assassinations provides a measure of justification for the suspicion that is directed at states as possible perpetrators of particular episodes of clandestine violence.

The collapse of the communist system in Eastern Europe in 1989 and 1990 uncovered new evidence of links between Western terrorist organizations and Eastern intelligence agencies.[19] In the case of particular organizations, this evidence may require some reassessment of the role played by Eastern intelligence agencies in their activities. However, it has stopped far short of establishing the case of those who argued that groups such as Red Army Faction in West Germany were controlled from the East. In general, the rather small number of cases in which it can be established that foreign intelligence agencies were implicated in terrorism do not justify the suggestion put forward by some writers on terrorism that there was a trend to state-directed and state-sponsored terrorism in the 1980s.[20]. What increased in the 1980s was simply Western awareness of the role that some states played directly or indirectly in relation to some campaigns of clandestine violence. This was particularly the case in relation to the long-standing involvement of a number of Arab states in the activities of various Palestinian organizations.

Modernity and terrorism

A number of writers have suggested that certain features of modern Western societies have increased their vulnerability to terrorism. A good example is the anonymity of modern cities, the fact that the mobile populations which inhabit the apartments in these cities frequently have no idea of the identity of their next-door neighbours, creating scope for cells to hide in such areas without attracting attention. That means that any group can resort to clandestine forms of violence without the need to rely on a measure of popular sympathy for their actions to provide a cloak over their activities. Further, the cosmopolitan character of Western cities and the ease of travel between them have enhanced the ease with which foreign groups can conduct clandestine campaigns of violence within such countries. It is an issue that xenophobic politicians in the West are able to exploit in their campaigns against migrant workers and immigration generally.[21]

However, it is easy to exaggerate the issue of setting. In particular, hijackings have originated from airports in all parts of the world. Similarly, assassinations and bombings have occurred in many different places. What is perhaps more to the point is that the clandestine violence associated with terrorism is one of the few forms of political violence, apart from rioting, that is possible in the modern industrial and post-industrial society. That is to say, the kind of political breakdown in which it is possible for large numbers of people to carry arms openly in a guerrilla army is likely to occur only in a society where a considerable proportion of the population still live in the rural areas. However, the militias that have appeared in the Balkans and in the southern republics of the former Soviet Union are an argument against the assumption that large-scale violent political conflict is possible only in the poorest countries of the Third World.

While individual acts of terrorism in the sense of the use of particular methods can occur almost anywhere, terrorism is most likely to be identified as a problem in countries where such acts are divorced from other forms of violence. In particular, acts of terrorism are usually seen as the acts of terrorists. Where such acts are carried out by the security forces of the state or by a guerrilla army, there is likely to be considerable inhibition about applying the term 'terrorism' to them. Precisely because the kinds of organized violence possible in a highly developed industrial society tend to be limited to forms of clandestine violence associated with terrorism, labelling those who use violence as terrorists tends to be less problematic, even solely on the grounds of method. The net result is to strengthen the impression that terrorism is a phenomenon that particularly afflicts Western societies, notwithstanding the fact that these societies suffer far less political violence than other areas of the world.

It might be argued that this is because of the special character in normative terms of the violence affecting Western societies. In particular, it might be suggested that what distinguishes terrorism in the West from, say, the conduct of guerrilla warfare is the killing, injuring, or threatening of innocent bystanders. It is a common enough impression, but one for which there is not a great deal of justification in reality. Indeed, in practice, other forms of violence tend to be just as, if not more, indiscriminate in their impact on innocent bystanders as the methods that tend to be associated with terrorism. The flood of refugees from areas of civil war is testimony to the terrorizing impact on civilians of high levels of conflict. The association of 'terrorism' with the lowest level of political violence links the term's use to situations where the actual risk to most civilians is generally extremely small. However, less important than the actual numbers of civilians killed, injured, or threatened by terrorism is the public's perception that terrorists deliberately target civilians and bystanders as part of their strategy. Of course, different publics, internal as well as external, may have different perceptions in this respect, and this may be a factor in how they label perpetrators of political violence.

Terrorism as pathological

The perception that terrorists seek to maximize the impact of their actions on society by the very randomness of their choice of victims is one of the factors underpinning the view of terrorism as a pathological phenomenon. Thus, terrorism is often seen as the product of minds that carry out actions on the basis of a crude calculation of their utility without reference to moral considerations. However, such a view is very often inferred from the consequences of a terrorist organization's actions without reference to the actual thinking of any terrorist. This is especially likely to be the case where there is a wide gulf between the public's conception of morality and of how the world works and that of the terrorist organization. The wider the gulf the less likely it is that the public will understand how the terrorist organization itself justifies its actions, not just in utilitarian terms but morally, and not merely in propaganda terms to the outside world but to its own members and supporters.

On the whole, governments faced by terrorist campaigns have little interest in seeing a narrowing of this gulf. Indeed, it is likely to be in the government's interest that the public should regard terrorists and acts of terrorism as devoid of moral content and incapable of being legitimized from any perspective. But governments can become victims of their own propaganda in this respect. In particular, if they fail to take into account the processes by which those engaged in terrorism justify their actions to themselves, they may unwittingly prolong campaigns of terrorism by taking actions that reinforce the terrorists' belief in the justification of their campaign.

Anger at a campaign of terrorism may be further intensified by the belief that the utility of the violence is dependent on how successful it is in the manipulation of the public's emotions. If it seems unlikely that the public will respond in the way demanded of it by the terrorists, the campaign of terrorism is likely to appear futile, if not senseless. The more senseless any campaign appears, the more reasonable it may seem to categorize it as pathological. Alternatively, terrorism's apparent reliance for its success on the manipulation of public emotions may be treated not as inevitably futile, but rather as placing a moral imperative on the public to resist its demands. In this case, terrorism is treated as a test of the moral fabric of the afflicted society, and terrorism takes on demonic rather than simply pathological connotations. Of course, few terrorists are likely to share the view that the campaign of terrorism they are involved in is either pathological or demonic, though they may take that view of the behaviour of other organizations, including those of the state. Indeed, such polarization of attitudes is commonplace in conflicts that have become institutionalized.[22]

Liberal-democracy's vulnerability

One of the most common propositions in the literature on terrorism is that it is a form of violence to which liberal-democracies are especially prone.[23] Liberal-democracy's vulnerability has been presented as, on the one hand, evidence of a conspiracy by its ideological enemies and, on the other, a consequence of the very freedom that liberal-democracy permits. Thus, Sterling argues that '[t]here is nothing random in this concentrated assault on the shrinking area of the world still under democratic rule. Not only is it easier and safer to be a terrorist in a free country than it is in a police state, it is ideologically more satisfying'.[24] Chronologies of acts of terrorism and statistics of acts of terrorism, particularly international terrorism, seem to bear out the proposition. However, if we focus on the meanings of terrorism rather than on what might make liberal-democracy more vulnerable to terrorism than other forms of government, it will be evident that the proposition has more to do with what types of violence are associated with terrorism than with any peculiar vulnerability of liberal-democracy as a political system.

Firstly, one of the reasons for the association of terrorism and liberal-democracy is, paradoxically, the success of liberal-democracy in maintaining political stability, particularly in industrialized societies. Most of these societies have been affected by only low-level conflict. In fact, the very effectiveness of government in these societies, in marked contrast to the debilitated political systems of the Third World, has prevented the outbreak of more serious conflict, and, as we saw in the last chapter, one of the ways of distinguishing terrorism from other forms of violence is as the lowest level of conflict. In short, the association of liberal-democracy and terrorism is due in part to the absence of more serious conflict in these societies.

Secondly, among those who share a belief in liberal-democratic values there is a much greater readiness on normative grounds to label acts of violence that occur in a liberal-democracy as terrorism than there would be in relation to similar acts under a different political system. Here again it is the very success of liberal-democratic values that accounts for the impression of the vulnerability of such systems to terrorism. A factor that helped to underscore the notion that liberal-democracy as a system was peculiarly vulnerable to terrorism was the apparent stability of the communist world during the 1970s and most of the 1980s and the rarity of any form of political violence behind the Iron Curtain. However, the political upheaval in these societies at the end of the 1980s has tended to undermine the force of this argument. In particular, it is no longer possible to attribute the relative tranquillity of these societies prior to the late 1980s to any inherent qualities of their political systems, and such tranquillity as existed in these countries appears to have been based on transient factors, such as the boost that the Soviet system received as a result of the Soviet Union's victory over Nazi Germany.

Democratization of violence

A more profound proposition, and one that has a bearing on upheavals in the communist world, is the notion that the trend towards mass participation in politics concomitant with modernization has brought with it the democratization of violence and that terrorism is a symptom of this process. One can identify a whole range of factors that have made resort to violence by the ordinary citizen easier: the decline of social hierarchy and of the capacity of local power-holders to control populations; the ready availability of weaponry and especially the ease with which small arms can be purchased in many parts of the world, with states dumping their arsenals of obsolescent weapons on the arms market; and other aspects of industrial and post-industrial society that have already been mentioned such as the anonymity of modern cities and access to transportation and communication. At a political level, the first of these is of particular significance. In the absence of local control, the issue of the legitimacy of the political system itself and of the judicial arrangements for the suppression and criminalization of violent dissent assumes crucial importance. In societies where sharp ethnic divisions exist, the process of democratization and of liberalization is often fraught with the danger of intercommunal violence, especially in circumstances of economic change giving rise to conflict over resources. The intercommunal violence that has accompanied the process of democratization in the southern republics of the former Soviet Union provides an illustration of such difficulties.

Societies that have successfully made the transition from a situation in which tranquillity is maintained by the force and influence of local power-holders to the control of men and women by laws deriving their legitimacy from popular participation, however indirect, in the processes that make those laws are often remarkably blind to the difficulties that less fortunate societies encounter in controlling violence. British attitudes towards Irish violence during the nineteenth century provide a significant example. Up to the mid-nineteenth century the scale of disorder in Britain and Ireland was more or less comparable,[25] but thereafter the experience of the two societies diverged, with Britain alone making the successful transition to a society characterized by the rule of law and a decline of disorder. In the process the violence of the past was rapidly forgotten, and the divergence prompted a tendency in Britain to attribute violence in Ireland to the peculiar mentality of its inhabitants, rather than to the substantial differences in the circumstances of the two societies. The specious view that the Irish are culturally endowed with an inherent desire to fight has even cropped up as an explanation of the most recent troubles in Northern Ireland in academic studies of terrorism.[26]

One reason for the prevalence of such explanations is an aspect of terrorism touched on earlier, the large distance that seems to exist between the means being used and the goals sought. This distance also provides part of the explanation for the characterization of terrorism as a strategy of desperation and as the weapon of the weak. The implication is that the strong are in a position to pursue both a more direct and a more certain route to their goals. Thus, to take the extreme case, military conquest is a much surer method of dictating policies than relying on a few bombs to elicit the required political response. Indeed, in most circumstances terrorism seems likely to elicit the opposite response to what it seeks, resistance to its demands precisely because of their identification with such methods.

The odds against success suggest desperation and weakness. However, here it is necessary to draw a distinction between strategic terrorism and tactical terrorism, a distinction made by Lawrence Freedman in an interesting analysis of the subject.[27] In the latter case, terrorism simply forms one of a number of instruments in a broader strategy, as, for example, when it is employed by states. In this context, it is hardly appropriate to characterize the use of terrorism as a weapon of the weak. As an example, Freedman refers to the use of terrorism by partisans in the Second World War in the overall context of the battle against Nazi occupation. In the former case, where terrorism, conceived in any of the three ways identified in the last chapter, is the sole or, at any rate, the primary means being employed, the generalization that terrorism is the weapon of the weak holds up much better. Freedman gives as an example of strategic terrorism ETA's campaign for an independent Basque homeland. He argues that dependence on terrorism tends to be a sign of strategic failure and he suggests that the successes of strategic terrorism tend to be largely negative, preventing outcomes opposed by the terrorists rather than achieving positive goals. Freedman has in mind the capacity of terrorism to polarize situations, thereby wrecking the possibility of compromise through negotiations.

Related to the notion of terrorism as the weapon of the weak is the common observation that terrorism kills relatively few people.[28] It is worth noting straightaway that this generalization rules out the inclusion of state terror within the conception of terrorism, as the notion of state terror is generally associated with cases of genocidal regimes, whose victims number in the millions. Indeed, the enormous disparity between the numbers killed in state terrorism and those killed in terrorism from below is reason enough to question their treatment as examples of the same phenomenon. At the same time, it is worth underlining the extraordinary implication that follows from treating the two together.

This is the implication that it is necessary for the state to kill very large numbers of people if it is to be successful in terrorizing a population, while terrorists from below are supposed to achieve or at least attempt to achieve the same result through the deaths of a handful of people. It underscores once more the inappropriateness of a literal interpretation of the term. It is very doubtful if any terrorist organization would expect to achieve its goals through the creation of a climate of fear in any way analogous to that in a totalitarian state, as described, for example, in Hannah Arendt's classic study of totalitarianism.[29] Little more needs to be added here about the proposition that terrorism kills few people, since the issue was discussed in Chapter 1. However, it should be noted that the proposition most closely fits the meaning of terrorism as low-level conflict.

Role of the state

The proposition that desire for revenge plays a part in the making of terrorists is discussed by Crenshaw in her article on the causes of terrorism and by Schmid in his survey of theories of terrorism.[30] They give a number of examples drawn from different periods. In particular, both mention the role that the desire for vengeance played in the anarchist violence of the 1890s. But perhaps the most striking case of all is the role that the unprovoked and unpunished killing of a student demonstrator by police during a visit to West Berlin by the Shah of Iran in June 1967 appears to have played in the development of terrorism in West Germany.[31] These examples – and, in fact, all the cases that Crenshaw and Schmid mention – involve vengeance against acts of violence (or force) by the state. They therefore would seem to provide support for the proposition listed above that terrorism is a response to violence by the state. The notion that violence from below is very often a reaction to pre-emptive action by the state forms the interesting thesis of John Walton's book on national revolts, *Reluctant Rebels*.[32] But how far Walton's ideas might be applied to cases of terrorism is a question that can best be answered empirically. The issue of revenge itself is best subsumed under the important question of motivation; this question is the subject of Chapter 5.

The notion that terrorism is a response to the failure of mass political movements has been put forward by Richard Rubenstein as an explanation of the current wave of terrorism.[33] He argues that the conditions for terrorism have been created by the growth in the size of the intelligentsia, the shattering of its hopes for social transformation, and the absence or weakness of mass parties capable of engaging its energies or commitment in a socially useful role. Thus, he characterizes terrorism as 'an isolated intellectual's dream of efficacy', and he argues that 'the most effective counter terrorist device yet discovered is popular mobilization for significant change'.[34] Of course, that answer presupposes the readiness of the state to tolerate such popular mobilization. In the cases that Walton examines it is precisely the unwillingness of the state to allow peaceful mass mobilization that creates the conditions for national revolt.

Clearly the more successful any state's strategy of repression is in dealing with mass movements, the more likely it is that the resulting violence from below will appear illegitimate and the more likely it will be to attract the label of terrorism, though the nature of the violent tactics employed will also have some bearing on this. Military rule in Latin America during the 1970s and 1980s provides the most obvious examples of states resorting to repression to crush left-wing or populist mass movements. However, in Western Europe, the disintegration of the left-wing mass movements of the 1960s clearly had other causes than state repression. In this context Rubenstein makes much of the swing to the right of left-wing parties as a cause of disillusionment that led to terrorism. But Rubenstein's thesis, like the previous proposition, is best examined empirically to see how far his model holds up across a range of cases.

The age of terrorism

This brings us finally to another issue that requires an examination of the historical evidence, the proposition that an age of terrorism began in the late 1960s. However, there is much more to this issue than the factual one of whether the incidence of political violence over the last two decades justifies that characterization. In this context the different ways we identified of distinguishing terrorism from other forms of political violence are particularly salient. For example, in so far as terrorism is identified with low-level conflict, one might argue that the description of the period since the 1960s as an age of terrorism was simply a rather convoluted way of saying that the present era is one of peace, at least for the West. Admittedly, the war in Vietnam overlaps with the beginning of the age of terrorism, but the involvement of American combat troops was being wound down during Nixon's first term as president of the United States and by 1973 the war was essentially over for the Americans. One might also point to the 1973 Yom Kippur War and the 1982 conflict in the South Atlantic over the Falkland Islands as other instances of wars involving states in the West, but neither war lasted long. Western states were prominent in the 1991 war in the Gulf to expel Iraq from Kuwait, but it too was of short duration.

Significantly, previous waves of terrorism, in the 1890s and the 1930s, have also been associated with periods of peace. The association is not as surprising as it might first appear. Only in circumstances of peace is the small-group violence associated with terrorism capable of attracting sufficient attention to appear to warrant the description of terrorism. In short, the shocking character of terrorism requires a background of tranquillity for maximum impact. It also derives its impact from another factor, which Cameron noted in 1970, that 'it has always seemed that the violence of the present was unexpected and, in a sense, undeserved'.[35] But eras of peace tend to be recognized only in retrospect, when there is a greater readiness to appreciate the inconsequential character of the violence that occurred during such a period.

From a normative interpretation of the concept of terrorism, the issue of an age of terrorism can be approached from two angles, from the perspective of widespread violation of existing norms governing the conduct of conflict or from the perspective that it is the development of such norms that has led to the characterization of the age as one of terrorism. A case can be made out for both perspectives. On the one hand, one might point to the taking of hostages as an activity which has become prevalent during the age of terrorism and very clearly violates established norms of warfare. On the other hand, it is evident that the term 'terrorism' is routinely applied today to acts such as political assassination that were as prevalent prior to the age of terrorism but were not categorized as terrorism. Finally, if we take 'terrorism' as a description of the types of violence that have threatened Western citizens during the last quarter of a century, the existence of an age of terrorism simply follows from current usage of the term. The word 'current' deserves underlining, for the general conception of what types of violence 'terrorism' encompasses is not static.

Here again it is worth noting that changes in the way certain acts are characterized have underscored the impression of a watershed in relation to acts of political violence in the late 1960s. That impression has been used to justify explanations of the age of terrorism in terms of a breakdown of moral constraints. Even more importantly, it has been used to justify the need for harsh policies in confronting the problem of terrorism and for the shedding of liberal illusions about human nature that the phenomenon of terrorism appears to contradict. Indeed, at one level, the fact that the present age is widely characterized as one of terrorism reflects the success of Western conservatives in changing the ideological climate in relation to political violence as much as it does actual patterns of violence. In fact, if we take the three types of violence most closely associated with the present wave of terrorism, bombings, assassinations, and hijackings, what is new is more their characterization as acts of terrorism than their prevalence.

This applies even to hijackings. For example, according to the chronology of terror compiled by Dobson and Payne, the first hijacking of a plane by Palestinians occurred in July 1968.[36] As it happens, it is the very first item in their chronology. It was also one of the first hijackings, if not the first, that was generally labelled an act of terrorism. However, it was very far from being the first hijacking of a plane. According to the American Federal Aviation Administration, worldwide a total of 79 hijackings occurred in the years from 1930 to 1967.[37] Admittedly, one reason why earlier hijackings did not attract the label of terrorism is that the aim of such hijackings was usually limited to forcing the pilot to fly the plane to a particular destination and did not involve attempting to gain more general political concessions through direct threats to the lives of the passengers, though of course any hijacking involves at least an indirect threat to the passengers.

But once Palestinian groups resorted to hijacking for the purpose of hostage-taking, attitudes towards hijacking for any purpose tended to harden, and, in particular, the somewhat jocular view that had been taken of hijackings between America and Cuba in the early 1960s became a thing of the past. In the present climate, any hijacking tends to be labelled an act of terrorism, regardless of its purpose. While passengers are far more conscious of the danger of hijacking than they were in the past, hijackings in fact constitute a far smaller proportion of total commercial flights today than they did prior to the age of terrorism.[38] This is only partly because of the counter-measures that were taken in response to the rash of hijackings by Palestinian groups in the late 1960s and early 1970s, when aircraft hijackings reached their peak. More fundamentally, it reflects the exponential growth in air traffic.

The current view of what the term 'terrorism' encompasses has not merely affected perceptions of contemporary violence. It has also started to change the perception of violence in the past. Thus, articles and chapters in books have begun to appear on the subject of terrorism in the 1950s and the first half of the 1960s that refer to acts of political violence that had not been called terrorism at the time they were committed.[39] Over time this process seems likely to lead to a revision of our picture of the past, and in the long run it may actually undermine the sense that the late 1960s marked a watershed in the employment of political violence, the main basis for the notion of an age of terrorism itself. In this respect, the study of terrorism may end up following a somewhat similar trajectory to that of imperialism. In that case, the very ideas that were applied to analyse the period of formal expansion of empire between 1870 and 1914, the so-called age of imperialism, led economic historians to insist on the importance of the creation of informal empires prior to actual colonial annexation, until eventually it became possible to suggest that the later period was actually one of the crisis of imperialism.[40] The notion that the present period will eventually come to be seen as one of the crisis of terrorism is perhaps a little far-fetched. But at the very least it seems likely that the concept of terrorism, including its absolutist overtones, is going to have an effect on people's view of the past for good or ill.

The ten generalizations that have been examined in this chapter represent some of the more common conclusions to be found in the literature on terrorism. The last three provide useful markers for the discussion of the history of terrorism and will be considered further in the next two chapters. However, while each of the generalizations touches on an aspect of the nature of terrorism in one conception or another, none seems to take us very far towards an explanation of why terrorism occurs, though some provide clues as to the conditions in which it occurs. Furthermore, if one bears in mind which conception of terrorism relates to which generalization, the large element of tautology in some of these propositions is evident.

Thus, given that the media identify terrorism largely with violence directed at stable liberal-democracies of the West, to say that terrorism largely affects societies with the characteristics of Western liberal-democracies is doing no more than identifying current usage of the term. One possible reason for the failure of writers on terrorism to produce more incisive explanations for the occurrence of terrorism may simply be that terrorism, however we choose to distinguish it from other forms of violence, does not represent a single phenomenon and that different explanations of different terrorisms will take us further. This is the task to which we must now turn.

4

Varieties of terrorisms

The onset of the age of terrorism in the late 1960s is often linked in
the literature on terrorism to watershed events in that decade, most
particularly the defeat of Arab states by Israel in the Six-Day War of
June 1967, the death of Che Guevara in October 1967, and the student
revolt in France in May 1968.[1] They provide a convenient starting
point for distinguishing among different terrorisms, though to complete the picture two further events should be added to this list, the
clashes between police and civil rights demonstrators in Londonderry
in October 1968 that marked the start of Northern Ireland's most
recent troubles and, perhaps somewhat less satisfactorily, the failure
of the National Democratic Party (NPD) to gain parliamentary representation in the West German federal election of 1969 after its earlier
success at state level. These events had little in common beyond the
significant fact that each represented a failure or a defeat. That is
self-evident in the first and last cases. Guevara's death was seen as
marking the failure of rural guerrilla warfare in Latin America. Left-
wing parties suffered a crushing defeat in the elections that followed
the May events in France, while the clashes in Londonderry were a
sign of the failure of reform in Northern Ireland.

Admittedly, in none of the cases is there a direct link between the
event and the outbreak of political violence that was seen as marking
the emergence of the age of terrorism. Indeed, it would be difficult to
establish an indirect link between these events and particular groups
that came to be labelled as terrorist or even particular categories of
terrorism. But each of these events was significant in the setting of
the political trends identified with one or other category of terrorism.
The categories of terrorism that can be identified from the five events
are, following the order of events given above: Middle Eastern, Latin
American, New Left, Separatist, and Neo-Fascist. The last three were
generally associated with the industrialized developed world. While
separatist movements resorting to violence existed in Africa and Asia
in this period, their activities played no part in the forging of the

concept of terrorism. Each of the categories will be discussed in turn, but to take account of the tendency of Neo-Fascist terrorism to be paired with New Left terrorism, the last two categories will be taken in reverse order.

Middle Eastern

Violence by Palestinians against Israel did not start in the aftermath of the Six-Day War. It goes back to the very foundation of the state. Further, violence between Arabs and Jews within Palestine, out of which Israel was created, even predates the establishment of the League of Nations mandate over the territory after the First World War. While such violence, especially when it involved attacks on civilians, has been labelled as terrorism in retrospect, it was the actions of right-wing Jewish paramilitary organizations, the Irgun and the Lehi, during their offensive against the British authorities between 1944 and 1948 that were most commonly singled out as terrorism at the time.[2] One incident in particular achieved notoriety throughout the world as an act of terrorism, the bombing by Irgun of the British headquarters in King David's Hotel in Jerusalem on 22 July 1946. Ninety people died in the attack.

The proclamation of the state of Israel by the representatives of the Jewish community on the eve of Britain's departure in May 1948 was followed by an invasion of the territory by Arab armies. Their defeat ensured the new state's survival. Israel's War of Independence was accompanied by a vast movement of population giving rise to the creation of large numbers of Palestinian refugees on the borders of the new state.[3] In the years following the defeat of the Arab states, infiltration of Israel by groups of Palestinians took place on a minor scale. After the revolution of 1952 in Eygpt, the government there took a hand in the organization of infiltration, recruiting Palestinian refugees into units of *fedayeen*. Israel's response to attacks across the country's borders was harsh retaliation. For example, after a grenade attack on a Jewish village killed a woman and two children in October 1953, the Israeli army bombarded and attacked the Jordanian village of Kibya, destroying 40 houses and killing 53 villagers. Ending *fedayeen* raids was one of Israel's principal objectives in the Suez War of 1956.

The Palestinians were slow to develop political organizations that were independent of the Arab states in which the refugees lived. The most significant first step in this direction was the formation of Fatah in 1956–7.[4] It was followed by the establishment of the Palestine Liberation Organization (PLO) in January 1964 at the initiative of the Arab states at a summit of the Arab League in Cairo. While the states claimed that the PLO's creation would allow Palestinians to play a role in the liberation of their own country, they also intended the organization to provide them with a mechanism for exercising control over Palestinian political mobilization. In fact, the PLO came into its own as an organization independent of the states and representative of Palestinian opinion only after the 1967 war. In 1969 Fatah gained control of the Executive Committee of the PLO, and it has dominated the organization ever since, under the chairmanship of Yasser Arafat.[5]

The Six-Day War was a massive blow to the Arab states. Egypt, Jordan, and Syria suffered humiliating defeat on the battlefield and large losses of territory. There was little sympathy for their plight in the West, where the outbreak of the war tended to be blamed on Nasser's brinkmanship. The loss of confidence in the Arab states as agents of their deliverance from Israel prompted Palestinians to rely on their own resources, leading to a flood of recruits into Fatah. At the same time, other, more radical Palestinian organizations sprang up, including the Popular Front for the Liberation of Palestine (PFLP) and the Democratic Popular Front for the Liberation of Palestine (DPFLP).[6]

In the year following the Six-Day War, Palestinians launched a number of attacks across Israel's enlarged borders. They achieved relatively little success, while prompting ferocious retaliation by Israel against neighbouring states, especially Jordan. Fatah gained considerable prestige throughout the Arab world by inflicting heavy losses on an Israeli force raiding its base at Karameh in Jordan in March 1968, but it was soon apparent that the conditions did not exist for the establishment of guerrilla warfare within the territories Israel had occupied as a result of its victory in the Six-Day War. The Palestinians' political and military weakness, coupled with their strong sense that they had been let down both by the Arab states and by the world at large, provided the impetus for the adoption of new tactics in the conflict with Israel, as did the desire of the new organizations to outflank rivals in proving their revolutionary credentials. On 23 July 1968 three members of the PFLP hijacked an El Al jet en route from Rome to Tel Aviv and forced it to land in Algiers. After protracted negotiations, leading to Israel's agreeing to free 16 Palestinians imprisoned for infiltration, the plane and its passengers and crew were released. While hijacking of airliners was not a new tactic, hijacking for the purpose of seizing hostages was.

The enormous impact of this first hijacking in drawing the attention of the outside world to the plight of the Palestinians while also extracting concessions from the Israeli government prompted a rash of further hijackings over the next four years. In August 1969 a

Trans World Airlines jet en route to Tel Aviv was hijacked by the PFLP and forced to fly to Damascus. The plane was destroyed and two Israeli passengers were exchanged for 13 Syrian prisoners in Israel. In September 1970 four planes were hijacked by the PFLP: a Swissair jet, a Pan Am jet and a TWA jet, all en route to New York from different European cities, and a BOAC jet en route to London from Bombay. Three of the planes were forced to land in Dawson's Field, a Second World War airfield in the Jordanian desert, where they were eventually blown up. The fourth was destroyed at Cairo airport. The passengers held hostage at Dawson's Field were released in exchange for Palestinians imprisoned or being held in custody in West Germany, Switzerland, and Britain.[7]

The new threat that hijackings represented to air travellers, who were by and large from peaceful and politically stable Western societies, previously untouched by events in the Middle East, gave a further international dimension to the Arab–Israeli conflict. To the potential danger of confrontation between the super-powers as a result of the conflict was added the further threat of spill-over of violence from the continuance of the conflict. But if the initial effect of the hijackings was to generate an awareness of Palestinian grievances, the persistence of the threat and the involvement of Palestinians in other, bloodier acts of violence in and outside of Israel cemented the identification of the Palestinian cause with terrorism. Among the actions that brought notoriety to the Palestinian cause in the early years of the age of terrorism were a PFLP car-bomb that killed 12 people in Jerusalem in November 1968; the destruction of a Swissair plane in February 1970 by a mid-air explosion with the loss of 47 lives, with suspicion falling on a Palestinian group, though its guilt was never proved; the ambush of a school bus in Israel in May 1970, in which nine pupils and three teachers were killed; an attack on Lod airport in Israel in May 1972 by three members of the Japanese United Red Army acting in association with the PFLP, resulting in the deaths of 28 people, 16 of whom were Puerto Rican pilgrims; and in the autumn of 1972 the attack on the Israeli quarters at the Munich Olympics by Black September, in which a total of 17 people died, including the five perpetrators.[8]

The Black September Organization had come into being following Jordan's bloody expulsion of the PLO that began in September 1970. Jordan's action was itself prompted by the impact on the society of persistent Israeli raids against Palestinian commandos employing Jordan as a base for their operations. Initially, Black September had directed its attacks at representatives of the Jordanian government. For example, it was responsible for the assassination of the Jordanian prime minister in Cairo in November 1971. But while the connection between Israeli retaliation and the establishment of Black September was indirect, the ferocity of Israel's response to violence directed against it, whether at home or abroad, in general tended to act as a spur rather than a deterrent to Palestinian violence.

Following the first attacks on El Al planes in 1968, Israel launched a commando attack on Beirut airport in December 1968 which destroyed 13 civilian planes belonging to three Arab airlines.[9] In the short term, such action simply served to validate the political effectiveness of the Palestinians' actions against civilian airliners, creating the basis for cycles of violence. In the longer term the destabilization of the political system in Lebanon as a result of the spill-over of the conflict between Israel and the Palestinians itself became a potent new source of violence emanating from the Middle East. The region's association with terrorism was further reinforced by the impact on Lebanon of the 1979 revolution in Iran.

Latin American

As in the case of the Middle East, political violence in Latin America in the late 1960s has to be viewed against the backdrop of a long history of violence and instability. From this perspective, there is little justification for singling out the late 1960s as a period when the continent was particularly beset by political violence. None the less, events in Latin America in this period did play a part in the development of the idea that the late 1960s constituted the beginning of an age of terrorism. During the first half of the 1960s Latin America had been much influenced by the example of Castro's revolution in Cuba. However, by the time of Che Guevara's death in Bolivia in October 1967, and after the defeat of other rural guerrilla movements in Venezuela, Peru, and Colombia, it was evident that the left could not achieve power in the rest of Latin America by imitating the Cuban model of revolution. One of the commonest explanations for the failure of the Cuban model was the urban orientation of the population.

Influential in arguing the case for urban guerrilla warfare to take account of this reality was the Brazilian Carlos Marighela. His *Handbook of Urban Guerrilla Warfare*, which he completed in June 1969, was translated into a number of languages after his death and had a considerable influence on the New Left in Europe.[10] Marighela broke with the Brazilian Communist Party in 1967 over his advocacy of a violent revolution to overthrow the military dictatorship that had seized power in Brazil by a coup d'état in 1964. He went on to found the ALN (Acao Libertadora Nacional – Action for National Liberation), committed to putting into practice his ideas for urban guerrilla warfare. Marighela was killed in an ambush in November 1969 in the wave of police activity that had followed the kidnapping by the ALN of the American ambassador to Brazil, Charles Elbrick, in September 1969. Elbrick was released in return for the freeing of 15 prisoners, who were flown to Mexico where they were granted political asylum. In the course of 1970 the Japanese Consul-General in Sao Paulo, the West German ambassador, and the Swiss ambassador were all kidnapped and released, in exchange for a total of 115 prisoners.

The targeting of diplomats was a feature of urban guerrilla campaigns in a number of other Latin American countries. In Uruguay the most well-known of the Latin American urban guerrilla movements, the Tupomaros (named after an eighteenth-century Inca resistance leader), kidnapped the British ambassador, Geoffrey Jackson, in January 1971. He was released nine months later, after over a hundred Tupomaro prisoners escaped from jail. At a lower level, the honorary British consul in Rosario in Argentina, who was also the manager of a local meat-packing plant, was kidnapped in May 1971 by the ERP (Ejercito Revolucionario Popular – People's Revolutionary Army). He was released after a week in captivity following the distribution of food to the poor in Rosario. More commonly, the ERP targeted the executives of multinational companies. The executive president of Fiat in Argentina was killed after being kidnapped by the ERP in March 1972. In March 1970 the West German ambassador to Guatemala, Count Karl von Spreti, was kidnapped by members of FAR (Fuerzas Armadas Rebeldes – Rebel Armed Forces). He was killed after the Guatemalan government refused to meet the kidnappers' demands for the release of prisoners. The refusal provoked strong protests from the West German government.[11]

The kidnapping of diplomats and foreign businessmen was the principal reason for the attention the urban guerrillas of Latin America received in the Western media. It was also the main reason for their characterization as terrorists.[12] However, the political context of these groups' violence varied very considerably, as a brief comparison of events in Brazil, Argentina, and Uruguay will make clear. The ALN in Brazil launched its campaign of violence against the military dictatorship in 1968. The beginning of the campaign, consisting of bombings against property and bank robberies, coincided with a wave of student protests provoked by the death of a student at the hands of the police during a demonstration in Rio de Janeiro. It followed the failure of attempts in 1967 to establish rural *focos* (nuclei) on the Cuban model as a basis for opposition to the regime.[13]

An early victim of the campaign was an American army officer, Captain Charles Chandler, shot dead outside his home in Sao Paulo in October 1968. But it was through the kidnapping of diplomats that the ALN and other minuscule groups operating in the urban areas of Brazil achieved their greatest impact. The seizure of a radio station in Sao Paulo and the broadcast of a speech by Marighela in August 1969 provided another high point of a campaign that began to fizzle out towards the end of 1971. The campaign had coincided with the most harshly repressive phase of military rule in Brazil between 1964 and 1985. Torture played an important role in crushing the campaign of the urban guerrillas, who were also pursued by unofficial vigilante organizations such as a group called the Commando for Hunting Communists. But the political ineffectiveness of the ALN and the other groups, despite their success in attracting world-wide headlines, was also due to their very narrow political base, the fact that they enjoyed little support outside the ranks of student activists.[14]

The political situation in Argentina in the late 1960s was very different from that in Brazil, despite superficial resemblances. Argentina too was under military rule, as a result of a coup d'état in 1966. As in Brazil, earlier attempts to establish rural *focos* had ended in failure. However, the military's hold on power in Argentina was much weaker, and by 1969 it was encountering widespread opposition to the continuance of its rule.[15] Consequently, from the outset, urban guerrilla movements in Argentina both attracted far larger numbers into their ranks and enjoyed more widespread popular sympathy than in Brazil. The largest grouping were the Montoneros, a left-wing nationalist movement that supported the return to power of the exiled former dictator Juan Perón, whom the army had deposed in 1955. It was formed late in 1969. The other main urban guerrilla movement was the Marxist ERP, which was founded in June 1970. Kidnappings netted the two organizations large sums of money with which to sustain their activities. In March 1971 the military government conceded defeat by announcing that it would hand the country over to civilian rule. In March 1973, the Perónist candidate Hector Campora was elected president. After 50 days in power he stood down to clear the way for Juan Perón's return to power. Perón duly achieved an overwhelming victory in the presidential election in September 1973. He died less than a year later in July 1974, and was succeeded by his widow Isabel.

The Montoneros suspended their campaign of violence during 1973 and 1974, though politically they soon found themselves at odds with Perón. However, the ERP continued its campaign throughout the period of transition to civilian government. There were 58 political murders during the course of 1973; 110 in 1974.[16] One factor in the escalation of violence was a violent right-wing response to the continuation of left-wing violence. The best-known of the right-wing paramilitary groups was the Triple A (Alianza Anticommunista Argentina – Argentine Anti-Communist Alliance). It had close links with the government and the police. After Isabel Perón was inaugurated as president, the Montoneros resumed their campaign of violence in response to 'aggression by police and para-police groups against the people's forces'.[17] This led to a further sharp escalation in the level of violence and particularly of political assassinations. The victims included not just politicians and journalists but rank-and-file trade unionists, teachers, and priests. To add to the government's difficulties, the economy was beset with rampant inflation, while production was stagnant. In March 1976 the military took power in a coup d'état. Military rule put an end to the activities of the urban guerrillas in the so-called dirty war between 1976 and 1979, in the course of which approximately 10–12,000 people 'disappeared'.[18] After defeat in the war with Britain over the Falkland Islands in 1982, the military once more returned the country to civilian rule.

Unlike Brazil and Argentina, Uruguay was a liberal-democracy in the late 1960s, though it was a democracy going through a severe crisis. Student unrest in 1968 had resulted in the suspension of the constitution and the declaration of a state of emergency. The crisis was partly political: Uruguay's antiquated two-party system had become unresponsive to public opinion. It was also partly economic: the country had been suffering the economically depressing impact of a large deterioration in its terms of trade with the outside world during the 1960s. The Tupomaros were formed in 1962. However, they only became active as urban guerrillas on a regular basis in 1968. To begin with, they cultivated a Robin Hood image by distributing the proceeds of supermarket and bank robberies to the poor. As a consequence, they succeeded in attracting a measure of public support. This was reflected in the support the Tupomaro-backed Broad Front attracted in the elections of November 1971, when the Front won 18 per cent of the vote, though this was less than the Tupomaros, who had suspended operations during the campaign, had hoped for.

In October 1969, in an operation intended to mark the second anniversary of Che Guevara's death, the Tupomaros took over the small town of Pando. The killing of three of the guerrillas by the police after they had surrendered and the torturing of others contributed to a bitter conflict between the Tupomaros and Uruguay's security forces. In 1970 an American adviser to the Uruguayan police was kidnapped and murdered. However, the highpoint of the conflict was in 1972. In April the Tupomaros killed three security officials whom they had identified as members of a state-supported death squad. The killings were followed by the declaration of a state of war by the government. In the next three months over a hundred members of the Tupomaros were killed and there were several hundred arrests by the security forces. By the time the military seized power in July 1973, the Tupomaros had already been virtually destroyed. A period of harshly repressive military rule followed, giving Uruguay the highest political-prisoner-to-population ratio in the world.[19] In the mid-1980s civilian rule was restored.

Of these three Latin American cases, only the Brazilian fits the notion of terrorism as low-level conflict. In both the Argentinian and Uruguayan cases, the situation verged on civil war. Further, in these two cases, attacks on foreigners were a very small part of the overall conflict, though it was this aspect of the insurgents' activities in all three cases that led to their being labelled terrorists internationally. But it was not the only reason why they were so labelled. Another was the nature of urban guerrilla activities, particularly in contrast to rural guerrilla warfare. Because there could be no question of establishing liberated zones in the urban areas outside the context of a full-scale revolution or civil war, the activities of urban guerrillas were necessarily clandestine. In particular, there was no possibility of establishing a *foco* in the city, which is why Castro and Guevara saw the city as the graveyard of the guerrilla.[20] From the outset the image of the urban guerrilla was of a person in a mask, a man or woman who was on the run. This contrasted unfavourably with the image of the rural guerrilla as a member of a large peasant army, carrying weapons openly and defending territories that had been liberated from security forces often less disciplined in the use of force than the guerrillas themselves.

If this image tended to romanticize the nature of rural guerrilla warfare, the very fact that such warfare seemed to pose no conceivable threat to ordinary Western citizens, whatever the concerns of Western governments, inevitably reinforced the rather benign attitude taken towards such warfare, despite the immense toll it took in lives. During the 1980s Western governments, as the sponsors of rural guerrilla warfare in a number of countries, such as Afghanistan, themselves came to develop a stake in the view that rural guerrilla warfare constituted a legitimate form of armed struggle, at least in certain circumstances. In particular, support for anti-communist insurgencies was a central feature of the Reagan Doctrine.

The view that there were fundamental differences between rural guerrillas and urban guerrillas was not without justification. Firstly, without a serious breakdown of the government's authority and widespread popular disaffection at least in the areas where the guerrillas established their operations, rural guerrilla warfare was unlikely to prove sustainable. Such exacting political preconditions did not apply to the covert acts of violence undertaken by urban guerrillas. Secondly, the relationship between means and ends was much clearer and more direct in the case of rural guerrilla warfare. It was to displace the government in the rural areas as a first step to the replacement of the whole political system.

The political rationale for the operations of urban guerrillas was much less straightforward. Thus, Marighela suggested that one of the objectives of the urban guerrilla was to prepare the ground for rural guerrilla warfare.[21] He is also associated with the view that urban guerrillas, by provoking reprisals from the authorities, could act as a catalyst for popular revolution. In his *Handbook of Urban Guerrilla Warfare*, Marighela argued that once the population took the activities of the urban guerrilla seriously his success would be assured.

> The government can only intensify its repression, thus making the life of its citizens harder than ever: homes will be broken into, police searches organized, innocent people arrested and communications broken; police terror will become the order of the day, and there will be more and more political murders – in short a massive political persecution. The population will refuse to collaborate with the authorities, so that the latter will find the only solution to their problems lies in having recourse to the actual physical liquidation of all their opponents.[22]

In this way, Marighela argued, the guerrillas would win mass support, paving the way to the overthrow of the dictatorship. It was an argument to which the New Left in Western Europe proved highly receptive, though the political conditions there could hardly have been more different from those that prevailed at the time in Brazil.

New Left

No event is more closely associated with the rise of the New Left in the 1960s than the student revolt in France in May 1968. Since many writers on terrorism also tend to associate the beginning of the age of terrorism with the ideological influence of the New Left, it is not surprising that the events of 1968 have found a place in the literature.[23] Yet, ironically, it is difficult to establish any more direct link between the events of 1968 and forms of political violence associated with terrorism. This is less surprising than it might seem at first sight. Support for revolutionary violence within Western societies was a minority view among adherents of the New Left. What was central to the New Left was rejection not only of the authoritarian structures that had grown up in the West as a result of the Cold War but also of the Soviet model of communism. Associated with this reaction against West and East was sympathy for the Third World and, particularly, for revolutionary figures in the Third World who appeared to offer a radical alternative. But support for anti-imperialist struggles in the Third World did not automatically translate into a belief in the utility of violence within the heartlands of capitalism.

In the decade after May 1968 France, in rather striking contrast to its two largest neighbours, West Germany and Italy, remained largely unaffected by extreme left-wing violence. Admittedly, France was affected to a limited extent in this period by separatist violence, but this posed rather less of a threat to the country's political system than had violence associated with the issue of Algeria at the beginning of the 1960s. Three countries stand out as the main sources of New Left violence during the 1970s, at least in terms of visibility, if not in terms of number of actual incidents. They are West Germany, Italy, and Japan.

As countries the three had quite a lot in common. They had all been (or been part of) fascist dictatorships in the 1930s. They were all defeated in the Second World War. Furthermore, they owed their liberal-democratic institutions in large part to the Western powers that had defeated them. Inevitably, therefore, the legitimacy of their institutions was to some extent bound up with the prestige of these powers, and most particularly with that of the United States of America. This was further underpinned by their subordinate relationship with the United States in foreign policy terms. Even within this framework they had to tread carefully in foreign policy matters so as to avoid raising spectres of the past. Such restraints gave rise to tensions in all three. The development that most obviously affected American prestige adversely during the late 1960s and early 1970s was the war in Vietnam. Opposition to the war played a major role in the rise of the New Left in the United States and many other countries. The obvious exception in this respect was France, and its absence as a factor is perhaps one reason why New Left terrorism did not emerge in the country until the end of the 1970s. Opposition to the war was most likely to spawn a violent fringe in those countries where the presence of American troops appeared to signify the country's subordination to the United States. It was hardly surprising that the principal New Left groups associated with terrorism in the three countries, the West German Red Army Faction (Rote Armee Fraktion), the Italian Red Brigades (Brigate Rosse), and the Japanese

United Red Army (Sekigun), should all at one time or another have carried out attacks on American diplomatic and military personnel.[24]

Hostility towards the United States also took a right-wing, nationalist form in all three countries. The most significant combination of left-wing and right-wing political violence took place in Italy, and the interaction of two categories of terrorism was one reason why Italy was by far the most seriously affected in terms of fatalities caused by political violence.[25] However, because of the domestic orientation of much of Italy's violence and perhaps because its position was not regarded as quite so sensitive in the context of European stability as that of West Germany, Italian political violence generally attracted less attention than the much lower level of violence suffered by West Germany. Why the rather limited violence that took place in West Germany should have raised such alarm is discussed further in Chapter 6. Of the three cases, the Japanese fits closest the thesis of the onset of an age of terrorism in the late 1960s and early 1970s.

The Japanese United Red Army (URA) was formed in September 1969, a radical offshoot from an organization of socialist students.[26] It emerged against the backdrop of two years of widespread and violent student unrest that had closed many of the country's universities. The organization first attracted international attention in March 1970, when nine of its members hijacked a Japan Air Lines plane and forced it to fly to North Korea. It next made an impact outside of Japan with the involvement of three of its members in a massacre at Lod airport in Israel in May 1972, though earlier that year the grisly story of the organization's execution of 12 of its own members in Japan over policy differences had also gained wide coverage.[27] In September 1974 three URA members seized hostages at the French embassy in The Hague. The attack secured the release of a URA member being held at the time by the French customs. All four were then flown to Damascus, Syria. The tactic was repeated with the seizure of hostages at the American consulate in Malaysia in 1975. That led to the freeing of five URA members imprisoned in Japan. In 1977 URA members hijacked a JAL jet to Algiers. After that the activities of the URA became episodic. In its 1987 report on terrorism the State Department estimated the strength of the Japanese Red Army at between 30 and 40.[28]

Neo-Fascist

A feature common to the various New Left groups that engaged in violence in the industrialized countries was their very narrow political base. This is the most obvious difference between these cases and most Latin American groups with similar ideologies. At the other end of the political spectrum, far right or Neo-Fascist groups have also operated at the fringes of popular opinion. Indeed, one explanation of the extreme right's resort to violence has been its lack of success at the ballot box. This is the justification for using the failure of the NPD to achieve parliamentary representation in the West German federal election of 1969 as a peg for discussing the contribution of violence by Neo-Fascist groups to the development of the concept of terrorism. Peter Merkl describes this explanation as the 'fire sale theory' of political violence, applying it to actions of the far right in West Germany after the 1969 election scuppered the NPD's electoral progress.[29]

> The fire of the movement is out and the disappointed militants embark on highly destructive, even suicidal and quixotic actions to rekindle it. But their desperate violence really sullies and cheapens whatever constructive left- or right-wing political ideals and actions may have inspired them before. The turn of a radical political movement in decline to scattershot violence is thus in a sense its final sellout, a fire sale of ruined noble intentions.[30]

Much of the violence of the extreme right in West Germany was directed at foreign workers. Prior to the unification of the two Germanies in 1990, this form of violence was at its peak in the early 1980s. However, the principal act of violence by the extreme right to attract international attention was the bomb at the Munich beer festival in September 1980, which killed 13 people, including its perpetrator. It is the only act of the extreme right in West Germany that one finds included in chronologies of terrorism. But while the perpetrator had once been a member of a Neo-Nazi group, the Defence Sports Group Hoffman, the evidence does not suggest that his action formed any part of an organized right-wing campaign of violence. Merkl compares the incident to such non-political mass murders as the shooting spree by a loner that killed 16 people in Austin, Texas, in 1966.[31]

The country in Europe most seriously affected by Neo-Fascist violence was Italy. Between 1969 and 1986 415 people died in Italy in acts of political violence.[32] Over a fifth of these died in a single incident, the bombing of Bologna railway station in August 1980. The incident was one of several *stragi* (massacres) attributed to the extreme right. The first of these took place in December 1969, when a bomb in a bank killed 17 people in Milan. In the first phase of the right wing's campaign of violence, between 1969 and 1974, the two main Neo-Fascist groups engaged in violence were ON (Ordine Nuovo – New Order) and AN (Avanguardia Nazionale – National Vanguard).

Both groups were formed well before the age of terrorism, ON in 1956 and AN in 1960. Indeed, acts of political violence, including murder, had been a feature of Italian society through the 1950s and the 1960s.[33] But in so far as the resort to *stragi* by the extreme right represented a qualitative escalation in political violence in the country, the Italian experience fits into the time frame of the age of terrorism. Furthermore, the indiscriminate nature of the extreme right's violence epitomized the association that was made between terrorism and the killing of innocent bystanders.

The aim of the Neo-Fascist campaign was to persuade the public through the very climate of insecurity its own violence created to accept the need for authoritarian government.[34] The threat to Italian democracy was magnified by the direct involvement of elements of the Italian intelligence service (SIS) in this strategy of tension.[35] The intermeshing of part of the state establishment with the far right gave right-wing violence in Italy a political seriousness that it lacked elsewhere in the industrialized world. In Latin America there was a similar overlap between elements of the security forces and right-wing death squads. However, the aim in the Italian case was the actual overthrow of the country's political institutions, whereas the role of Latin American death squads was generally directed towards the defence of the *status quo*.

In the late 1970s a new generation of Neo-Fascist organizations appeared, of which the most significant were NAR (Nuclei Armati Rivoluzionari – Armed Revolutionary Nuclei) and TP (Terza Posizione – Third Position). A factor in the growth of Neo-Fascist groups both in this period and earlier was the growing popularity of the Italian Communist Party (PCI) and the possibility that it might get into government through sharing power with the Christian Democrats, the right-wing party that had dominated Italian politics since the end of the Second World War.

Paradoxically, that was also a factor in the growth of left-wing political violence. Elements on the left saw the increasing reformism of the PCI as a betrayal of its revolutionary mission. A number of left-wing organizations committed to the use of violence came into being in the late 1960s and early 1970s against a backdrop of student protest and industrial unrest. The most important of these organizations, the Red Brigades, was launched in Milan in 1970. To begin with, its violence was limited to sabotage and kidnapping of short duration for propaganda purposes. In June 1974 members of the organization killed two party officials in a raid on the Neo-Fascist Italian Social Movement (MSI). The raid followed the bombing of a trade-union rally by the extreme right in which eight people had died. The killing of the two MSI officials represented the crossing of an important threshold. Henceforth, the Red Brigades became an organization ready to justify, and to carry out, the murder of political opponents. It was most active in the years 1978 to 1980, the so-called years of lead.[36]

Leonard Weinberg identified a number of common factors behind the rise of both Neo-Fascist and New Left political violence in Italy. He argued that the sharp contrast between the ideological style of Italian politics and the actual reality of bargaining within the political system was a factor in prompting disgruntlement with the political process. Further, both right wing and left wing could hark back to a time in the relatively recent past of the use of violence against the other. Neo-Fascists harked back to the aftermath of the First World War, when Mussolini's fascists, as they perceived it, saved the country from a communist revolution, while the New Left glorified the actions of the Italian resistance in the final stages of the Second World War. 'Each side', wrote Weinberg, 'has been armed with a historical example of its victory through violence over the other'.[37] The third factor identified by Weinberg was pervasive popular dissatisfaction with the functioning of the Italian state. This was compounded by the hegemonic position of the Christian Democrats within the political system, which had given the party a dominant position in all of Italy's governments since 1945, and by the widespread perception of the political system as the embodiment of a gerontocracy because of the age of the leading figures in government.[38]

Separatist

The final source of political violence in the late 1960s and early 1970s underpinning the perception of the dawn of an age of terrorism was separatist nationalist violence within the developed world itself. Nowhere were political strains over the question of national identity more apparent than in Northern Ireland with the onset of inter-communal violence in 1968 and 1969. But while the situation in Northern Ireland gave rise to the most intractable of all the conflicts within the West over the question of nationality, initially the connection between terrorism and regional nationalism was forged elsewhere. In October 1970 a cell of the FLQ (Front de Libération du Québec – Quebec Liberation Front) kidnapped the British trade commissioner, James Cross, and demanded, among other things, the release of prisoners, money, and the publication of the FLQ's manifesto.

When the Canadian government refused to meet these demands, apart from giving publicity to the manifesto, another cell of the FLQ kidnapped Pierre Laporte, a minister in the provincial government of Quebec. He was murdered after an attempted escape. According to one of the members of the FLQ cell, the motive for kidnapping Laporte was the FLQ's unwillingness to carry out the threat to kill Cross as an outsider to the conflict, and, in fact, Cross was ultimately released in December 1970 in exchange for free passage out of the country for his kidnappers. Laporte's killers were caught and sentenced to long prison terms. In response to these events, the Canadian government enacted draconian emergency measures. These were allowed to lapse at the end of April 1971. Arrests of FLQ members continued during 1972, and by the end of that year the campaign of separatist violence was effectively over.[39]

While the FLQ first gained international prominence as a result of the 1970 kidnappings, its campaign of violence was at its peak in 1968 and 1969. The organization had actually been founded in 1963. Its campaign had begun with bombings against military targets. In all the different phases of its campaign of violence, FLQ actions resulted in the deaths of seven people.[40] While the murder of Laporte produced a strong backlash and a loss of public support for the organization, the main reason for the FLQ's decline seems to have been the success of constitutional separatism in the form of the Parti Québecois (PQ). It achieved an electoral breakthrough with 23 per cent of the vote and second place in the provincial elections in Quebec in December 1970.

PQ's success led to the defection in 1971 of a former leader of the FLQ. He called for the abandonment of violence and the transfer of the struggle to the electoral plane. Ironically, it later transpired that a communiqué supposedly issued by an FLQ cell in response to this call, which urged the continuation of the campaign of violence, was the work of the Royal Canadian Mounted Police and was put out with the intention of creating disunity within the organization.[41] But PQ's success, culminating in its victory in the 1976 provincial elections in Quebec, simply made the FLQ irrelevant. Even the inability of the PQ to carry a referendum in 1980 on its proposal for sovereignty-association for Quebec failed to revive separatist violence.

In retrospect, it is evident that the attention the FLQ received during its brief heyday was utterly out of proportion to the organization's actual political significance. There were other violent separatist organizations in the developed world that posed a far greater threat to their respective central governments. An example was ETA (Euzkadi ta Askatasuna – Basque Homeland and Liberty). ETA was founded in 1959, a militant breakaway group from the youth section of the Basque Nationalist Party (PNV). The PNV itself had been in existence since 1895. After Franco's victory in the Spanish Civil War between 1936 and 1939, Basque culture and Basque nationalism were ruthlessly suppressed as a threat to the unity of Spain. However, by the time of ETA's formation, the situation was beginning to ease somewhat. ETA did not start out with a commitment to pursue its goal of Basque independence by violence. That developed in the mid-1960s, partly as a result of the adoption of the theory that political progress would come through a spiral of action followed by repression leading to further action and partly through the influence of the success of national liberation movements in the Third World.

To begin with, ETA's campaign of violence consisted mainly of acts of sabotage and bank robberies. The first death occurred in 1968, the year from which ETA's campaign is most usually dated. In 1970 a military tribunal sentenced six members of ETA to death in connection with this killing, the assassination of a local security police chief. Franco commuted the sentences after the release of the honorary West German consul in San Sebastian, whom ETA had kidnapped during the course of the trial. The effect of the Burgos trial was to win ETA international attention and to provide a flood of recruits to its cause.[42] ETA's campaign has spanned the last years of Franco's rule to the dictator's death in November 1975, the period of transition to the June 1977 elections, and democratic rule after the 1977 elections to the present day. In fact, the achievement of democratic rule saw an escalation in the level of Basque separatist violence, and it reached a peak in 1980 coinciding with the first elections for the parliament of the Basque autonomous region.[43]

In 1986, the number of deaths attributed by the Spanish government to ETA in all its various manifestations and factions reached 500, making it far and away the most important source of political violence in Spain. In the early years of ETA's campaign, the nature of the Franco regime encouraged sympathy for the organization's cause and inhibited the use of the term 'terrorism' in connection with its campaign. The establishment of democracy has diminished external sympathy for separatist violence in Spain, though democracy has also provided ETA with the opportunity to demonstrate that its activities enjoy substantial, if minority, support among the Basques themselves. For example, in the elections for the Basque regional parliament in 1990, the militant Basque party associated with ETA, Herri Batasuna (HB), won 18 per cent of the vote.[44]

While the chronology of ETA's separatist campaign fits the thesis of an age of terrorism from the late 1960s well, there are other cases that do not. A few separatist campaigns actually preceded the age of terrorism and were over before it began. An example is the campaign by German-speakers in South Tyrol for greater autonomy from Rome.

South Tyrol became part of Italy as a result of the First World War. After the Second World War, the area was promised a measure of autonomy in recognition of the language and culture of its inhabitants. After the failure of the Italian government to meet the expectations of the German-speakers for a new deal, their campaign against Rome took a violent turn in the late 1950s and early 1960s. There were a total of 20 fatalities during the course of the campaign, though for the most part the violence in what was called the war of the pylons was directed against property.[45] The conflict was defused by concessions made by the Italian government to the German-speakers in 1969. However, tensions still existed between Italian- and German-speaking inhabitants of South Tyrol, and these gave rise to minor acts of violence in the area in the late 1980s.[46]

However, the case of South Tyrol was the exception rather than the rule. In many of the peripheral areas of the developed world, there was an upsurge of separatist nationalism in the 1960s and 1970s that coincided with the onset of the age of terrorism. Where such separatist nationalism was accompanied by organized violence, it provided one of the strands in the development of the current concept of terrorism. Two questions arise: why did earlier examples of separatist violence not attract the attention achieved by organizations such as ETA and the IRA in the 1970s and why did violent separatist and/or nationalist movements in the Third World play so little part in the shaping of the concept? Northern Ireland provides a very clear illustration of the issue raised by the first question. In sharp contrast to the onset of the troubles in 1968, the IRA's border campaign between 1956 and 1962 made virtually no impact on the outside world. In regard to the second question, it may be objected that Palestinian groups should be seen as Third World movements, not least because the Palestinian cause has enjoyed such widespread support in the Third World. However, if the Palestinian case can be seen as an exception, it is a partial exception, since Israel, the object of the Palestinians' campaign, was not regarded and did not regard itself as part of the Third World.

An attempt to answer the two questions themselves at this point would take us beyond the scope of this chapter, the purpose of which was simply to identify the different categories of political violence that were forged together in the making of the modern concept of terrorism. What, hopefully, is evident from necessarily brief descriptions of the political context of the various categories of violence is that the development of the concept of terrorism involved the glossing over of considerable differences among these categories. Indeed, it can be argued that there were relatively few points of commonality to be found among the different campaigns. The political aims of the groups and the level of popular support they enjoyed varied very widely. Where they could be compared was in the methods adopted and in the targeting, though to very different degrees, of foreigners. But treating the different campaigns as part of a single phenomenon even exaggerated the similarity of their methods. For example, the hijacking of planes was generally not a feature of the campaigns of either separatist nationalists or Neo-Fascists.

With the passage of time the concept has come to span an even wider field with the arrival of new terrorisms such as Islamic terrorism and narco-terrorism and the extension of the term to some of the conflicts in the Third World. Further, some academics in the field have continued to press for the inclusion of state terrorism.[47] Popular recognition of the extent to which people are terrorized by governments has grown, particularly as a result of the work of Amnesty International.[48] However, confusion among the terms 'terrorist state', 'state-sponsored terrorism', and 'state terrorism' has discouraged use of the last term outside the academic world. But while this extension of the concept was motivated in large part by a desire for more even-handed analysis of the problem of political violence, it has tended to obscure rather than illuminate the foundations of the modern concept. These are examined further in the next chapter, in which the question of the legitimization of the different categories of violence identified in this chapter is addressed.

5

The legitimization of terrorism

Before examining how groups seek to justify resort to organized violence, it is helpful first to consider the reasons why people usually obey the political authorities that rule over them. Five reasons are commonly put forward. Firstly, habit is suggested as a powerful reason for people's day-to-day acceptance of existing political authority. Secondly, the capacity of political authority to provide a framework of security, of law and order, constitutes another motive for accepting existing political authority, whatever its character in other respects. Thirdly, fear of the consequences of disobedience or negative sanctions plays a part. Fourthly, inducements or positive sanctions provide a motive for at least some people in the society to support the regime. Finally, it is commonly argued that people obey political authority because they recognize the legitimacy of its claim to rule over them. The last is also generally seen as the most important reason for people's obedience and consequently the most durable basis for the establishment of stable government in any society.[1] Most of the world's governments today claim that they are legitimate by reason of being representative of the people over whom they rule. While this claim is open to question in the case of many of the world's governments, the fact that the vast majority of governments pay at least lip-service to the notion of popular sovereignty matters politically.

Legitimacy and popular mobilization

If the opposition in any country is able to demonstrate unambiguously that the government does not represent the majority of the population, through, for example, mobilizing large numbers of people on the streets against its rule, the existing government will be placed in jeopardy. There have been some striking examples of the fall of regimes over the last 25 years owing to their failure to match mobilization by opposition groups. The fall of the Shah of Iran in 1979 provides one such example. Attempts by the regime's security apparatus, SAVAK, to orchestrate demonstrations in the Shah's favour failed to reach the scale or intensity of opposition protests against the regime, despite the regime's forceful discouragement of such protests with consequent fatalities among the demonstrators. It was this failure that prompted defections from hitherto loyal armed forces, precipitating the regime's complete collapse.[2]

President Marcos of the Philippines owed his downfall in 1986 not merely to his inability to convince domestic and world opinion that he had prevailed, as he claimed, at the ballot box, but also to 'people's power', which allowed the opposition to control the streets. As in the Shah's case, defections from the armed forces finally put an end to the existing regime's hold on power.[3] But the most dramatic demonstration of the power of popular mobilization to change governments was provided by the events in Eastern Europe in the second half of 1989. In this case the most important factor facilitating the process of change lay outside the individual countries. It was the Soviet Union's disavowal of any intention to intervene to shore up the continuation of any local communist party's monopoly of power. Significantly, the changes in Eastern Europe followed the holding of elections on a competitive basis inside the Soviet Union itself, indicating that Gorbachev's commitment to pluralism was real and not simply rhetorical.

Even governments that have come to power as a result of competitive elections within a liberal-democracy have proved on occasion to be vulnerable to political mobilization on the streets. In particular, the events of May 1968 in France clearly threatened the survival of President de Gaulle's government. However, unlike Marcos or the Shah of Iran, de Gaulle was able to match the mobilization by his opponents by bringing his supporters on to the streets in numbers even greater than they had been able to muster.[4] Popular mobilization against the government should not be confused with popular mobilization over particular policies of the government. In general, the latter does not pose a threat to the existence of an elected government. Indeed, such mobilization may not even prevent the government from carrying through unpopular policies in a particular area of government. Consequently, provided there is little likelihood that the mobilization of opinion over a particular issue will lead to the questioning of its legitimacy, government has little reason to suppress such mobilization. Indeed, it generally has every incentive not to do so, since a policy of suppression, however successful in preventing protest from getting off the ground, will exact some price from the government in terms of loss of legitimacy, whether internally or externally.

However, in some cases the issues over which popular mobilization is taking place may be too closely bound up with the basis of the government's legitimacy to be ignored by the power-holders. Two striking examples of popular mobilization within liberal-democracies being met by attempts at suppression were the response of southern states within the United States to the civil rights movement of Martin Luther King in the early 1960s and the reaction of hardline Protestant opinion, supported by elements in the province's security forces, to the Northern Ireland civil rights movement in the late 1960s.[5] In both cases it was local power-holders who were tarnished by the attempts at suppression, though with some knock-on political effects on the central governments as well.

If government is determined to suppress popular mobilization and provided it has good reason to believe that it can rely on the loyalty of those given the job of putting down by force any manifestation of popular protest, it may prove virtually impossible for the opposition to organize effective demonstrations against the government. An example was the incapacity of the opposition in Panama to sustain street protests against the government's decision to cancel the results of the May 1989 elections.[6] Monitoring of the election by independent entities which indicated that the opposition candidate had achieved a clear victory had ruled out the government's preferred option of rigging the outcome. However, in the end the Noriega government fell, not because of popular mobilization against the regime, but as a result of American intervention in December 1989. Another reason, apart from suppression, why a strategy of popular mobilization may fail is the difficulty of staging mass protests outside urban areas. Where the vast majority of people live in urban areas, this does not present a major obstacle to the strategy. However, in countries in which the majority of the population live in the rural areas, it may be difficult to establish that mass protest in the cities is representative of opinion in the country at large.

A weakness of the pro-democracy movement in China before its suppression by the authorities in June 1989 was the apparent absence of active support for it in the Chinese countryside.[7] In practice, that meant that the Chinese government could consider the option of suppression at a far later stage in the process of political mobilization than could a regime where urban opinion could not be isolated and its significance dismissed. The danger of such isolation explains in part why opposition elements in many Third World countries turn to the countryside in the first place to mount a challenge to the *status quo*. However, unlike the strategy of mass mobilization in the urban areas, which in the right circumstances may succeed in bringing about change non-violently or, at any rate, with a minimum of violence, and which may indeed be able to make play of the opposition's non-violence in the face of provocation and even violence by the government, rural strategies for change almost inevitably involve the use of violence against the agents of the government in the countryside. In other words, they usually take the form of guerrilla warfare. Before examining the political implications of guerrilla warfare further, more needs to be said about how ideas on what constitutes legitimate government have evolved since 1945.

Mobilization against colonial rule

Popular sovereignty as a near-universal basis for the legitimacy of government is comparatively recent. At the beginning of the post-war era and the formation of the United Nations, most of the 175 or so sovereign independent states that currently make up the international political system were colonies of European powers or, in a very few cases, of the United States. However, as the dominant power in the world, the United States opposed the continuation of colonialism after the war. American influence and, more importantly, the increased cost, politically and economically, of sustaining overseas empires persuaded the European powers to embark on a process of decolonization. However, the commitment to decolonize was by no means unconditional. At the outset, the process was selective. In a number of cases the colonial power resisted nationalist demands for independence. The result in most of these cases was violence against the colonial power to force it out.

Portugal alone of the European colonial powers attempted to hang on to the whole of its empire and, apart from Goa, an enclave on the Indian sub-continent which India took over by force in 1961, it succeeded in doing so until the mid-1970s. However, by the mid-1960s the Portuguese were confronted with guerrilla warfare against their rule in their three colonies on the African continent. In the case of the two main European colonial powers, Britain and France, strategic considerations and political commitments were the main reasons why they resisted decolonization in particular cases. Strategic considerations were usually of two kinds. The location of the territory coupled with the existence of military bases provided one of the strategic imperatives for wishing to retain a colony. The ideological orientation of the principal nationalist movement towards communism was another reason why a colonial power might resist decolonization on strategic grounds. The main political factor complicating decolonization was the presence in a number of colonies of white settlers. They were invariably opposed to independence under majority rule, while at the same time their well-being and security was an issue capable of rousing domestic opinion within the metropolitan country itself.

The two cases that caused most difficulty to France were Vietnam and Algeria. Japan's occupation of Indochina during the Second World War had been a major blow to French colonial rule throughout the region, because it destroyed one of the central pillars on which the legitimacy of colonial rule rested, its capacity to provide security for its subjects against external attack. Japan's sudden surrender in August 1945 created a power vacuum in Indochina. This was partially filled by Ho Chi Minh's proclamation of an independent Democratic Republic of Vietnam in September. However, this ran contrary to what had been agreed by the major Allied powers at Potsdam, and in accordance with the decisions made at Potsdam, Nationalist Chinese troops occupied the north of the country, while British troops occupied the south.[8] They were followed by French troops dispatched by the new government of France, intent on making clear its determination to re-establish colonial rule in Vietnam. This was to prove beyond France's power.

Between 1946 and 1954 the Viet Minh, nationalist forces loyal to Ho Chi Minh, fought a guerrilla war against French colonial rule. For the French, defeat at Dien Bien Phu in May 1954 was the final straw. It was quickly followed by the French government's agreement to independence for all the countries of Indochina. However, in Vietnam's case the country was partitioned between north and south, with the communist Viet Minh in control of the north. American determination to prevent the south from falling under communist rule resulted in their costly and unsuccessful intervention in Vietnam as they took over the defence of the fragile political entity France had created in the south of the country to deny the Viet Minh total victory.

The fusing together in Vietnam of social revolution and anti-colonial nationalism helped to establish a political formula, en-capsulated by the concept of national liberation, that was to prove immensely influential not just in the Third World but in the First World as well. Many of the violent movements that appeared in the First World in the late 1960s and early 1970s proclaimed national liberation as their aim. This was especially true of separatist groups. In fact, they frequently incorporated the term 'national liberation', or its equivalent in an apposite language, in their name.[9]

Vietnam was by no means the only example of the success of the idea of national liberation in the Third World. As significant in establishing the influence of the concept was the war in Algeria, France's other major colonial confrontation. France's reluctance to grant independence to Algeria stemmed from the presence in the colony of a million white settlers. The result was a protracted confrontation with nationalists from the colony's Muslim majority organized in the FLN (Front de Libération Nationale – National Liberation Front). It began in November 1954 with the launch of a guerrilla campaign by the FLN and ended with the country's independence in July 1962. But whereas Vietnam was unambiguously identified with the success of tactics of rural guerrilla warfare (despite the role of conventional forces in the latter stages of the conflict), rural guerrilla warfare was seen as only one component of the Algerian war.

In particular, the battle of Algiers in 1956 and 1957, when the FLN carried out an urban bombing campaign in the country's capital, exerted a powerful influence on perceptions of the war, as did the bombing campaign in 1961 and 1962 of the pro-settler OAS (Organisation Armée Secrète – Secret Army Organization). The consequence has been to identify the war in Algeria with the use of 'terrorism', an association reinforced by the intercommunal character of much of the violence that occurred during the war.[10] By contrast, the term 'terrorism' has rarely been applied to any phase of the conflict in Vietnam.[11] This has little to do with perceptions of the legitimacy of the parties, since the FLN enjoyed far wider support in the international community for the cause of Algerian independence than the Vietnamese communists were ever able to attract to their cause.

Before turning to cases in which Britain faced violent anti-colonial campaigns, the problem France still faces in the Pacific territory of New Caledonia should be mentioned. While the issue of New Caledonia could not begin to give rise to the difficulties France encountered in Vietnam and Algeria, if only because the total population of New Caledonia is barely 150,000, the near-equality in size of the indigenous and the settler populations, with neither constituting a majority of the population, makes the problem as politically intractable as any that France has encountered in its overseas territories. Indeed, the intractability of the situation prompted British newspapers to compare New Caledonia to Northern Ireland.[12] Tensions between the local Melanesians, known as Kanaks, and the French settlers or Cadoches had grown during the 1970s. These led to violence between the two communities in 1984 and 1985, prompting the French government to declare a state of emergency.

The immediate cause of the violence was Kanak opposition, organized through the FLNKS (Front de Libération Nationale Kanak et Socialiste – Kanak Socialist National Liberation Front), to the holding of a referendum on independence. There was further violence involving the FLNKS in the run-up to France's presidential election in

1988, making New Caledonia an issue in the campaign. The conservative candidate for the presidency, Prime Minister Jacques Chirac, approved the use of force to rescue hostages held by members of the FLNKS. He hoped to boost his chances of election by this demonstration of his commitment to strong action against terrorism. Following the return to power of the French Socialist Party in June 1988, a compromise agreement was reached between the FLNKS leader, Jean-Marie Tjibaou, and the leader of the settlers, entailing the division of the territory into three self-governing provinces and the postponement of a referendum on independence to 1998. The agreement survived Tjibaou's murder in 1989.[13]

Britain and decolonization

Violence played a prominent role in the transition to independence of five British colonies: Malaya, Kenya, Cyprus, Aden, and Southern Rhodesia. In the last case, nearly 20,000 people died in a guerrilla war lasting seven and a half years.[14] However, the war did not involve the colonial power directly. In fact, it began several years after the settlers had unilaterally declared independence to resist evolutionary progress towards majority rule. The situation in Malaya bore some similarities to that in Vietnam. As in that case, Japanese occupation was a crippling blow to the legitimacy of colonial rule. As in Vietnam, communists played a leading role in the organization of resistance to the Japanese. However, in Malaya guerrilla warfare against the colonial power did not commence immediately after the defeat of the Japanese, though soon enough afterwards to owe much to the networks established during the war. The Malayan Communist Party (MCP) launched its offensive against the colonial power in 1948. In June of that year the colonial authorities imposed a state of emergency. It was lifted only in 1960, three years after Malaya became independent in 1957. However, the insurgency had effectively been defeated by the end of 1955. The main reason for the failure of the MCP's campaign was its inability to attract significant support outside the ethnic Chinese community, which formed a minority of the country's population.[15]

The presence of a small but economically and politically powerful community of white settlers constituted the main obstacle to a peaceful transition to independence in Kenya. The Mau Mau insurgency, which began in 1952, was a product of agitation over the land question, aggravated by demographic pressures in the African reserves, and of African nationalist demands for political rights that Britain was reluctant to grant because of settler opposition. The settlers rather than the colonial authorities formed the main target of the Mau Mau campaign, though, in practice, the actual number of white farmers killed in the course of the campaign was very small, particularly in comparison with the casualties among the African population.[16] A state of emergency was declared from the outset and British troops were dispatched to the colony. A significant effect of their arrival was to weaken the political bargaining power of the settlers, since it underlined their dependence on the colonial power to maintain law and order. After the troops had brought the insurgency under control, the British government introduced political reforms. The state of emergency was lifted in 1960 and elections conceding the principle of African majority rule were held in 1961. By the time that independence was granted in 1963, the country's prime minister was Jomo Kenyatta, the African nationalist leader whom the colonial authorities had held responsible for the Mau Mau rebellion and had imprisoned throughout the emergency.

In Cyprus the British colonial authorities faced not a campaign for independence but a demand from the island's Greek majority for union with Greece that was fiercely opposed by the Turkish minority. While the Turkish minority constituted only 20 per cent of the population, the island's proximity to Turkey made its wishes politically impossible to ignore. However, the possibility of ethnic conflict was of secondary importance in Britain's reluctance to withdraw from Cyprus, which was principally due to the strategic importance Britain attached to the military bases it maintained on the island. This was underlined by an ill-considered ministerial statement in 1954 that Britain would never give up sovereignty for this reason.[17]

By the end of 1955, Britain faced a guerrilla war against colonial rule. A state of emergency was declared in November 1955, and in March 1956 the leading figure in the Greek campaign for *enosis* (union with Greece), Archbishop Makarios, was deported. The driving force behind the insurgency was EOKA (Ethniki Organosis Kyprion Agoniston – National Organization of Cypriot Fighters). Its campaign was a mixture of classical guerrilla warfare, conducted from the Troodos mountains, and covert operations, including bombings in the towns. A further dimension of the conflict was intercommunal violence between Greeks and Turks. After a ceasefire by EOKA at the end of 1958, Makarios as the leader of the Greek Cypriots accepted a compromise solution whereby Cyprus became an independent state in 1960 with special constitutional guarantees for the Turkish minority, while Britain retained two military bases on the island. Makarios became the first president of the new state.

The conflict in Aden arose out of Britain's desire to retain a naval and air base it had built at a port that had once formed a key link in the defence of the British empire east of Suez. While decolonization had reduced Aden's importance in this respect by 1960, Britain still wished to maintain a strategic role in the Indian Ocean, and it had significant economic interests in the Arabian peninsula that it wished to protect. With demands for decolonization growing, Britain attempted to shore up its position in Aden through the creation of the Federation of South Arabia. This attached Aden to conservative sheikhdoms that looked to Britain for their protection. The arrangement was designed to provide a way of justifying Britain's continuing presence in Aden itself. Resentment at Aden's inclusion in the federation provided the impetus for the establishment in 1963 of the National Liberation Front (NLF). The British colonial authorities declared a state of emergency in December of that year after an attack on the High Commissioner.

A sustained campaign of urban guerrilla warfare against the British presence followed. A notable feature of the campaign was the active support the insurrection received from the city's residents.[18] In this respect, the campaign was very different in character from the urban guerrilla campaigns of groups such as the Tupomaros and the Montoneros in Latin America. A complicating factor in the situation was division in the ranks of the nationalists with the formation of the Front for the Liberation of Occupied South Yemen (FLOSY) in 1966. However, like the NLF, FLOSY was committed to the violent expulsion of the British from Aden. Mutiny by the Aden Armed Police in 1967 graphically demonstrated the strength of hostility to continuing British rule. By this time, Britain had abandoned any intention of maintaining a military presence in the federation after independence, but too late to save the federation. In November 1967 Britain withdrew unilaterally from Aden. The NLF emerged as the dominant force in the territory and set up the People's Democratic Republic of Yemen.

Violence played a more minor role in the path to independence in many other countries. In these as in the cases described above, the colonial powers fiercely contested the political legitimacy of those who resorted to violence against colonial rule. Indeed, only towards the very end of the process of transition did the colonial powers concede that the principle of decolonization had near-universal applicability. As long as they intended to maintain colonial rule in significant cases, they were bound to defend the legitimacy of colonial rule as a general principle, both to justify their presence in those territories and to counter the claims to legitimacy of any anti-colonial forces they faced. Consequently, during the process of decolonization itself there was little disposition on the part of the colonial power to validate anti-colonial movements by acknowledging that they enjoyed popular support. This was especially the case where an anti-colonial movement resorted to violence against colonial rule. Thus, it was common for successful nationalist leaders to be dismissed by the colonial authorities as political extremists out of touch with opinion in their own community, before the actual process of transition to independence began. Where violence formed a component part of the struggle for independence, the leaders of the nationalist movement were likely to be anathematized as terrorists by the colonial authorities, as happened to Makarios in Cyprus and Kenyatta in Kenya.[19]

The most effective way for nationalist movements to counter such propaganda was through action that demonstrated to the outside world the extent of their popular support. Covert actions such as bombings and assassinations that did not depend on the existence of popular support for the nationalist cause were of little value from such a perspective. Consequently, whatever value such actions might have in the overall context of a violent campaign, their political value in terms of demonstrating the legitimacy of the nationalist cause was limited. It is therefore not surprising that covert actions of the armed propaganda type that anarchists pioneered during the nineteenth century played relatively little part in the colonial conflicts of the 1950s and 1960s. However, at the end of the colonial era which was reached in the late 1960s with the completion of the process of decolonization in most areas of the world, the logic of the situation changed fundamentally.

Once the process of decolonization was more or less complete, virtually everyone, and not least the former colonial powers themselves, had an interest in the legitimization of the new post-colonial order. That even entailed the support by the former colonial powers of nationalist leaders who had once taken up arms against them. In the case of Britain the acceptance of the leaders once anathematized as terrorists was signalled by the ritual of tea with the Queen. In the short term this reversal of attitudes tended to rob the term 'terrorist' of some of its sting, since it created a precedent for the transformation of former terrorist leaders into statesmen and of former terrorists into freedom fighters.

Self-determination

For the leaders of the newly independent states themselves, often presiding over fragile political systems and faced with a revolution of rising expectations, it was vitally important that there should be no question-mark over their position as rulers. Shoring up their position involved glorifying the anti-colonial struggle and their role in it. It also entailed the representation of colonial rule as not just a fundamental denial of the principle of self-determination, but an affront to the human dignity of the people ruled over. Henceforth, colonial rule was presented as illegitimate in principle. The logical corollary of this proposition was that violence directed at the overthrow of colonial rule and at enabling the people to exercise their right to self-determination was legitimate. Since the former colonial powers themselves had a stake in the stability of the new post-colonial order, both because they still had significant economic interests in their former colonies and because the new order could be presented as a testimony to the success with which they had managed the process of decolonization, there was little disposition on their part to contradict such propositions. The new international consensus on the interpretation of the principle of self-determination was incorporated in the 1970 *Declaration of Principles of International Law concerning Friendly Relations and Co-operation among States in accordance with the Charter of the United Nations.*[20] It was passed by the United Nations General Assembly without a vote under a special 'consensus' procedure which reflected unanimity or near-unanimity among the members and which gave extra legal authority to resolutions adopted under it.

The declaration placed a duty on every state to refrain from any forcible action that deprived people of their right to self-determination. It proclaimed that those seeking to exercise their right to self-determination had not merely the right to resist but the right to seek external assistance for their struggle. While the declaration allowed for the possibility that people might not seek to exercise their right to self-determination through the creation of an independent state, it insisted that the option of independence should remain available to any territory that did not form an integral part of an existing sovereign independent state. The right of secession from such a state was explicitly denied. The world the declaration envisaged was one that would be wholly made up of sovereign independent states, equal in status, and possessing permanently fixed boundaries. By implication, the declaration attached a presumption of illegitimacy to any political arrangement that stood in the way of the achievement of such a world. It was made clear in the declaration that 'the people' entitled to self-determination should be interpreted simply as the will of a majority of the population living within a particular territory. In practice, there remained considerable scope for argument over how this seemingly clear-cut principle should be applied in particular cases. And in any event, the restriction of the right of self-determination to territorial majorities was contestable.

For the most part, the declaration simply represented a *post hoc* endorsement of the new order that had been created as a result of decolonization. However, there were a few situations in which its implications were more radical. In particular, it gave added international legitimacy to the struggles against white minority rule in southern Africa and against Portuguese colonial rule. In this context, neither Portugal's redefinition of the terms of its rule by proclaiming its overseas territories provinces nor South Africa's claim that it was implementing the principle of self-determination through the creation of independent homelands cut much ice internationally. At the same time, the dawning of the post-colonial order did not make an immediate practical difference to the situation in southern Africa or in other parts of the Portuguese empire. By this time, guerrilla warfare was taking place in all of Portugal's territories on the African continent. It had also begun in South West Africa. In these territories, the form that the anti-colonial struggle would take had already been determined. In South Africa and in Rhodesia, the form of African nationalist opposition to white rule still remained to be determined. At this point (the end of the 1960s and the beginning of the 1970s), no serious challenge existed to the continuation of white rule.

While white minority rule in southern Africa and the Portuguese empire stood out as the most obvious examples of political arrangements that violated the international community's interpretation of the norm of self-determination, the end of the colonial era created opportunities for the exposure of other situations as anachronistic or anomalous in a post-colonial world. However, their exposure depended on those opposed to the *status quo* being able to seize the moment to attract the attention of the world to their particular cause. At the same time, the logical implication of the propositions that colonial rule was illegitimate in principle and that violence directed at its overthrow was justified was that it was sufficient to define a situation as colonial to provide a justification for violence directed at the overthrow of the *status quo*. In particular, groups committed to the use of organized violence were freed from the imperative of demonstrating mass support for their actions as a way of legitimizing their activities.

However, the disappearance of this imperative proved a distinctly double-edged development for the remaining anti-colonial movements. Groups with a very narrow or even non-existent popular base could grab the headlines through covert acts of violence that could be justified as striking a blow against colonialism and thereby outflank well-established anti-colonial movements with long records of organizing opposition to the colonial power. Such tactics tended to devalue the currency of anti-colonial violence in general. There was the further danger that a conflict fought at the level of covert action would favour the state, since almost all states had agents trained in appropriate skills for such a campaign.

After colonialism

Most nationalist movements in the post-colonial age faced another difficulty. This was to secure international acceptance of the proposition that the situation they faced was a colonial one. Given the link that had been established between the existence of colonial rule and the justification of political violence, it was hardly surprising that there should be considerable reluctance for any but the most clear-cut cases to be defined as examples of colonial rule. In this context a further factor intervened. While the passing of the colonial era marked the end of an age of formal, constitutional domination of much of the Third World by major Western powers, it did not usher in an era of equality among nations except in the most formal, legal terms. Quite apart from the vast differences in power and wealth among states, the West still dominated the Third World both economically and politically.

It did so in part through its influence over the elites of Third World societies. In this context the leading power was not Britain or France but the United States. For example, although most of the states of Latin America had been independent for more than a hundred years, the United States still exercised a considerable measure of informal control over their political development. Both economic interests and strategic considerations were factors in how this control was exercised. The effect was to align the United States with right-wing and authoritarian elements in societies characterized by extreme inequality in their distribution of wealth and power. In the 1950s the term *gorilas* was coined in Latin America to describe pro-American and extremely right-wing factions within the military.[21]

The ending of colonial rule naturally tended to put a spotlight on other forms of subordination. The contradiction between the claim of the new post-colonial order to embody relationships of equality between states and the reality of the dependence of much of the Third World led inevitably to the questioning of the legitimacy of other forms of subordination. The concept that best encapsulated the existence of non-legal and non-constitutional forms of domination was imperialism. One consequence was a burgeoning of interest in theories of imperialism both in the West and in the Third World. This growth of interest in theories of imperialism itself played a part in a more general intellectual revival of Marxism as a form of analysis, since the most sophisticated explanations of imperialism as a force structuring relationships between the West and the Third World tended to be rooted in Marxism.[22] The issue that gave political resonance to the concept of imperialism in this period was the war in Vietnam.

It provided a striking example of the lengths to which the United States was prepared to go to impose its will on a Third World society. To all but the most blinkered supporters of US policy, the resistance the Americans encountered suggested that their efforts to create an alternative to communist rule enjoyed little popular support in South Vietnam. The lack of legitimacy of American intervention in Vietnam naturally led to a wider questioning of America's role in the Third World. At the same time, the incapacity of the United States to prevail in Vietnam underscored American weakness and vulnerability. In these circumstances, it hardly seemed absurd to suggest that further Vietnams might bring about the collapse of the whole structure of American domination over the Third World.

Violence against imperialism

Further, if violence against colonial rule was justified, it hardly seemed unreasonable to suggest that violence against imperialism was too. Indeed, the obvious inference to be drawn from most theories of imperialism was that it represented a deeper and more fundamental system of domination than the formal structures of colonialism itself. It was therefore a short step in theory to justify violence against imperialism. Thus, nationalists who were concerned primarily with changing formal structures of power through secession from an existing First World state often found it expedient to couch both their demands and their resort to violence against the central state in anti-imperialist terms. Revolt in the peripheries of the First World was another dimension of the questioning of the legitimacy of structures of domination, for the Third World's subordination to the West was not the only structure of domination exposed by the passing of the colonial era.

Hierarchy within the West itself and particularly America's domination of the Western alliance also represented such a structure. It too became a target of the attack on imperialism. Not surprisingly, the notion that the Western alliance itself was a function of imperialist domination proved most persuasive in countries such as West Germany and Japan that had been forced by reason of historical circumstance to play a largely passive and subordinate role within the alliance during the 1950s and 1960s. By contrast, there were few even on the left of the political spectrum in Britain who did not believe that the country's special relationship with the United States was fundamentally the product of free political choice, however much they might have deplored it. This was one reason why Britain was so little affected by organized violence from New Left groups. A group called the Angry Brigade operated briefly in the late 1960s and early 1970s and was responsible for a few, very minor acts of violence, but its political impact was negligible, even within the far left of the political spectrum.[23]

Readiness to resort to political violence in this period did not simply reflect the influence of theories of imperialism on the legitimization of violence. It was also a reflection of the transitional character of the period between a colonial and a post-colonial world. In general, one would expect transition to weaken the effectiveness of a number of the usual restraints on the employment of violence. Habit provides an unpersuasive argument for passivity during a period of change, while the calculation of negative and positive sanctions becomes more uncertain. The turbulence that often accompanies a process of transition also tends to make the argument that the *status quo* provides a framework of security less convincing. At the same time, the supposition during times of transition that anything may be possible, if only the moment is seized, creates a climate conducive to the appearance of groups ready to gamble on the outcome of the use of violence to effect change. Admittedly, these arguments apply with more force to transition at a domestic level than to transition at a global level, as the impact of change at a global level is much more variable in its effect on behaviour at a domestic level. None the less, there seems good reason to connect the onset of the age of terrorism with the transition taking place in world politics during the period of the late 1960s and early 1970s.

Just as the rhetoric of anti-imperialism was used to justify the use of covert violence by a very wide variety of groups with divergent objectives and differing levels of support and in vastly different political contexts, so the concept 'terrorism' was employed to give coherence to a multitude of very different challenges to the *status quo*. However, there was slightly more to the term than simply a useful umbrella under which different strands of contemporary political violence could be included. Firstly, it contained a clear and explicit implication that the violence so described was perceived as utterly and absolutely illegitimate. In effect, it represented the clear drawing of a line between contemporary political violence and the violence of the colonial era. Secondly, the use of the term across Western societies to apply to particular tactics of covert violence, such as hijacking, hostage-taking, and attacks on diplomats, provided an early indication of a consensus in the West not to accord legitimacy to such methods, even if it meant altering previous practice such as the leniency shown in the past to hijackers from Eastern Europe. This consensus still allowed room for disagreement in the West on how the political conflicts giving rise to violence should be dealt with. This was to be most apparent in relation to the issue of the Palestinians. But these differences remained slight compared with the measure of concord there existed to face down the different manifestations of violence that made their appearance under the banner of anti-imperialism in the late 1960s and early 1970s.

Small groups thought they could justify the use of violence by claiming that they were striking a blow against imperialism, but this proved to be a snare. Fighting imperialism was not like fighting colonial rule. In the struggle against colonial rule, the relationship between means and ends was relatively clear. Colonial administrations formed concrete targets. Further, it was clear what the political boundaries of the contest for legitimacy were. In the battle against imperialism, both the relationship between means and ends and its political limits were anything but clear. Grotesque inequality in living standards between the First World and the Third World was a concrete reality, but imperialism as a theory of how such inequality was maintained was an abstraction from that reality. Depending on the theory, virtually anyone or anything could be presented as a legitimate target in the campaign against imperialism. The problem was that for the wider public to accept that such and such was a legitimate target required them to accept the theory. The obsession of groups engaged in covert violence with the propagation of lengthy manifestoes justifying and explaining their actions reflected a recognition on their part that their actions did not speak for themselves.

However, in practice, such manifestoes tended to be written in such abstractly ideological terms as to be incapable of striking a political chord with the wider public. That is still the case. For example, when the Red Army Faction wounded a senior official in the German Ministry of the Interior in 1990, it issued a statement that the attempted assassination was the 'beginning of a long phase of struggle against the newly established Greater German/West European world power'.[24] Further, the very association of such manifestoes with acts of violence provided the public with the strongest possible motive for rejecting any political message they contained. By contrast, violence that tackled the inequality in society directly, such as the actions of the Tupomaros in Uruguay in literally stealing from the rich and giving to the poor, did manage to secure a measure of public understanding and sympathy. But action of this sort was the exception rather than the rule.

Of course, some of the violent groups that incorporated an anti-imperialist perspective in their programmes were also engaged in the pursuit of more concrete nationalist or local political objectives. Indeed, in practice, these objectives often played a more important role in their activities than the abstract battle against imperialism. Such groups were also often able to generate a measure of popular support on this basis. The attraction of putting an anti-imperialist gloss on their campaigns was that it provided a universalist basis on which they could appeal for support in the outside world. However, it also carried the danger of universalizing the basis of opposition to their objectives. This was especially likely to happen if a group acted on its anti-imperialist rhetoric by attacking Western businessmen or diplomats. The publicity that could be gained by such action made it a particularly tempting course to follow. However, association with such attacks also provided part of the explanation as to why separatist and nationalist groups using violence should have attracted the label of terrorist in this period, whereas previously they had not. Attacks on foreign nationals came to be perceived as the essence of international terrorism.

However, the label of terrorism was also applied to violence within the confines of a single political system in a variety of political circumstances, though it tended to be used with least reservation in relation to violence within the context of long-standing liberal-democracies. The next two chapters examine two very different cases of organized violence within a liberal-democratic framework. They provide more specific illustration of the process of the legitimization of terrorism, in the sense both of how groups attempted to justify their use of violence and of how opinion was mobilized against them.

6

On the fringe: political violence in stable democracies

Few organizations have been more closely identified with the concept of terrorism than the RAF (*Rote Armee Fraktion* – Red Army Faction) or Baader-Meinhof group in West Germany. The story of the Baader-Meinhof group itself is easy to summarize. In April 1968, Andreas Baader, Gudrun Ensslin, and two accomplices planted fire bombs in two Frankfurt department stores, timed to detonate at midnight. Their arrest, trial, conviction, and imprisonment on charges of arson followed. In May 1970, during a visit to a library outside prison, Baader was sprung from custody by a group that included the journalist Ulrike Meinhof, an event that in retrospect was seen as marking the birth of the RAF. After a brief sojourn in June at a Palestinian training camp in Jordan, which was arranged through contacts in Fatah, the group returned to West Germany and began its underground activities, in the process attracting new recruits to its ranks.

Much of the early activity of the group consisted of bank robberies. They caused a wave of hysteria through West Germany and a massive police operation to track down the perpetrators. In April 1971 the group published a manifesto, the Concept of the Urban Guerrilla, in the name of the Red Army Faction. It marked the first use of the term to describe the group. The manifesto proclaimed that the strength of the authorities' reaction to the group's activities was a proof of its success. At the same time, it derided chatterers in the fight against imperialism.

The first death to arise out of the group's underground activities occurred in July 1971, when a member of the RAF was shot dead in a shoot-out with a policeman. In October a policeman died when challenging two members of the group. The campaign reached a peak in May 1972, when two US army bases in Frankfurt and Heidelberg were bombed, killing four American soldiers. The bombings were carried out by the RAF in response to the escalation that month of

American military action against North Vietnam, including the mining of Haiphong harbour. In the same month, the RAF bombed the headquarters of Axel Springer's right-wing publishing empire in Hamburg, injuring 17 print workers and office staff. In this case, there were telephone warnings that bombs were about to go off and the building should be cleared, but they were not believed by the telephonists who received them.

The following month saw the arrest of the RAF's leading members. However, it was May 1975 before the main trial of the group on a wide range of charges, including murder, began. The trial reached a conclusion nearly two years later in April 1977, when Baader, Ensslin, and Jan-Karl Raspe were sentenced to life imprisonment. By then two out of the five core figures in the organization were dead. Holger Meins died in the course of a hunger strike in November 1974, while Ulrike Meinhof committed suicide in prison in May 1976 after falling out with other members of the group during the course of the trial. An indication of the conflict within the group was Ensslin's disavowal in court of the attack on Springer's headquarters, an attack with which Meinhof was identified.[1]

Second generation

By the mid-1970s a second generation of the RAF and organizations associated with it, such as the 2 June Movement, had come into being. Much of the violence of the second generation was directed at freeing prisoners or supporting their protests against the conditions under which they were being held. In February 1975, the Christian Democrat candidate for mayor of West Berlin, Peter Lorenz, was kidnapped. His kidnappers identified themselves as members of the 2 June Movement and demanded the release of six prisoners. None of the prisoners the kidnappers listed had been accused or convicted of murder. A statement issued by the kidnappers amounted to an acknowledgement that they had carefully pitched their demands at a level they thought the state was likely to meet. Their calculation proved correct. Five of the six prisoners the kidnappers had named were flown to South Yemen, where they were granted asylum (the sixth prisoner had refused to be part of the arrangement). Lorenz was released.

In April 1975 six people armed with pistols and explosives seized the West German embassy in Stockholm in Sweden, taking 12 hostages in the process. They identified themselves as members of the Holger Meins Commando of the RAF. Their principal demand was the release of 26 prisoners, including the leading figures in the Baader-Meinhof group. It was flatly rejected by the West German government.

By this time the embassy's military attaché had already been murdered. His murder was followed by that of the economic attaché, prompting the Swedish police to make preparations to storm the building. At this point, a series of explosions set off accidentally from within brought the siege to an end. One of the gunmen was killed outright by the explosions. Another died later from his injuries.

Attempts to secure the release of RAF prisoners reached a peak in 1977. In September 1977 the president of the employers' association, Hans-Martin Schleyer, was kidnapped by members of the RAF. The kidnappers outlined their demands in a letter; their principal demand was the release of 11 RAF prisoners, including Baader, Ensslin, and Raspe. In October 1977 further pressure was put on the West German government by the hijacking of a Lufthansa airliner. The central demand of the four hijackers claiming to represent an organization styling itself the Struggle against World Imperialism was, in the words of 'Captain Mohammed', their leader, 'the release of our comrades in German prisons'.[2] 'Mohammed' turned out to be a known member of the Popular Front for the Liberation of Palestine (PFLP). After stops at several airports, the plane ended its journey at Mogadishu in Somalia, where it was stormed by members of GSG9, a special anti-terrorist unit of West Germany's Border Police. Three of the hijackers were killed and the fourth seriously wounded in the operation, which was successful in securing the release of the plane's remaining 86 passengers and crew. At an earlier point in the hijack, the plane's pilot had been murdered by the hijackers. Shortly after the news of the outcome of GSG9's storming of the plane was broadcast, Baader, Ensslin, and Raspe committed suicide. The following day, Schleyer's body was discovered in the boot of an abandoned car in a town in France close to the country's border with West Germany.

The events in the autumn of 1977 did not mark the end of organized violence by the RAF and other groups. Acts of violence by such groups continued through the 1980s. Opposition to the deployment of American Cruise and Pershing missiles was one factor in the revival of organized left-wing violence, with much of it directed at American military personnel or property. Two Americans were killed by a car-bomb in August 1985 in an attack on an American air force base. Prison conditions also continued to provide a focus for mobilization of support for the RAF, with a series of hunger strikes by prisoners through the 1980s. The RAF also attacked prominent figures in West Germany's political and business establishments. A senior foreign ministry official and a director of Siemens were murdered in 1986.

A leading West German banker, Alfred Herrhausen, chief executive of the Deutsche Bank, was killed by a bomb attack on his car at the

end of November 1989. The RAF letter admitting responsibility attacked the wartime record of the Deutsche Bank as justification. It
also demanded that RAF prisoners should be brought together in a
single unit.[3] The campaign continued after German reunification. On
1 April 1991, the RAF shot dead Detlev Rohwedder, the head of the
Treuhand holding company, charged with the task of privatizing East
German industry, at his home in Düsseldorf.[4] However, a year later
the RAF issued a statement to the press, acknowledging that 'we have
not been able to achieve a breakthrough in our combined international
struggle'.[5] The RAF declared that it would cease its attacks on leading
representatives of industry. At the same time, it made a complete end
to its campaign of violence conditional on the release of some prisoners
and free association in one prison for the rest.

The relatively muted reaction in Germany to the RAF's statement
was a reflection of the fact that it had long since ceased to be seen as
a serious threat to the country's political stability. In fact, 1977 was
the turning point in this respect. Stefan Aust, the author of the most
detailed account of the activities of the Baader-Meinhof group, summarized their outcome at that point as follows:

> By the autumn of 1977, sometimes called 'German Autumn', twenty-
> eight people had lost their lives in RAF attacks or shooting incidents.
> Seventeen members of the urban guerrilla movement were dead. Two
> wholly innocent persons had been accidentally shot by the police in the
> course of their investigations. Forty-seven dead: that is the balance of
> seven years' underground fighting in the Federal Republic. They were
> seven years that changed West Germany.[6]

There is relatively little disagreement in the literature about the
basic story itself, notwithstanding inevitable controversy about some of
the details of particular violent events, including the suicides. However,
there is much less agreement about the significance of these events.
Explanations range from full-blown conspiracy theories that treat these
events as part and parcel of a covert war by Moscow against the
Western liberal-democracies to accounts which suggest that the group's
activities were more the product of the personal circumstances of its
members than of their particular political convictions.

Before different explanations are examined, it is useful to consider
what needs to be explained. While it is important that the roots of the
violence itself should be understood, it is perhaps as important in this
case to explain why events that involved relatively few people, whether
as participants or as victims, should have had such an enormous
impact on the political life of West Germany. Indeed, the most
puzzling aspect of the whole story is why the war of 'six against sixty

million', as Heinrich Böll put it in an article at the beginning of 1972,[7] should have caused such political panic. Before considering these wider issues, let us start by looking at the motivation of the principal participants.

Explanations

Klaus Wasmund has argued that personal factors played an important role in the slide into terrorism of the first generation of the RAF, though he also treats the radicalization of the student protest movement during the late 1960s as a factor in the precipitation of political violence. He argues that the act of arson by Baader and Ensslin in 1968 which marked the first step on the path to resort to organized violence was a personal gesture on their part against bourgeois society, though he accepts that it was a politically motivated protest against the Vietnam war and the political situation in West Germany as well. He continues:

> The second step, however, the liberation of Baader with the aid of firearms, was by no means politically motivated but was based on private or personal interests: namely Gudrun Ensslin's desire to free her boy-friend from prison. The political justification for this act was provided much later.[8]

But it was the seriousness of this crime that committed everyone involved in it irrevocably to the underground, though the actual planning of the escape itself had been made hurriedly by a group brought together spontaneously for the purpose by Ensslin. Little thought was given to the possible consequences. In the course of springing Baader from custody, a library official had been shot and seriously wounded, and the day after the escape 'Wanted' posters went up across West Germany with a large photograph of Ulrike Meinhof under the heading of 'Attempted Murder in Berlin' and offering 10,000 DM reward for her capture. According to Astrid Proll, who was a member of the group involved in Baader's escape but who later broke with the RAF,

> It was the first wanted campaign of this kind to be run in post-War Germany. It was an early indication of the tragic pattern of escalation and entanglement in which the state and the faction have been embroiled ever since, and where each has persisted in its illusions about the enemy in order to justify its own merciless actions.[9]

One does not have to accept Proll's implicit equation of the actions of the state with those of the RAF to accept the force of the argument she is putting forward. The demonization of groups such as the RAF meant that once individuals had crossed the threshold of illegality, their prospects of ever rejoining normal society were virtually non-existent. The logical alternative was to escalate their conflict with society, while seeking political rationalizations for their actions. In practice, the extremely exaggerated reaction of the state, which treated their activities as a serious threat to the country's political system, which they never were, simply lent credence to these rationalizations and encouraged more of the same. Once underground, the individual became dependent on the group for survival and subject to its overpowering influence. Even in prison there was no escape, as the isolation imposed upon RAF prisoners, on the grounds of the danger they posed to society, cut them off from other possibilities. The point was actually made in court by Ulrike Meinhof herself.

> How can a prisoner kept in isolation show the authorities, always supposing he wanted to, that his conduct has changed? How? How can he do it in a situation from which every expression of life has already been cut out? The prisoner kept in isolation has only one possible way of showing that his conduct has changed, and that's betrayal.[10]

Wasmund makes much of the importance of group dynamics in his account of the political socialization of West German terrorists.[11] The obvious analogy is with the deviant behaviour of a criminal gang. Much of the behaviour of the RAF fits such an analogy very well: the concern with the survival of the gang, with avenging the deaths of gang members, and the priority given to operations aimed at securing the release of comrades from prison as opposed to action to further RAF's political aims.

Political motivation

But where the Baader-Meinhof group clearly differed from an ordinary criminal gang was in the political motivation of its members, though admittedly RAF's political aims were somewhat vague. Two themes ran through the political pronouncements of the RAF's leading members. They were opposition to American imperialism and the subordinate position of West Germany within an imperialist system and the characterization of the response of the authorities to their activities as fascist. At the trial in 1974 for her part in Baader's escape, Ulrike Meinhof explained the organization's aims as follows: 'The anti-imperialist struggle, if it is to be more than mere chatter, means annihilation, destruction, the shattering of the imperialist power system – political, economic and military'.[12]

This was typical of the RAF leader's bombastic rhetoric and her tendency to speak in generalities which failed to establish any clear relationship between means and ends. At the beginning of 1975 the leading figures in the organization provided written answers from prison to questions from *Der Spiegel*. Asked how they saw the political situation in the Federal Republic of Germany, they replied: 'An imperialistic centre. U.S. colony. U.S. military base. Leading imperialistic power in West Europe, in the EC. Second strongest military power in NATO. Representative of the U.S. imperialistic interests in Western Europe.'[13]

In the same interview they identified themselves as Marxists rather than anarchists. But their Marxism was much more a crude tool of analysis than a guide to the kind of society they wished to see. In particular, there is little evidence to suggest that there was any admiration in the RAF for the Soviet model of government as practised anywhere in Europe. Indeed, on the contrary, the philosophy of action espoused by the New Left with which the RAF identified stood in direct opposition to the political stance taken by orthodox communists. Further, at an early stage they gave up any expectation that their activities might attract support in the West German working class, which they wrote off in Marxist terms as a labour aristocracy. It was among students and marginal groups in society that they looked to recruit supporters, while they identified politically with Third World liberation movements. This was most clearly reflected in the RAF's links with various Palestinian groups.

In the early years of their activities, the RAF placed a great deal of emphasis on the Vietnam war as a justification for their actions. The similarity between American actions in Vietnam and Nazi atrocities was a persistent theme of the defence lawyers during the main trial of the leading members of the first generation of the RAF. Further, the defence attempted to call witnesses who could testify that the American bases in West Germany attacked by the RAF had played an important role in the American war effort in Indochina. However, the judges trying the case ruled consideration of such evidence inadmissible on the ground that the conduct of the Vietnam war was not relevant to the charges the defendants faced.

The issue of the Vietnam war had also played a part in the 1968 trial of Baader and Ensslin for arson. They claimed that they had committed the offence as a protest against indifference to the killing in Vietnam. Their claim then to have acted out of conviction was rejected by the presiding judge because it had taken them seven months to confess to the crime.

Widespread opposition to the Vietnam war, especially among the younger generation of West Germans, was a factor in the popular sympathy that existed for the group when they first went underground. Such sympathy was at its peak after the death of Petra Schelm in a shoot-out with police in July 1971. Ten days after this episode, the Allensbacher Institute of Public Opinion published the results of a poll on public attitudes to the group's activities. Eighteen per cent of the sample accepted the proposition that the group was acting mainly out of political convictions. One in four respondents under the age of 30 admitted to sympathy for the RAF. Five per cent of the sample said they would be willing to shelter wanted members of the group overnight from the police.[14] The poll was a striking indication of the degree of alienation from the political system that still existed at this time in West Germany, despite the fact that a reformist coalition of the Social Democrats (SPD) and Free Democrats (FDP) was in office, having come to power in 1969 with a pledge to introduce greater democracy into all areas of social and political life. The existence of such sympathy also in part explains why the activities of the RAF had caused such political panic in the establishment. However, at this point the RAF had not carried out any acts of premeditated murder. Once this line was crossed, sympathy for the group very quickly evaporated, leaving the RAF with a minuscule political base on the fringe of society.

West Germany in the 1960s

To understand the political roots of the first generation of the RAF, it is necessary to examine the political situation in West Germany before the group went underground. The late 1960s were a period of widespread student unrest in West Germany, as they were elsewhere in the industrialized world. In West Germany's case, conflict between the generations was a particularly important aspect of the unrest, exacerbated by the suspicion with which the post-war generation viewed their parents' record during the Nazi era, usually at best passivity and at worst complicity. The fact that former members of the Nazi Party were to be found in prominent positions in the liberal-democratic structures of the Federal Republic was a contributory factor to alienation from the political system among the younger generation. Questioning of the authenticity of the country's conversion to liberal-democracy was by no means confined to the young of left and right in West Germany. That democracy had shallow roots in West Germany was a common prejudice elsewhere in the West.[15] It was reflected in popular culture and in the cinema, in particular; for example, the implication that demons lurked just beneath the surface calm of West German life formed the highly effective basis of a successful British spy thriller, *The Quiller Memorandum*.[16]

Another factor in the alienation from the political system was the existence from 1966 of a grand coalition between the country's two main parties, the Christian Democrats and the SPD. This was made possible by the SPD's moderation of its political stance on a whole range of issues in order to advance its acceptability as a party of government. The formation of the coalition made debate within the system even more constricted, and such debate as still took place seemed increasingly out of touch with the tides of popular opinion outside parliament. An economic recession in 1966 and 1967 and the passage of emergency legislation in 1968 intensified dissatisfaction with the functioning of the political system.

One consequence of the belief that parliament no longer represented the full range of opinions in the country was the formation on the left of the Extraparliamentary Opposition, while the Neo-Nazi NDP became the beneficiary of right-wing protest votes against the system. Its rise was particularly unwelcome to the political establishment since it prompted foreign concern over the future of the democratic system in West Germany. Disaffection was particularly marked among students. In a poll of student opinion at the end of 1968, only 35 per cent of the respondents declared themselves satisfied with the existing political parties. The disaffection existed at both ends of the political spectrum, with 19 per cent of students wanting to be able to vote for a party to the right of the Christian Democrats, while 28 per cent wanted to be able to vote for a communist party or other party to the left of the SPD.[17]

Support for the student protest movement was especially strong in West Berlin. In the 1960s West Berlin, with relatively cheap accommodation and an exciting lifestyle in comparison with the provinces, acted as a magnet for young people. Residence in West Berlin offered young men the further advantage of a means of escaping military conscription. A radical youth subculture grew up there that was reflected in the size and frequency of student demonstrations in the city in 1967 and 1968. The response of the authorities to such expressions of dissent was not gentle. In a notorious episode in June 1967 a student demonstrator, Benno Ohnesorg, was shot dead by a policeman during a protest against the visit to the city of the Shah of Iran. This episode was mentioned by a number of people who later turned to violence as an influence on their decision to join the underground. According to Astrid Proll, it was a watershed in Ulrike Meinhof's life.[18] The event gave its name to the 2 June Movement.

The shooting was not an isolated incident. Large numbers of

students were injured in aggressive police action during the course of the visit and, incredibly, agents of the Shah's own security police, SAVAK, were permitted to weigh into the protesters with cudgels that included steel bars. The torrent of abuse directed by the Springer press against the student movement was a factor in the polarization of opinion underlying such violence. When a young right-wing house-painter shot the student leader Rudi Dutschke in West Berlin in April 1968, there were demonstrations against the Springer press by angry students who blamed the newspapers for the attempt on Dutschke's life. Violent clashes between the police and students ensued when students attempted to block distribution of Springer's papers.[19]

While the student protest movement was a formative influence on many of those who joined the RAF in the 1970s, the relationship between the radicalization of the student movement in this period and the resort to organized violence was by no means direct. From some of the statements made by leading figures in the first generation, it would appear that disappointment at the subsidence of the protest movement provided the real trigger for the move towards violence. For example, Ulrike Meinhof described the reasons for RAF's formation in 1970 as follows:

> Nauseated by the proliferation of the conditions they found in the system, the total commercialization and absolute mendacity in all areas of the superstructure, deeply disappointed by the actions of the student movement and the Extraparliamentary Opposition, they thought it essential to spread the idea of armed struggle. Not because they were so blind as to believe they could keep that initiative going until the revolution triumphed in Germany, not because they imagined they could not be shot or arrested. Not because they so misjudged the situation as to think the masses would simply rise at such a signal. It was a matter of salvaging, historically, the whole state of understanding attained by the movement of 1967/1968; it was a case of not letting the struggle fall apart again.[20]

Meinhof's account fits nicely Merkl's 'fire sale theory' of political violence discussed in Chapter 4. Merkl applied it to the actions of the far right following their disappointment when the NPD failed to break through the 5-per-cent barrier to representation in the West German parliament, but it can as easily be used to explain the turn towards organized violence by elements of the left. Richard Rubenstein's notion of terrorism as 'an isolated intellectual's dream of efficacy'[21] would also seem to be an apposite description of the case of Ulrike Meinhof herself.

Institutionalization of the RAF

What the political situation in West Germany in the 1960s does not explain is the capacity of the RAF to attract new generations to its ranks. It can be explained in part in terms of a knock-on effect of the original campaign, with the deaths of members of the first generation providing the emotional impetus for new recruits to the RAF from among the larger pool of the group's sympathizers and so on. As a result of the research that has been carried out on the social and psychological attributes of people convicted of involvement in the RAF's activities, it is also possible to make some generalizations about the type of person who joined it. Members of the RAF were mainly drawn from the upper middle classes, with an above-average level of education, though only a minority ever held full-time employment. Conflict at home was a frequent feature of their family background. Personal connections often played an important role in drawing the individual into the underground. Not merely was there a large number of couples in the RAF; brother-and-sister pairs were also common.

Wide publicity has been given to these findings and there has been a tendency to extrapolate them to other situations where they emphatically do not apply, such as Northern Ireland, where membership of paramilitary organizations is overwhelmingly working class in terms of social background. It has also encouraged the belief that it is possible to construct a psychological profile of the terrorist. The very fact that those engaged in organized violence in West Germany lacked any political base of substance within the society itself does perhaps suggest that such violence may be a pathological phenomenon, at least in part. In support of this proposition can be cited the contribution that the Socialist Patients Collective in Heidelberg, a group experimenting with new methods of therapy, made to the development of the RAF.[22]

However, such explanations have some very obvious limits. Social and psychological similarities among members of violent organizations are in practice not that telling as factors, simply because the actual numbers engaged in any kind of political violence have been so small. In fact, they would form an infinitesimal proportion of people who shared all the most typical social and psychological characteristics of convicted members of the RAF.[23] Further, if social and psychological factors were so important, one would expect that countries with a social structure similar to that of West Germany would face a similar pattern of political violence. But while other developed countries in Western Europe have also, to varying degrees, been afflicted by small-group violence, there have been very large differences in the patterns of political violence in the countries affected. The differences suggest the primacy of political factors. The problem of explaining the survival of the RAF even simply as a fringe phenomenon remains.

The obvious implication that might be drawn from the RAF's survival through the 1980s is that profound alienation from the political system continued to exist on the margins of West German society and that this resulted in the institutionalization of terrorism. Reaction on the left to new political developments, such as the NATO decision on the deployment of Cruise and Pershing missiles and the nuclear sabre-rattling of the Reagan administration in the early 1980s, are one possible explanation for such alienation. From this perspective, one might argue that the end of the Cold War has so profoundly changed the German political environment as to remove what had been a potent source of alienation on the left of the political spectrum, the relationship between the United States and West Germany in the context of the Cold War system.[24] Alternatively, it can be argued that more permanent factors lie at the root of such alienation. Thus, the RAF can be treated as the product of the long-term influence on German society of traditions of political thought, particularly anarchism, that deny the state's legitimacy and that have previously given rise to political violence. From this perspective, it is the tranquillity of German society during the 1950s that is exceptional and requires explanation. Certainly, fear that the emergence of the RAF represented a revival of traditions of political violence that had destabilized government in Germany in the past was an important factor in the political reaction to the initial activities of the Baader-Meinhof group.[25]

Incomplete legitimacy

Another approach is to suggest that a factor underpinning both left-wing and right-wing political violence in West Germany was the incomplete legitimacy of the Federal Republic of Germany: incomplete because of the partition of West and East Germany and because of the restraints imposed on its policies as a legacy of the Nazi era. The collapse of democratic institutions under the Weimar Republic owing to the system's deficiency in legitimacy provides the obvious historical precedent for this view, and, indeed, the exaggerated reaction to the appearance of organized violence in West Germany owed much to the anxiety that history was repeating itself. In fact, at no stage did the level of political violence in West Germany ever provide any justification for such fears about the durability of the country's democratic institutions, explicable as the fears are as a response to the burden of the past and the political establishment's own inner doubts about the legitimacy of the Federal Republic. One might have expected the reunification of Germany in 1990 to have ended all such fears, but they have been kept alive by new problems, in particular the economic difficulties and the rise of xenophobia and attacks on foreigners that have accompanied reunification.

If the thesis of 'incomplete legitimacy' by itself does not provide a convincing explanation of organized left-wing violence in the 1970s, it was certainly the case that political violence gained credibility from the fact that the state itself treated such violence as a serious threat to the political system. To provide a comparative perspective on this point it is useful to compare West Germany's reaction to 47 deaths in seven years stemming directly or indirectly from the Baader-Meinhof group's campaign with the reaction of a more secure liberal-democracy to a much higher level of violence over a shorter period. Using the *New York Times Index*, Jeffrey Ross and Ted Gurr have compiled figures for three categories of terrorism in the United States during the 1960s. According to their figures, there were six reported deaths between July 1968 and December 1970 as a result of white supremacist attacks against blacks and civil rights workers. This category includes 'clandestine bombings, arson, shootings, beatings, and major cross-burning incidents but excludes mob attacks and riots'.[26] In the same period there were 49 deaths as a result of black activists' attacks on whites and shoot-outs with police. This category excludes violent acts during ghetto riots. Four deaths resulted from the third category of anti-war and anti-establishment bombings and arson. In short, there was a total of 59 reported deaths in a matter of two and a half years as a result of what would now be classifed as terrorism. However, the figures for deaths tend to understate the extent of such violence. For example, in evidence to Congress, the Assistant Secretary of the Treasury reported that there had been a total of 4,330 bombings in the United States in the period from January 1969 to April 1970.[27]

However, while there was widespread concern in the United States in the late 1960s over the much broader issue of violence in general, bombings and the like were not conceptualized as a separate problem of terrorism, nor was terrorism *per se* seen as a serious threat to the political system. In short, what Gurr has carefully separated out was seen as only part of a much wider problem of violence in the society. Further, the need to address the social, economic, and political issues underlying violence in a broad sense was accepted. Indeed, it was recognized that the health of the country's political system was at stake. It is interesting to speculate what the political consequences would have been if clandestine violence had been separately conceptualized as a problem of terrorism and the organizations and individuals responsible systematically labelled as terrorist.

It seems reasonable to suggest, firstly, that it would have been more difficult for any reforms to be carried through and, secondly, that America would be facing today a qualitatively much more serious problem of organized violence of all types. The United States is fortunate that its most notorious terrorist organization, the Symbionese Liberation Army (SLA), and its most notorious terrorist, the exceptionally unfortunate Patty Hearst, owe their reputation to events in the mid-1970s, by which time much of the violence associated with the civil rights movement and protest over the Vietnam war had burnt itself out.[28] Of course, the very fact that this was a period of relative domestic tranquillity in the United States made it much easier and much more likely that the violence of a group like the SLA would be singled out in this way.

The argument that the problem of political violence in West Germany was exacerbated by the overreaction of the authorities and their treatment of it as a much greater threat to the political institutions than it was ever capable of being helps to explain the durability of political violence in the 1970s. However, it is not quite so helpful in explaining its persistence through the 1980s, since after the freeing of hostages at Mogadishu the belief that such violence posed a serious threat to the survival of democratic institutions in West Germany clearly subsided. The collapse of communist rule in East Germany has uncovered some evidence of assistance to West German terrorists by the Stasi, but not on a scale or of a character to account for the persistence of the violence in West Germany.[29]

A more significant factor was the fact that the problem of political violence continued to be conceptualized as one of terrorism. The effect has been to give disparate violent events a coherence and a continuity they would otherwise lack. For example, the Munich beer festival bomb in September 1980 is typically treated as the very centrepiece of right-wing terrorism in West Germany, notwithstanding the absence of evidence that the perpetrator was acting as a member of any group committed to the use of violence and the difficulty of divining his intentions from the circumstances in which the bomb actually exploded. Ironically, there would seem good reason to suppose that both the continuity and the coherence imposed on events by the concept of terrorism have been factors in the legitimization of political violence by removing from individuals joining underground organizations or even acting independently of any organization the psychological burden of justifying such violence *ab initio*.

From the histories of many violent organizations it would seem that the burden of justifying murder in practice and not simply in theory is a very considerable one, but once that threshold is crossed very few restraints on what is accepted as permissible survive. Whereas it took nearly two years from the birth of the RAF to the organization's involvement in what were unambiguously acts of premeditated murder, no such inhibition has been evident in the behaviour of the second and subsequent generations of the RAF, a fact reflected in an increase in serious offences by left-wingers during the 1980s.[30] The West German case is quite typical. Even in the far more violent conditions of Northern Ireland, more than a year passed between the formation of the Provisional IRA, committed to fight the British military presence in the province, and the death of the first British soldier in the conflict.

In the case of the Italian Red Brigades (Brigate Rosse – BR), launched in 1970, 'the first occasion on which the BR carried out a premeditated act of cold-blooded murder'[31] was in June 1976, with the killing of the chief procurator of Genoa and his two bodyguards. It clearly becomes easier for members to carry out acts of murder and to justify such acts to themselves when the organization has already crossed that threshold or where a new group is able to claim more or less direct descent from such an organization. Notwithstanding the extremely negative overtones of terrorism as a term, the state's conceptualization of political violence as a problem of terrorism is likely to assist such a process of legitimization by placing fresh outbursts of violence in such a framework of purposeful action. This does not only apply to the behaviour of groups on the fringe of the political spectrum. The relative ease with which agents of any state can be persuaded to kill, even outside the context of self-defence or war, illustrates just how important the framework in which acts of violence or force are carried out generally is.

In this chapter, organized left-wing violence in West Germany has been examined in some depth, with only a few allusions to other cases. But this case is sufficiently typical of covert small-group violence in the industrial liberal-democracies to provide the basis of some generalizations about the nature of political violence in such societies. However, one qualification is necessary. The West German case is by no means typical of industrial liberal-democracies in which the main political cleavages are territorial and ethnic rather than ideological. Situations in which ethnic divisions co-exist with conflict over what constitutes the legitimate territorial boundaries of political authority are capable of generating violence on a qualitatively different scale from those in which class and ideology provide the main basis of political divisions. These situations are examined in the next chapter through a case study of the Northern Ireland conflict. But apart from such cases, it is evident that organized political violence in long-standing liberal-democracies in the industrialized world is almost invariably a fringe phenomenon, though in a few cases the actual level of violence as measured by fatalities has been higher than occurred in West Germany. The basic reason why it is a fringe phenomenon and seems likely to remain so is the difficulty groups resorting to covert violence have encountered in attracting and retaining significant levels of support for their activities.

Protest and liberal-democracy

In a liberal-democracy in an industrialized society there are many more opportunities for participation in politics than simply casting a ballot every four or five years, though for many people that provides a sufficient justification for according legitimacy to government in such a society. As discussed in the last chapter, liberal-democracies generally permit the peaceful mobilization of popular opinion through the holding of mass demonstrations, and mass demonstrations as expressions of public opinion often exert considerable influence on government policy. However, such demonstrations rarely challenge the legitimacy of government as such. In principle, it is possible for an elected government to ignore even the largest demonstrations, though the danger exists, if it does, that the legitimacy of the political system itself may be called into question by at least some of the participants in such demonstrations, thereby creating the basis for small-group violence.

For example, the decision of Western European governments to proceed (temporarily, as it turned out) with the deployment of a new generation of American medium-range missiles in the face of huge protests against the policy in the early 1980s was widely seen as a factor in the revival or the initiation of small-group violence on the left in a number of these countries. However, with good reason, governments are usually far more concerned about the electoral consequences of ignoring public opinion than they are about the danger of small-group violence as a by-product of resisting demands backed by mass demonstrations. This is because it usually takes much more than the disregard by government of public opinion over a particular issue to produce a violent reaction even from small groups on the fringe of society.

The myth of popular sovereignty still remains sufficiently strong that there is very great reluctance right across the political spectrum to challenge the legitimacy of the decisions of an elected government in a liberal-democracy through covert violence. In practice, the influence of anarchist ideas rejecting the whole framework of the state and the state system remains extremely slight. It is in relation to issues where that myth of popular sovereignty is most difficult to sustain that political violence is most likely to arise, and that is in the field of international relations. Thus, if it appears that an elected government's decision is the result not of the free will of its members but the consequence of the country's subordination to a foreign power, its legitimacy will be compromised to the extent that covert violence may occur. But, as the frequency with which American installations and personnel have been attacked in Western Europe suggests, the target in the first instance is likely to be the foreign power perceived as being behind the decision.

However, the option of non-violent forms of protest in a liberal-democracy makes any kind of political violence very difficult to justify and underpins a general perception in liberal-democracies of covert violence as illegitimate and lacking in any significant measure of popular support. Indeed, so strong is this perception that there is a tendency in liberal-democracies to believe that covert violence lacks popular support wherever it occurs, even outside the context of a stable, liberal-democratic framework of government. Quite clearly, this is not necessarily the case. Because ideologically based covert violence is for the most part accurately perceived as lacking a political base in a liberal-democracy, such violence often appears not merely wrong for that reason but also quite incapable of bringing about any political change for the same reason. Consequently, it may appear virtually devoid of political meaning. Indeed, the horror such violence evokes has as much to do with public perception of its apparent irrationality as it is a response to its lethal consequences. In fact, even in the most severely affected of the industrialized countries, ideologically based covert violence kills extremely few people in comparison with other causes of violent death. The impression that such violence is irrational derives from the huge distance that appears to exist between the means used and the ends sought, in so far as these are discernible at all. Ironically, it is from the state's reaction that it tends to derive its political significance.

7

Bomb culture: the case
of Northern Ireland

The case of Northern Ireland has frequently been cited in books on terrorism.[1] Indeed, it was rare for books that dealt with terrorism on a global basis not to refer to it. In many edited works, political violence in Northern Ireland was considered a sufficiently important example of terrorism to rate a chapter, or even two, on the particulars of Northern Ireland's experience.[2] The fact that the most recent wave of violence in Northern Ireland dated from the late 1960s, coinciding with the onset of the age of terrorism, and the international perception of the United Kingdom as a model liberal-democracy were two factors that underpinned the association of the province with terrorism. By contrast, the impact of the literature on terrorism on the study of the Northern Ireland conflict has been slight. The term 'terrorism' did not even appear in the index of John Whyte's magisterial survey of the literature on the conflict.[3]

The reason for this was not sympathy among analysts of the conflict for the proponents of violence in either community in Northern Ireland. Rather it was principally because few academic analysts of the conflict were prepared to endorse the assumptions that use of the term tended to imply, in particular that a legitimate political order existed that was being challenged by the violence of a tiny minority of extremists. The weakness of such a characterization of the violence in Northern Ireland, in sharp contrast to the criticism to be made of such a characterization of political violence in West Germany, was that it underestimated the gravity of the conflict in Northern Ireland and the extent to which the violence was embedded in the deep sectarian division in the society between Protestants and Catholics.

Official discourse has used the terms 'terrorism' and 'terrorists', as have the mass media, though sometimes newspapers, particularly outside the British Isles, have employed the term 'urban guerrillas' as a way of signalling the seriousness of the conflict. Both governmental and media use of these terms have been profoundly affected by the paramilitary ceasefires of 1994. The British government has made the inclusion of the political representatives of paramilitary organizations in formal negotiations on the future of Northern Ireland dependent on permanent cessations of violence and is continuing to seek a surrender of their weapons as proof of such a commitment. This position underlined the government's stance on the illegitimacy of the use of violence for political ends, but it also treated violence as a tactic that the paramilitaries could be persuaded to abandon in favour of the pursuit of their political ends through negotiations. That profoundly altered the connotations attached to the continuing use of the term 'terrorist'. Further, seeking the inclusion of the political representatives of paramilitaries was an acknowledgement of the link between their violence and the long-standing conflict between the two communities in Northern Ireland that went back to the province's very creation as a political entity.

Partition

Northern Ireland, comprising six of the 32 counties of colonial Ireland, was established in 1920 as an autonomous political entity within the United Kingdom to accommodate Protestant opposition to Irish home rule. That opposition reflected the intensity of sectarian divisions in Ireland, especially in the north-east of the island, where Protestants formed a majority of the population. The divide as a source of conflict on the island went back to the beginning of the seventeenth century, when Protestant plantations were established in Ulster to secure the territory for the British crown under King James I. The settlements and the land confiscation that accompanied them prompted a revolt by the Catholic native population in 1641, which was marked by atrocities against Protestants, such as the drowning of 100 men, women, and children at Portadown.

The period of Protestant weakness was relatively short-lived. A consequence of the victory of (Protestant) King William over (Catholic) King James II at the Battle of the Boyne in 1690 was Protestant political predominance in Ireland. A century later, following sectarian conflict in the Ulster countryside, the Orange Order was founded to commemorate King William's victory and to ensure the maintenance of Protestant predominance. In the nineteenth century, Belfast, with a rapidly growing population as a result of the industrial revolution, became the main focus of sectarian conflict. There were riots in the city as a result of antagonism between the two communities in 1835, 1843, 1857, 1864, 1872, 1884, 1886, and 1898.[4]

After partition, Northern Ireland elected 12 members to the House of Commons in London. They formed for the most part a barely noticed contingent on the Conservative benches, particularly as discussion of the province's affairs in Westminster was not permitted in deference to the existence of a Northern Ireland parliament and government. For almost 50 years the British political system was insulated from events in Northern Ireland and successive British governments turned a blind eye to the way the Unionist Party ran Northern Ireland. This was on the self-fulfilling basis that only Protestants could be trusted to support the link with Britain. Catholics, constituting over a third of the province's population, were regarded as rebels at heart who had to be kept in their place. Their unsuccessful resistance to partition provided a ready justification for discrimination against them in the new political entity. Their subordination was further underlined by emergency legislation exclusively directed against the Catholic community and retained through long periods of tranquillity.

Origins of the present troubles

This system remained unchanged until the 1960s when deteriorating economic conditions in the province, due in part to the decline of its traditional industries, provided the impetus for reform during the premiership of Terence O'Neill. Politically, reform acted as a stimulus to Catholic demands for equality of treatment within Northern Ireland, which was reflected in the emergence of the civil rights movement. It also prompted a backlash among Protestants, who blamed reform for the ending of Catholic acquiescence in their subordination. Hardline Loyalists regarded the civil rights movement as a plot to bring about a united Ireland, the traditional aim of Irish Republicans. Their fears were also aroused by the social and economic trends of the period, particularly the erosion of residential segregation between the communities, which they saw as a threat to Protestant dominance.

Disorder grew out of the conflict between Catholic hopes and Protestant fears. The most recent phase of 'the troubles', the colloquial term for periods of unrest in Ireland, is generally dated from October 1968 and violent clashes between the police and civil rights demonstrators, who defied a government order banning them from marching through Northern Ireland's second city, Londonderry. In August 1969 British troops were dispatched to the province to aid the civil power after prolonged rioting in Londonderry and Belfast had exhausted the resources of the local security forces. Initially, Catholics welcomed the arrival of British troops, not merely because they protected Catholic housing estates from attacks by Loyalist mobs, but because their presence enhanced the British government's responsibility for how Northern Ireland was governed. At the same time, the international attention that the situation in Northern Ireland was attracting raised Catholic expectations of far-reaching reform.

However, at the outset, the British government attempted to limit the scope of its involvement in the affairs of Northern Ireland to reform of the security system. In particular, it wished to maintain the existing Unionist government's political autonomy. A major weakness of the policy was that from the perspective of the Catholic minority it looked like a programme for the restoration of the *status quo ante*. Disappointment at the narrow scope of British policy provided the context for a radicalization of Catholic opinion, especially in areas where conflicts with the British army over such sensitive issues as the routes of Orange Order marches provided an additional source of alienation from the British authorities. The enthusiasm with which Catholics had greeted the arrival of the troops gradually gave way to disillusionment and even hostility.

Events in Northern Ireland took the Republican movement by surprise. In 1956, the Irish Republican Army (IRA) had launched a border campaign in support of a united Ireland, but in 1962 it had been forced to call off its campaign, in which six police officers were killed, because of lack of support from the Catholic minority in Northern Ireland. In the 1960s the Republican movement came under the influence of left-wing intellectuals who blamed the failure of the movement in the past on its political isolation and its elitist militarism and persuaded the movement that it should concentrate its energies on campaigning on social and economic issues. The violent turn of events in Northern Ireland in 1968 and 1969 was a contingency for which the leadership of the Republican movement was manifestly unprepared.[5]

The birth of the Provisional IRA

The Republican movement split, leading to the formation at the end of 1969 of Provisional IRA and shortly thereafter of its political wing (Provisional) Sinn Fein. The Provisionals embodied a revival of the creed of physical-force Republicanism and quickly attracted support among Northern Ireland Catholics, especially in areas where there had been sectarian clashes. The Provisionals' paper *An Phoblacht* described the movement's aims as being:

to end foreign rule in Ireland, to establish a 32-county Democratic Socialist Republic, based on the proclamation of 1916, to restore the Irish language and culture to a position of strength, and to promote a social order based on justice and Christian principles which will give everyone a just share of the nation's wealth.[6]

The fact that the Provisionals presented the conflict as a classical anti-colonial liberation struggle in which the enemy was British imperialism tied in with the disposition of much of the world, including even some people in Britain, to see Northern Ireland as a remnant of empire, a colonial problem in a post-colonial age.

Initial operations of the Provisional IRA were justified in terms of defending the Catholic ghettoes. This applied even to the bombing of commercial premises in the city centre of Belfast, which began in 1970, because, as one of the Provisional leaders, Joe Cahill, explained, it stopped the army from concentrating its resources on the ghettoes.[7] The other justification the Provisionals advanced for the bombing campaign was that it added to the economic burden of British occupation, as the cost of compensating businesses fell on the British taxpayer.[8] The resort to the tactic of bombing reflected the ready availability of industrial explosives, such as gelignite, in contrast to a shortage of other weapons.[9] The tactic contributed to external perceptions of the Provisional IRA as a terrorist organization, because, although the bombing campaign at this juncture was directed at property and warnings were given, accidents and mistakes occurred that led to fatalities. The long history of the use of explosives in previous campaigns by Irish nationalists, going back as far as the Clerkenwell prison bombing carried out by Fenians in 1867, meant that there was no inhibition for the leadership to overcome on the use of such a tactic.

Indeed, even before the start of the present troubles bombs were seen as part and parcel of the culture of Irish Republicanism, and this was reflected in the portrayal of Irish Republicans in British popular culture, as in the 1967 film *The Jokers*, which featured a bomb hoax conveyed to the police by one of the principal characters putting on a thick Irish accent.[10] By contrast, the Provisionals were restrained from attacks on the army by public opinion in the ghettoes. However, as relations between the army and the Catholic community deteriorated, the stance taken by the Provisionals became increasingly aggressive. At the beginning of 1971, the Provisional IRA Army Council approved offensive operations against the British army. In February a soldier was killed in a gun battle with a Provisional IRA unit. He was the first army fatality of the current troubles. The bombing campaign was also stepped up, leading to a rising toll of civilian casualties as a result of bungled warnings or even no warnings at all. In 1970 there were 153 explosions in Northern Ireland; in 1971 1,022.[11]

In response to the escalation of the Provisional IRA operations, the Unionist government introduced internment (providing for detention without trial) on 9 August 1971. It produced an explosion of Catholic anger and resentment, resulting in a massive increase in support for the Provisional IRA in the ghettoes and a sharp jump in the level of violence. At the time of the introduction of internment, 34 people had died in political violence in the course of 1971. A further 139 people had died by the end of the year.[12] The reaction of the Catholic community to internment contributed to a Protestant backlash, reflected in the establishment in September 1971 of the Ulster Defence Association (UDA), which brought together local Loyalist vigilante organizations that had grown up in a number of working-class Protestant estates. The spiral of violence was given further impetus by 'Bloody Sunday', 30 January 1972, when 13 unarmed demonstrators were shot dead by British troops after an illegal civil rights march in Londonderry. 'Bloody Sunday' also triggered off anti-British violence in the Republic of Ireland during which the British embassy in Dublin was burnt down. Internationally, the episode prompted fierce criticism of British rule in Northern Ireland, particularly in the United States.

Direct rule

A change in the direction of British policy followed. On 24 March 1972 the British government imposed direct rule on Northern Ireland, taking charge from the local Unionist administration and suspending Northern Ireland's parliament at Stormont. The imposition of direct rule prompted Protestant protest on a scale that matched Catholic reaction to the introduction of internment. At the time most Protestants regarded the existence of a local administration and parliament at Stormont as their guarantee that they would not be forced into a united Ireland against their will. Inevitably, therefore, there was widespread suspicion among Protestants that direct rule had been imposed in order to pave the way for Irish unification. But if many Protestants saw the downfall of Stormont as a betrayal, most Catholics remained too suspicious of British intentions to celebrate the event as their victory, though it was welcomed by the main nationalist party, the Social Democratic and Labour Party (SDLP), in a statement which appealed to 'those engaged in the campaign of violence to cease immediately'.[13]

The call was ignored by the Provisionals, who presented their own

proposals for a ceasefire linked to British withdrawal and the establishment of a federal Ireland. They had already dubbed 1972 'the year of
victory'.[14] The SDLP's hopes of an early end to internment to defuse
the situation were also dashed. Catholic fury over internment and
'Bloody Sunday' and Protestant fears of a sell-out by Britain in response to what they saw as rebellion formed an extremely potent
mixture. In the course of 1972, there were 467 fatalities in political
violence, the highest number of deaths in any year of the troubles (see
Table 7.1). A significant factor in the high level of civilian fatalities in
the course of 1972 and the four subsequent years was a campaign of
random sectarian assassinations carried out by members of Loyalist
paramilitary organizations, principally the UDA. It resulted in the
deaths of hundreds of Catholic civilians. The practice of the Loyalist
paramilitaries was to let the killings speak for themselves and at the
beginning of the campaign, claims of responsibility for particular
murders were rarely made, providing the tenuous basis of the police's
initial description of the killings as motiveless. However, the Catholic
community had little difficulty in discerning the intimidatory intent
behind the campaign, and the killings strongly reinforced the trend
towards residential segregation as Catholics fled to the safety of their
own ghettoes. Occasionally, Republican paramilitaries responded in
kind to the Loyalist campaign. However, publicly, the Provisionals in
particular disdained sectarian warfare, emphasizing that their campaign
was directed against British imperialism and not Protestants as such.
In fact, the Provisionals' view of the conflict disposed them to suspect
British involvement in the Loyalist campaign.[15]

In its publications, the UDA proclaimed that a state of war existed
in Northern Ireland and described Catholics as being, virtually without
exception, 'on the side of murder, terrorism, intimidation, and the
total destruction of all loyalists'.[16] From the perspective of the UDA,
Protestants were a community under siege, entirely reliant on their
own resources for survival. A forceful statement of this viewpoint was
given in a 1973 UDA press statement:

> We are betrayed, maligned and our families live in constant fear and
> misery. We are a nuisance to our so-called allies and have no friends
> anywhere. Once more in the history of our people, we have our backs to
> the wall, facing extinction by one way or another. This is the moment
> to beware, for Ulstermen in this position fight mercilessly till they or
> their enemies are dead.[17]

At its peak, the UDA had 'about 25,000 dues-paying members'.[18]
Only a small minority of the membership were involved in the campaign of random sectarian assassinations. For most, membership meant

Table 7.1 Deaths in Northern Ireland arising out of the security situation, 1969–94

Year	RUC[1]	RUCR[2]	Army	UDR/RIR[3]	Civilians[4]	Total
1969	1	–	–	–	12	13
1970	2	–	–	–	23	25
1971	11	–	43	5	115	174
1972	14	3	103	26	321	467
1973	10	3	58	8	171	250
1974	12	3	28	7	166	216
1975	7	4	14	6	216	247
1976	13	10	14	15	245	297
1977	8	6	15	14	69	112
1978	4	6	14	7	50	81
1979	9	5	38	10	51	113
1980	3	6	8	9	50	76
1981	13	8	10	13	57	101
1982	8	4	21	7	57	97
1983	9	9	5	10	44	77
1984	7	2	9	10	36	64
1985	14	9	2	4	25	54
1986	10	2	4	8	37	61
1987	9	7	3	8	66	93
1988	4	2	21	12	54	93
1989	7	2	12	2	39	62
1990	7	5	7	8	49	76
1991	5	1	5	8	75	94
1992	2	1	4	2	76	85
1993	3	3	6	2	70	84
1994	3	0	1	2	55	61
Totals	195	101	445	203	2229	3173

Notes: 1. = Royal Ulster Constabulary. 2. = Royal Ulster Constabulary Reserve. 3. = Ulster Defence Regiment and Royal Irish Regiment. The Royal Irish Regiment was formed out of amalgamation of the Ulster Defence Regiment and the Royal Irish Rangers on 1 July 1992. 4. = Including members of paramilitary organizations.
Sources: *Chief Constable's Annual Report 1993*, Royal Ulster Constabulary, Belfast 1994, p. 96, and staff at *Fortnight* (Belfast) for 1994 figures.

taking part in patrols guarding Protestant neighbourhoods and participation in the military parades the organization staged to demonstrate the force at its disposal. In 1974 the mass membership of the UDA played a key role in the success of the Ulster Workers Council strike by setting up road blocks, building barricades, and otherwise physically discouraging people from going to work. The strike brought down the power-sharing Executive, the heart of an ambitious British effort to achieve a settlement of the Northern Ireland problem through political accommodation between Unionists and nationalists. Loyalist hostility towards the settlement focused on the provision for the establishment of a Council of Ireland, which many Protestants feared might become a stepping stone to a united Ireland.

The failure of the power-sharing experiment was a devastating blow both to British policy and to the middle ground of political opinion in Northern Ireland. In its wake the British government briefly considered the option of withdrawal before deciding on a further effort to promote political accommodation through the election of a constitutional convention charged with reaching agreement across the sectarian divide on a new political dispensation. After the predictable failure of the convention, the British government gave up for the time being its attempts to devolve power to Northern Ireland and adopted direct rule as a long-term policy, promoting it as the form of government which was the least unacceptable to both communities.

Criminalization

The policy of direct rule was accompanied by significant changes in security policy. Internment was ended; so too was the privilege of special-category status for prisoners whose crimes were politically motivated. The government also closed down the incident centres which had provided a channel of communication between the authorities and the Provisional IRA during the latter's 1975 ceasefire. It became the proclaimed policy of the government that it would not negotiate with 'terrorists' in future. What the changes amounted to was a policy of criminalizing political violence and playing down the notion that Northern Ireland was in a state of civil war that urgently required a political solution. At the same time, primary responsibility for security was shifted to the police, and reliance on troops from the UK mainland was reduced.

Initially, the new approach was quite successful. It met a widespread desire in both communities for a return to normality and a lessening of the extreme political tension that the violence had given rise to. Protestants in particular felt reassured that they would not be forced into a united Ireland against their will. That fear had been a significant element in the perceptions of the Loyalist paramilitaries. Another element in the perceptions of Loyalist paramilitaries was the assumption that Catholics as a community supported the Provisional IRA. This perception also began to change, in large part due to the rise in 1976 of the Peace People, a mass movement demanding an end to political violence that for a time attracted a wide measure of support in the working-class ghettoes of both communities.[19]

The changes in Protestant perceptions were reflected in a sharp fall in the level of Loyalist paramilitary violence. Whereas, on Michael McKeown's calculations, Loyalist paramilitaries were responsible for 40 per cent of the 924 fatalities between 13 July 1973 and 12 July 1977, they accounted for 12 per cent of the fatalities in the following quadrennium between 13 July 1977 and 12 July 1981.[20] The level of Republican violence also fell, though not as sharply. That too reflected changes in Republican perceptions in response to the change in the British government's approach. The Provisionals' expectation of imminent British withdrawal evaporated. As a consequence there was a change in the strategy of the Provisional IRA's campaign, which an internal staff report explained as follows: 'We must gear ourselves to Long-Term Armed Struggle based on putting unknown men and new recruits into a cell structure.'[21] This implied a radical reorganization of the Provisional IRA from its existing quasi-military structure of territorially based brigades and battalions. In practice, the switch to a cell structure was not fully achieved.[22]

Preoccupation with sustaining the campaign on a long-term basis led to efforts to conserve resources. The number of actual operations declined very sharply. Careful planning went into the operations that took place so as to maximize fatalities among those the Provisionals considered legitimate targets, though the concept of a legitimate target itself came to encompass an ever wider category of people, wide enough to justify attacks on off-duty or even retired members of the security forces, Unionist politicians as well as British ministers, prison officers, judges, and even commercial contractors supplying services to the security services. However, the somewhat greater selectivity of both the Loyalist and the Republican campaigns of violence led to a fall in the proportion of civilian fatalities among total deaths as a result of the troubles. There was also a decline in the number of innocent civilians killed by the security forces, both in absolute numbers and as a proportion of the total of all those killed by the security forces.[23]

Politicization of the paramilitaries

At the same time, the Provisional IRA and the UDA both began to place greater emphasis on political activity. In the case of the UDA, disillusionment with Loyalist politicians, particularly after the failed 1977 strike against British security policy, resulted in a decision by the leadership that the organization should develop its own distinctive political position on the conflict. To this end, the New Ulster Political Research Group was set up in January 1978. In March 1979 it published *Beyond the Religious Divide*, arguing the case for an independent Northern Ireland as a context in which the sectarian divisions of the society could be overcome and as 'the only proposal which does not have a victor or a loser'.[24]

However, the UDA leadership found little support for this message of political accommodation either among Loyalists in general or even among rank-and-file members. Despite this, politicization was a restraining influence on the violent activities of the UDA throughout the 1980s. In the case of the Provisional IRA, the failure of the organization to gain anything from its 1975 ceasefire led to the displacement of the Southern leadership of the Provisionals by Northerners. The change in leadership was reflected in three trends within the movement after 1976: secularization, radicalization, and politicization.[25] An early indication of the change in the Provisionals' approach was a speech by Jimmy Drumm at Bodenstown in June 1977 in which he warned of the danger of 'the isolation of socialist republicans around the armed struggle'.[26]

A major drawback of the policy of direct rule was that internationally it made Northern Ireland look like a colony, a perception that worked to the advantage of the Provisionals, while the continuation of the Provisional IRA's campaign of violence blighted hopes within Northern Ireland of a return to normality. A further difficulty for the British government was that constitutional nationalists disliked the policy of direct rule. Lobbying by the SDLP and the Irish government generated international pressure, particularly from the United States, for a change of policy. It came shortly after the election of the Conservative government in May 1979.

The government launched a fresh political initiative aimed at establishing a devolved administration in Northern Ireland. To encourage an internal settlement across the sectarian divide, the government threatened to impose its own solution if the parties failed to reach an agreement among themselves. But the government's bluff was called and the initiative failed. To add to the government's woes, it faced a crisis in the prisons. As part of the policy of criminalization, special-category status for prisoners convicted of politically motivated crimes had been abolished. This had led to protests in the prisons. In 1980 a number of Republican prisoners went on hunger strike in support of five demands, including the right to wear their own clothes and the right to free association within the prison. Their campaign was supported by mass protests on the streets in Catholic areas, underlining the failure of criminalization to achieve its objective of the political isolation of those resorting to violence. Indeed, the protests bore out a politics lecturer's warning to the government in 1978:

> The limited but nonetheless real bond of sympathy between the agents
> of political violence and a large part of the people who support their
> objectives but not their means will be strengthened rather than weakened
> by the official denial of political status of the former.[27]

The government's difficulties prompted a further change of direction. In December 1980, at a summit between the British and Irish prime ministers, the two governments agreed to enter into dialogue on 'the totality of relationships'[28] within the British Isles. The announcement was warmly welcomed internationally, particularly in the United States. However, the initiation of the Anglo-Irish process did not solve the prisons crisis in Northern Ireland. There was a further hunger strike by Republican prisoners in 1981, in the course of which ten hunger-striking prisoners died.

The prisoners' campaign attracted mass support from Catholics in Northern Ireland, its breadth underlined by the by-election victory of Bobby Sands, the first of the hunger-striking prisoners, in a parliamentary constituency with a narrow Catholic majority. Two prisoners were also elected to the Irish Dail in a general election in the Republic in June 1981. However, while the impact of the hunger strikes on opinion in the Republic of Ireland turned out to be temporary, the effect on Catholic opinion in Northern Ireland proved to be more long-lasting. The British government's handling of the crisis attracted generally adverse comment internationally,[29] though the favourable reaction to the initiation of the Anglo-Irish process helped to limit the damage, especially in the United States, and President Reagan resisted the pressure for American intervention over the issue.

The electoral success of the campaign on behalf of Republican prisoners persuaded the Provisionals that the impact of the campaign of violence could be enhanced through electoral participation by the movement's political wing, Sinn Fein. A fresh British initiative involving the election of a Northern Ireland Assembly in October 1982 gave the Provisionals an early opportunity to put their new policy into practice. With 10.1 per cent of the first preference vote, Sinn Fein achieved an immediate breakthrough, celebrated by the Provisionals as the 'ballot bomb'.[30] In the UK general election of June 1983, Sinn Fein did even better, with 13.4 per cent of the votes in Northern Ireland, prompting speculation that at a future election Sinn Fein might overtake the SDLP. However, in elections in 1984 and 1985 there was a slight decline in the Sinn Fein vote compared with 1983. None the less, the challenge that Sinn Fein posed to constitutional nationalism in the form of the SDLP gave a significant impetus to the Anglo-Irish process, helping to pave the way to the Anglo-Irish Agreement of November 1985.

The Anglo-Irish Agreement

The essence of the Anglo-Irish Agreement was that it allowed the Irish government to put forward, through the mechanism of an intergovernmental council, views and proposals in relation to how Northern Ireland was ruled.[31] Following the agreement there was a further swing of Catholic opinion towards the SDLP and away from Sinn Fein. However, virtually the entire Protestant community was opposed to the Anglo-Irish Agreement, and this was reflected in a pact between the two main Unionist parties to co-operate to bring it down. Unionist protests against the agreement took the form of mass demonstrations, civil disobedience, and shows of strength, both on the streets and through the ballot box. In a few areas where some erosion of residential segregation had taken place and partially mixed estates had grown up outside of traditionally integrated affluent sub-urbia, there were a number of instances of Catholics being intimidated out of their homes. A number of police officers were also forced to move from their homes as the Royal Ulster Constabulary (RUC) came under attack from militant Loyalists who accused the police of enforcing Dublin's diktat.

The crisis in the prisons in 1980 and 1981, the electoral rise of Sinn Fein, and the Anglo-Irish Agreement helped to revive Loyalist suspicions both of Catholics and of the British government. The former was reflected in a recurrence of assassinations by Loyalist paramilitaries, which had virtually ceased during the late 1970s. Despite the polarization of the two communities, the leadership of the UDA maintained its commitment to political accommodation, while justifying the campaign of the Ulster Freedom Fighters (UFF), a *nom de guerre* used by the UDA's own members, as being directed at the removal of 'active Republicans and active nationalists who are trying to overthrow what exists here in the form of a government'.[32] As Andy Tyrie, the UDA's Supreme Commander, put it, 'the only way to defeat the IRA is to terrorise the terrorists'.[33] In practice, the UFF's notion of a legitimate target, like that of the Provisional IRA, encompassed a very wide category of people. Furthermore, the police frequently disputed UFF claims about the Republican paramilitary connections of its victims.

However, the level of Loyalist paramilitary violence remained low compared to what it had been in the mid-1970s. Part of the reason was the paramilitaries' experience of being abandoned by Unionist politicians when Protestant fears of betrayal by the British government abated after the adoption of the policy of direct rule in 1976. They feared that they might be abandoned yet again if there was a further switch in British policy that was as favourably received by Unionist political opinion. That possibility exercised a strong influence on the strategy of the paramilitaries. The UDA in particular devoted much of its energies to preparation for a 'doomsday' situation, while placing the onus squarely on the leaders of the two main Unionist parties to make it clear when the moment for civil war had arrived.[34]

At the same time, the UDA's lack of confidence in the Unionist political leadership was forcefully expressed by one of the UDA's leading figures, who declared: 'If some of the present Unionist leadership had been in power in 1912, Northern Ireland would never have come into existence.'[35] John McMichael was alluding to the fact that the threat of organized violence by the Protestant community in Ulster, in the form of the Ulster Volunteer Force (UVF), had deterred the British government from implementing home rule before the outbreak of the First World War. For Unionists 1912 had much the same significance as 1916 and the Easter rebellion had for nationalists. Inevitably, the fact that violence or the threat of violence played such a significant role in the creation of the political order in the two parts of Ireland was used by both Republican and Loyalist paramilitaries to legitimize their current activities. It may fairly be objected that the origin of almost all polities could ultimately be traced back to violence of some kind. However, in contrast to Ireland, in the great majority of cases that fact has little bearing either on the people's current perception of the legitimacy of the political order or on the nature of contemporary political divisions.

The failure of the Unionist campaign to bring down the Anglo-Irish Agreement through protests in the streets forced the two main Unionist parties to change their strategy to one of seeking to secure the abrogation of the agreement through negotiation. To be credible, the new policy required a willingness on the part of the Unionist parties themselves to make concessions. The point was readily embraced by the leadership of the UDA as vindicating its advocacy of political accommodation. In January 1987 the UDA's Ulster Political Research Group published proposals for the establishment of a Northern Ireland administration, which accepted what the two Unionist parties had hitherto rejected, power-sharing with the SDLP.[36]

A task force appointed by the two Unionist party leaders to examine Unionist options followed the UDA's lead and reported that many Unionists would be willing to contemplate SDLP participation in government provided the link with Dublin was severed.[37] From a very different perspective, Sinn Fein published a discussion paper, entitled 'A Scenario for Peace', in May 1987.[38] It advocated elections to an all-Ireland constitutional conference in the context of a declaration of intent by Britain to withdraw. The paper argued that partition was a violation of the right of self-determination as laid down in the United Nations' 1966 Covenant on Civil and Political Rights. This initiative was followed by an exchange of views between Sinn Fein and the SDLP during 1988. In the course of the talks, the SDLP pressed, to no avail, for an end to the Provisional IRA's campaign of violence.[39]

Indeed, the summer of 1988 was marked by a resurgence of the Provisional IRA's campaign, fuelled by large arms and explosives shipments from Libya dating back to August 1985.[40] On 20 August eight soldiers died in a bomb attack on a bus at Ballygawley in County Tyrone, prompting a wide-ranging review of the government's security policy. In October the Home Secretary, Douglas Hurd, announced a ban on the broadcasting of direct statements by spokespersons for Sinn Fein or the UDA. However, the broadcasters could still report the words of the spokespersons, and the effectiveness of the ban was reduced further by the employment of actors to mouth the words of interviewees as they talked on film. Nevertheless, the broadcasting ban did have an inhibiting effect on the media's coverage of the political views of Sinn Fein and the UDA. This was most apparent in the case of the UDA. The murder of John McMichael in December 1987 and Andy Tyrie's resignation in March 1988 had already deprived the UDA of its two most articulate spokesmen.

The ban added to the UDA's political marginalization. While a candidate of the political party directly associated with the UDA, the Ulster Democratic Party (UDP), won election to the Derry City Council, the UDP, like its predecessor, the Ulster Loyalist Democratic Party (ULDP), otherwise fared poorly, securing few votes and little attention. Sinn Fein also lost ground politically. In the 1989 local council elections the party lost seats, though its overall share of the first preference vote fell only slightly compared to 1985. It fared worse in the elections to the European Parliament, with its candidate's share of first preference votes falling below ten per cent. At the same time, there was a decline in the level of support for the Reverend Ian Paisley and the Democratic Unionist Party in both the local and European elections.

The Brooke initiative

The shift in the political mood was reflected in a narrowing of the differences among the main parties, particularly between the Protestant Official Unionist and Democratic Unionist parties, on the one hand, and the party that represented a majority of Catholics, the SDLP, on the other. This convergence encouraged the Secretary of State for Northern Ireland, Peter Brooke, to launch a fresh political initiative in January 1990. Its basis was that there was common ground among the constitutional parties – the two Unionist parties, the SDLP, and the non-sectarian Alliance party – that three sets of relationships needed to be addressed in any negotiations: the relationship between the communities in Northern Ireland; relations between Northern Ireland and the Republic of Ireland; and the links between the United Kingdom as a whole and the Republic of Ireland. Despite this measure of agreement, finding a formula that would permit formal negotiations among the parties presented considerable difficulty, especially in view of Unionist insistence on the suspension of the operation of the Anglo-Irish Agreement.

It took the Secretary of State over a year to get agreement on the terms for negotiations. He eventually succeeded in arranging that negotiations among the parties would take place in a gap of 11 weeks between meetings of the intergovernmental council from the end of April to mid-July 1991. The prospect of talks among the constitutional parties raised expectations of an end to 20 years of stalemate.[41] The breakthrough elicited from a new umbrella organization for Loyalist paramilitaries, the Combined Loyalist Military Command, a commitment to maintain a ceasefire during the duration of the negotiations. However, in the event, little progress was made and talks hailed as historic failed to live up to their billing. Disagreement among the parties on procedural questions held up discussion on the substantive issues, and by the time the talks petered out over the issue of the resumption of meetings of the intergovernmental council there had been precious little engagement among the parties on any questions of substance. Because of the difficulties the Unionists raised over procedural issues, they tended to be blamed for the breakdown of negotiations by much of British opinion.[42]

The failure of the first round of talks among the constitutional parties was followed by an upsurge in Loyalist paramilitary violence. In 1991 as a whole, 40 of the 94 deaths as a result of political violence were attributed to Loyalist paramilitaries, far and away the highest level of Loyalist violence since the mid-1970s.[43] The escalation in Loyalist violence continued through 1992. A large part of the explanation was the emergence of a younger and more militant set of leaders in the UDA. The murder of McMichael and the ousting of Tyrie were followed by further changes in the membership of the UDA's Inner Council, partly as a result of a backlash against corruption within the organization and partly as a result of the exposure of an agent for Military Intelligence in a key position in the organization. The new leadership was determined to demonstrate its effectiveness in comparison with the old guard. Its measure of effectiveness was its capacity to match the violence of the Provisional IRA blow for blow. A substantial arms shipment from South Africa at the beginning of 1988 provided the Loyalist paramilitaries with the means.[44] While McMichael continued to be revered, it was as a military figure rather than as an advocate of political accommodation. In August 1992 the British government responded to the organization's new militancy by banning it. That made the UDA an illegal organization like the Provisional IRA.

While in practice a considerable number of the victims of Loyalist violence continued to be Catholics with no known associations with Republican paramilitaries, the fact that the Loyalists targeted prominent members of Sinn Fein and others with Republican paramilitary connections of one kind or another as a highly publicized part of their campaign elicited a 'tit for tat' response from Republican paramilitaries, including the Provisional IRA, which targeted Protestants it accused of involvement in the Loyalist campaign. One consequence of the war between the paramilitaries was that fewer members of the security forces died as a result of the troubles in 1991 than in any year since 1970. In the areas most affected by the paramilitary war, such as Belfast, fear grew among the public at large of a return to the random sectarian killings that had occurred in the mid-1970s.

Ceasefire

A second round of talks among the constitutional parties was held after the British general election in April 1992. These negotiations too ended in stalemate, though there was greater engagement with issues of substance in the course of the talks. Further, blame for the failure of the talks tended to be put on the SDLP rather than the Unionists. In the election itself, Sinn Fein suffered a substantial setback when its president, Gerry Adams, lost his West Belfast seat. At the same time, the potent threat the Provisional IRA's campaign posed to the British economy was demonstrated by a bomb in the City of London a day after the general election which did a billion pounds' worth of damage. (There was a further attack on the City of

London in April 1993 that caused a similar amount of damage.) Despite this, within the Republican movement itself, there were increasing doubts about the effectiveness of the Provisional IRA's campaign of violence. These had been made explicit in an interview given by one of its members as far back as 1990 who acknowledged that while the Provisional IRA could not be defeated, it had become increasingly difficult to persuade nationalists that it could win.[45]

A speech by a leader of Sinn Fein, Jim Gibney, in June 1992 gave a further indication of evolution in political attitudes within the Republican movement in its acknowledgement of the reality of Unionist aspirations and in its support for negotiations.[46] Another indication was the publication by Sinn Fein of a fresh document setting out its position on the ending of the conflict. It was titled *Towards a lasting peace in Ireland*.[47] These developments gave encouragement to the holding of talks in 1992 between Sinn Fein and church leaders, who were seeking to persuade all the paramilitaries to end their campaigns of violence. The possibility that the British government itself might enter into negotiations with Sinn Fein at some time in the future had been raised by Peter Brooke in 1989, shortly after his appointment as Secretary of State for Northern Ireland.[48] In April 1993, the resumption of negotiations between the SDLP and Sinn Fein, through the party leaders, became public knowledge.

But the first substantial indication that Sinn Fein's talks with other groups or individuals might pave the way to a Provisional IRA ceasefire came in September 1993, when the leaders of the SDLP and Sinn Fein agreed on a document containing proposals for the ending of the conflict, which they put to the Irish government. The SDLP leader John Hume claimed that the document held the key to peace. The claim was greeted with considerable scepticism by the British and Irish governments. However, they were put under considerable pressure to test the prospects for a ceasefire through a joint initiative of their own. Despair in the two communities in Northern Ireland as a result of sectarian massacres added to the pressure, as did the revelation in November 1993 that the British government had itself been exchanging messages with the Provisional IRA, contrary to its declared policy of not negotiating with terrorists.

The result was the Downing Street Declaration of 15 December 1993, a joint statement by the British and Irish governments. It set out the context in which Sinn Fein might be included in negotiations on the future of Northern Ireland. The reaction of Unionists to this initiative was surprisingly muted. The main reason was the underlining by the British government that there would be no change in the constitutional position of Northern Ireland without the consent of a majority in the province. In fact, in policy terms, the statement contained little that was new. In July 1994 a conference of Sinn Fein rejected the Downing Street Declaration. However, that was followed by an announcement on 31 August of 'a complete cessation of military operations'[49] by the leadership of the Provisional IRA. This was followed in October 1994 by a ceasefire by the Loyalist paramilitaries.

The most surprising aspect of the ending of paramilitary violence in the second half of 1994 was that it occurred in the absence of any political settlement. Indeed, while there has been a measure of convergence over the years in the positions of the Unionists and nationalists, no settlement is in prospect. Further, the expectations of Republican and Loyalist paramilitaries as to the political consequences that are likely to flow from the ceasefires are sharply at odds. That places a question-mark over the long-term durability of the present truce. None the less, it seems likely to last long enough for it to be seen as ending the phase of Northern Ireland's troubles that began in 1968.

Conclusion

While the number of people in each community directly involved in violence remained a very small proportion of the total population, political violence in Northern Ireland was far from being a fringe phenomenon. Though it is reasonable to characterize those who supported violence as a relatively small minority in each community, the violence shaped the attitudes and behaviour of the two communities in such fundamental ways that it was impossible to separate the question of relations between the two communities as a whole from the issue of the violence. One of the main objections to applying the term 'terrorism' to the situation was that it carried the implication of a pathological phenomenon that could be divorced from ordinary politics and led to an underplaying of the pervasive influence of the violence on the society. The highly segregated nature of the society, residentially and educationally, the extraordinarily high level of identification by individuals of themselves as Protestants or Catholics,[50] and the almost complete absence in the society of Protestant nationalists or Catholic Unionists[51] in part reflected that influence as well as providing the context in which sectarian tensions were amplified by political violence.

In political discourse in Northern Ireland the term 'terrorism' tended to be used to demonize the violence of the other community. Because of its identification with the language of vilification it was a term that those who acknowledged the need for political accommodation between the communities tended to avoid. Another reason why those in the middle ground of politics adopted the somewhat inappropriate term 'paramilitary' to refer to organizations engaged in violence was the association of the terrorist label with political rhetoric justifying retaliatory violence against the neighbourhoods from which the 'terrorists' emanated. In a society in which fears abound of an escalation of violence as a result of cycles of retaliation, this was a potent consideration.

Further, the potential for violence in Northern Ireland has by no means disappeared. Many factors have been adduced to explain the decisions of the Provisional IRA and of the Loyalist paramilitaries to cease their campaigns of violence. For example, in the case of the Provisional IRA, much has been made of the influence of the Irish-American lobby. What no one has suggested is that the paramilitaries ceased their violence because they lacked the means to sustain it. Thus, it would appear that they had the material to sustain their campaigns more or less indefinitely if they had so wished. In short, violence in Northern Ireland was not brought to an end by the direct actions of the security forces, though this is not to underestimate the importance of the role played by the British government in containing the conflict.

Indeed, in terms of the potential seriousness of conflict in Northern Ireland, this case has more in common with the various ethnic conflicts in Eastern Europe and what was formerly the Soviet Union than it does with that of West Germany. While the level of violence has been very much lower in Northern Ireland than in, say, Yugoslavia, without the restraining presence of British authority the potential existed in Northern Ireland for an intercommunal conflagration of considerable, if not quite comparable, proportions. A further restraining factor in the case of Northern Ireland was the absence of any strong external interest in the outcome of the conflict. Both the British government and the government of the Republic of Ireland sought to contain the conflict and to avoid confrontations with each other over the issue of Northern Ireland's future constitutional status. Republican para-militaries obtained weapons and explosives from Libya and a measure of financial support from Irish-American organizations, while Loyalists received arms from South Africa and support from Scotland and Canada. However, the scale of external involvement did not funda-mentally affect the course of the conflict. What made the Northern Ireland case different from instances of political violence in basically stable liberal-democracies was not the external dimension, but the connection of the violence to deep divisions in the society.

8

Violence, inequality, and the Third World

Never before in human history has the gulf in living standards among the different peoples inhabiting the planet been as enormous as it is today. Its relevance to the subject of this book is the common assumption in the literature on political violence of a close link between violence and inequality.[1] In historical terms, the great divide between rich and poor in the world is relatively recent. It has come into being in a matter of 200 years or so. In 1750, before the start of the industrial revolution, what is today referred to as the Third World accounted for 73 per cent of world manufacturing output, while Europe, Japan, and the United States together accounted for 27 per cent. By 1900, Europe, Japan, and the United States accounted for 88 per cent of world manufacturing output.[2] This massive shift of economic power has been reflected in living standards. Indeed, the gap in living standards between rich nations and poor has grown steadily wider in the course of the twentieth century.

Global inequality

The World Bank analyses the economic performance of the world's states each year in its *World Development Report*. It divides them into three categories: low-income, middle-income, and high-income economies. The Bank's *World Development Report 1994* classified 42 countries as low-income economies. While they represent a minority of the world's states, these countries contained almost 60 per cent of the world's population in 1992. According to the report, together they had an average *per capita* income in 1992 of 390 dollars. By contrast, the report concluded that the average *per capita* income of the Bank's 23 high-income economies, with about 15 per cent of the world's population, in 1992 was 22,160 dollars, in other words about 57 times that of the low-income economies.[3]

In the period 1980 to 1992, the *per capita* income of the high-income economies grew by an average of 2.3 per cent a year.[4] As may easily be calculated from these figures, that means that the average *increase* in the income *per capita* of the rich countries *each year* comfortably exceeded the *total* income *per capita* of the low-income economies. To complete the picture, the *World Development Report 1994* classified 67 countries as middle-income economies, with an average income *per capita* of 2,490 dollars in 1992 and holding approximately a quarter of the world's population.[5] From these figures, it is possible to calculate that the rich countries of the world, with about 15 per cent of the world's population, secure almost 80 per cent of total world income.

This scale of inequality is far greater than the level of inequality in any individual country, even the most unequal, such as Brazil or South Africa. Admittedly, the availability of information on the distribution of income within countries is far from satisfactory. For example, the figures on the distribution of household income given in the World Bank's report cover only a minority of countries, and these are for a variety of years. Among the countries for which there are figures, Brazil stands out as the place with the most unequal distribution; there the richest 20 per cent of households received 67.5 per cent of total income in 1989.[6]

It has become fashionable in South Africa itself to refer to the country as two worlds, First World and Third World. Income in South Africa is extremely unequally distributed in terms of race. Thus, whites comprising 14 per cent of the population received approximately 62 per cent of total personal income in the country in 1987.[7] However, not merely is economic inequality at the global level more extreme than that prevailing within South Africa, but there seems to be much less prospect of a radical reduction of global inequality than there is of a shift in the racial shares of income in South Africa, even on the assumption that whites continue to maintain a large amount of influence under a new political dispensation in South Africa. For most of the developing countries, the 1980s constituted a disastrous decade of falling living standards, exacerbated by the debt crisis. By contrast, the 1980s were a decade of rising living standards for the rich countries. At the same time, official development assistance, measured as a percentage of the Gross National Product of the donor countries, actually seems to have declined during the course of the decade.[8] The prospects for the poor countries and for the poor generally during the 1990s seem bleak. In particular, it seems unlikely that China, containing a fifth of the world's population, will equal in the 1990s the exceptional growth rates it was able to achieve during the 1980s.[9]

Inequality and instability

Economic inequality between states, inequality within states, and indeed the relationship between these two levels of inequality have been examined by political scientists respectively, as a source of political differences between states, as a cause of violence and political instability within states, and as an explanation of how the division of the world between rich and poor is maintained. While the second of these provides the most obvious link to the issues under consideration in this book, each in fact is relevant to the conceptualization of political violence in the Third World. The American political scientist Seymour Martin Lipset examined the question of the relationship of economic development to democracy in his 1959 study of political behaviour, *Political Man*.

His point of departure was the Aristotelian proposition that poverty made the masses susceptible to demagoguery and that the self-restraint necessary for the functioning of democratic institutions was possible only in a wealthy society. To test it, he looked at the relationship between various measures of affluence and of industrialization and the stability of democracy as reflected in the longevity of democratic institutions and the absence of significant support for parties opposed to the democratic system. He found that there was a strong correlation between stable democracy and affluence and a similiar relationship between stable democracy and a high level of industrialization.[10]

A second edition of *Political Man* was published in 1981. In it Lipset reviewed evidence from the 1970s of the relationship between democracy and wealth. In particular, he cited in support of his position a study by Larry Diamond on the correlation between the existence of liberal-democratic institutions and *per capita* incomes. Diamond examined how 31 countries he identified as functioning liberal-democracies were distributed among 123 countries in terms of wealth. He arranged the latter into quintiles according to their *per capita* incomes in 1974. All but four of the democracies fell into the two richest quintiles, with 19 of the democracies in the richest quintile of 25 countries.[11] In short, his study showed a remarkably high measure of correlation between democracy and affluence.

However, it would be difficult to replicate these results using current data, as the fall of several military dictatorships in Latin America and the restoration of democracy in a number of Asian countries such as the Philippines and Pakistan during the course of the 1980s have increased the number of liberal-democracies among the poorer nations of the world. Admittedly, the durability of many of these new democracies is very much in doubt. Even more importantly, it is already apparent that democratic government in many of these poorer societies has not achieved the same degree of effectiveness or legitimacy as it has secured in the richer countries. In particular, the existence of democratic institutions has not prevented the emergence or persistence of guerrilla warfare in a number of these countries, contrary to Guevara's dictum that guerrilla warfare was unsustainable in any country where there was even the semblance of democratic elections.[12] Ironically, it is in a neighbouring state to Bolivia, Peru, that his dictum has been most clearly refuted.

Lipset's original formulation of a correlation between affluence and *stable* liberal-democracy remains substantially true. Of course, correlation is not the same as cause and the existence of the correlation does not prove the proposition that the failure of democracy in Third World countries is due, in whole or in part, to the susceptibility of the poor to demagoguery. In fact, this explanation of the correlation has not proved persuasive, not least because it is apparent that what matters is not the absolute level of affluence but relative affluence. If the absolute level was the determining factor one would expect that the rise of living standards during the twentieth century would have produced a steady rise in the number of stable democracies. It has not.

Further, the current shift towards democracy in various parts of the world can hardly be ascribed for the most part to rising living standards. Rather the reverse is so in most cases, though it should also be said that political rather than economic factors have been the main cause of the current trend. However, recognition of the existence of a correlation between democracy and affluence has itself played a part in the demand for democracy. Thus, during pro-democracy demonstrations in Shanghai in December 1986, students repeatedly linked the demand for democracy to the achievement of higher living standards.[13] The implication was that democracy could transform China into a wealthy country, a miracle that is almost certainly beyond the capacity of any political system to achieve. As the case of India shows, there is little reason for supposing that liberal-democracy causes affluence.

Reversing the direction of causation and suggesting that affluence causes stable democracy is scarcely more persuasive. The imperfect nature of the correlation suggests a more complex basis of causation. In practice, it is not easy to identify factors that might form the basis of a causal connection between affluence and stable democracy, as there are no very obvious answers to the question of where relatively affluent societies with stable liberal-democratic systems differ from the rest of the world in other respects. However, it is clear that these countries do differ in two very significant ways from societies in the Third World and that is in respect of their level of industrialization and in the relative equality of their income distribution. Admittedly, neither factor is helpful in explaining the divergent political fortunes of Western and Eastern Europe. It is possible that with the end of communism there will be greater convergence between Western and Eastern Europe, at least in outward political forms. But in any event, one should not expect the stability or otherwise of a particular type of political system to be simply explicable in terms of the economic conditions prevailing in the countries in question. Of the two factors, industrialization and economic inequality, the latter is the more obviously relevant to the analysis of political conditions in the Third World.

Despite the gaps in the World Bank's figures for income distribution, it is evident from the information given that, as a general rule, income is distributed much more unequally in the Third World than in the First. Thus, on the Bank's data, with very few exceptions the richest 10 per cent of households in the Western liberal-democracies account for a lower share of total household income than their equivalents in Third World countries.[14] As the Swedish economist Gunnar Myrdal has observed, 'it is indeed a regular occurrence endowed almost with the dignity of an economic law that the poorer the country, the greater the difference between rich and poor'.[15]

Income distribution is by no means the only way of measuring economic inequality in the Third World. Distribution of land provides another. Indeed, partly because of the greater availability of data on land distribution, the political implications of this aspect of economic inequality have been studied extensively. In an article in the April 1964 issue of the journal *World Politics*, Bruce Russett examined the relationship between land tenure and instability, using data for 47 countries. He used three different indices to measure instability and three different indices to measure the equality of land distribution. The strongest correlation was between deaths from internal group violence in the period 1950 to 1962 and the Gini index of land distribution, which measures the deviation of the size of farms from the average. This showed that 'inequality of land distribution does bear a relation to political instability but that relationship is not a strong one, and many other factors must be considered in any attempted explanation'.[16]

One such factor was the relative importance of agriculture in the country's economy, since where alternative sources of wealth existed besides agriculture, inequality of land distribution was unlikely to be a politically sensitive issue capable of generating violence. Taking such factors into account, Russett put forward a more complex hypothesis, including data on the percentage of population engaged in agriculture and the income level of the society, and, with these and other refinements, produced a much stronger correlation between his two primary indices.[17] Subsequent efforts to replicate Russett's results using more recent data on political violence have achieved mixed results, while prompting considerable argument, much of it extremely technical, over how inequality of land distribution, in particular, may best be measured.[18] At the same time, research correlating inequality in income distribution and political violence has led to a debate on which measure of inequality yields the more significant results.[19]

Imperialism

A further issue that needs to be addressed is the relationship between economic inequality within states and inequality between states. It forms the basis of Johan Galtung's structural theory of imperialism, first outlined in an article in the *Journal of Peace Research* in 1971. His point of departure was 'two of the most glaring facts about this world: the tremendous inequality, within and between nations, in almost all aspects of human living conditions; and the resistance of this inequality to change'.[20] He argued that the maintenance of inequality at the global level could not be explained simply by the balance of military forces in the world. Instead, he suggested that inequality was built into the structure of relations between rich and poor states.

His basic idea was that the rich, developed world had been able to dominate the Third World through the establishment of bridgeheads within the developing countries themselves. He argued that the bridgeheads were provided by the elites of the Third World with their Western standards of living and lifestyle. By contrast, the huge gulf in living standards between the poor in the rich world and the poor of the Third World underscored their lack of any common interest in changing the nature of the system. He concluded that 'only imperfect amateurish imperialism needs weapons; professional imperialism is based on structural rather than direct violence'.[21]

In practice, it is open to question whether the relationship between the First World and the elites in the Third World should be seen as primarily a political alliance generating inequality between and within nations. In fact, it seems more reasonable to attribute the success of elites in the Third World in securing Western standards of living to the operation of market forces at a global level, enabling an extremely privileged as well as very narrow sector of Third World society to achieve such living standards by its role within a market that the mass of the population does not have access to. Medical doctors provide an example of a group that often enjoys a standard of living that reflects the high value that is placed on such skills globally. Notoriously, the geographical distribution of doctors in the world has an inverse relationship to actual medical need.

But however such inequality arises, it is clear that it generates political interests and, in particular, that Third World elites have an interest in ensuring that no obstacle is put in the way of their own integration into a global division of labour where incomes are determined by the standards of the very richest countries. How far this interest can be reconciled with those of society as a whole is a matter of debate. But that there is an intimate relationship between the global and internal levels of inequality is evident from how closely the lifestyles of the elites mirror those of the rich within the First World.

The interest of elites in the Third World in the maintenance of their access to a privileged existence economically might lead one to expect a common political approach by the elites to relations with the rich nations to underpin their position. In practice, the political stance of elites in different countries of the Third World to relations with the First World varies considerably. Their differing stances can partly be explained in domestic terms. To secure their position, the elites need at least a modicum of domestic political legitimacy. How that can best be achieved varies from country to country. Thus, if a country achieved independence only after a violent anti-colonial struggle, the elite's room for manoeuvre in its relations with the former colonial power may be limited. In such circumstances the elite may give its support to a government pursuing a foreign policy vigorously in-dependent of the West. Further, the elite itself is frequently divided on regional, ethnic, or other lines, according to the country's particular circumstances.

Changing international political conditions have also played a part in causing alterations in the relationship between the First World and Third World elites. During the heyday of the Pax Americana in the 1950s and 1960s, the allegiance of the elites to authoritarian govern-ments proclaiming their anti-communist credentials in justification of their policies and enjoying the support of Washington formed a typical pattern, especially in Latin America. This changed when President Carter made adherence to human rights norms one of the criteria for American support for any regime. The consequence was that authorit-arian governments were no longer able to count on unconditional backing from the United States simply through adopting a strongly anti-communist stance. This forced elites to recognize that meeting at least the formal requirements of a liberal-democracy, through, for example, the holding of competitive elections, was necessary if they wished to secure American support in confronting violence from below. The same consideration meant that states were less inclined to abandon liberal-democratic forms even in the midst of civil war.[22] It remains to be seen how the demise of communism will affect relations between the First World and the Third World and how they are conceptualized.

Western perceptions

The presumption that there is a link between political violence in the Third World and economic inequality has had a powerful influence on Western perceptions of turmoil in the Third World. Particularly during the 1960s, with the fading of Cold War attitudes in the West following the resolution of the Cuban missile crisis in 1962, there was a widespread tendency in the West to see the political violence in the Third World as part of a more general drive for greater social justice in the world. It led to a romanticization of the guerrilla, in particular. There was an assumption that outbreaks of political violence, and, particularly, rural insurgency, were an indication of the political illegitimacy of the government of the country in which such events occurred.

The corollary was that Western liberal-democracies by virtue of their proven political legitimacy were immune to the organized political violence affecting Third World states. The discovery towards the end of the 1960s that the West and Westerners were not protected by the mere existence of liberal-democracy from organized political violence, particularly clandestine violence, came as a considerable shock to Western public opinion. By the end of the 1970s, if not earlier, opinion had shifted to the extent that it became possible to present Western liberal-democracies as especially vulnerable to terrorism, as clandestine violence in Western liberal-democracies, or directed at Westerners abroad, was by this time invariably described. With the change of perception in relation to Western vulnerability went a marked hardening of attitudes towards all forms of anti-system violence.

At the beginning of the age of terrorism in the late 1960s and early 1970s, political violence in the Third World was not a significant factor in the interpretation of the concept of terrorism. Initially, such violence continued to be seen as a response to inequality or lack of democracy within the states affected by it and was generally not called terrorism, except by the political authorities in the country concerned. There were two major exceptions to this proposition: violence carried out by Palestinian organizations and the attacks of urban guerrillas in Latin America on diplomats and foreign businessmen.

Both had a significant influence on how the term 'terrorism' came to be used. In each case the international or transnational dimension to the violence was central to its labelling as terrorism. Thus, it was largely as a result of hijackings that Palestinian clandestine violence of all kinds came to be labelled as terrorism. Similarly, it is unlikely that the term 'terrorism' would have been used in relation to clandestine violence directed against the military dictatorship in Brazil if all the targets of the campaign had been Brazilian. Indeed, given its small scale, it seems unlikely that it would have attracted the attention of the Western media at all if that had been the case.

Over the last 20 years, the term 'terrorism' has gradually come to be applied to at least some of the instances of domestic political violence within the Third World, though in this context its use remains far more contentious than in an international context or in relation to violence within a Western liberal-democracy. Reservations about the use of the concept are reflected in the way it is applied in this context. In particular, perpetrators of acts of terrorism are much less likely to be labelled as terrorists or the organizations responsible called terrorist. The factors encouraging the extension of the term to domestic violence within the Third World and the reasons for the qualifications applied to its use both merit examination.

The simplest basis for the extension of the term to domestic political violence was the involvement of organizations that had carried out acts of international or transnational terrorism. Thus, because groups associated with Fatah, such as Black September, were involved in hijackings and other armed attacks outside the Middle East, Fatah itself and, indeed, the larger umbrella organization of which Fatah was a central part, the Palestine Liberation Organization (PLO), also came to be labelled as terrorist. This applied to all forms of violence in which these organizations engaged, even attacks explicitly directed at Israeli military personnel in a combat situation, as in cross-border raids. However, there were contexts that strained the credibility of the application of the term 'terrorist' to the PLO, such as its use to refer to large PLO military formations in Lebanon, since the whole notion of thousands of terrorists runs counter to assumptions about the nature of terrorism, particularly the assumption of its lack of any political legitimacy.

Similarly, the term 'terrorist' has been applied by extension to the domestic political violence of various of the contending parties in

Lebanon, by virtue of the involvement or suspected involvement of groups such as Hizbollah in hijackings and the taking of hostages. However, in this case too, writers analysing the political situation in Lebanon in any depth have tended to avoid the term, partly because of its misleading connotations, but also partly because of the simple recognition that the word's emotive overtones constitute an obstacle to the dispassionate assessment needed to convey the complexity of Lebanon's conflicts.

Lebanon also illustrates another form of the application of the concept by extension, and that is its application to methods associated with terrorism in the West, such as car-bombs and the assassination of important political figures. In the Third World the use of such covert methods is quite commonly referred to as terrorism, and instances of the use of such methods are often described as acts of terrorism, but responsibility for such acts is much less likely to be attributable to perpetrators who can be labelled as terrorists than in similar occurrences in the West. One reason is that in a Third World context responsibility for such action is much more likely to lie with the agents of governments than in the West. Governments, unlike small groups engaged in clandestine violence within Western liberal-democracies, generally do not proclaim publicly their responsibility for such deeds.[23] Further, the state involved may be a foreign power and not necessarily the state of the territory in which the act has taken place. The vulnerability of Third World states to such covert intervention is a significant point of distinction between these states, virtually regardless of ideology, and Western liberal-democracies.

Terrorism and the Third World

In the Introduction, it was pointed out that an implication of the emotive power of the term 'terrorism' was that it applied to violence that was absolutely illegitimate. Whereas it is possible to speak of justified violence or even legitimate violence, there can be no question of justified terrorism or legitimate terrorism. The difficulty in judging the legitimacy of government in many Third World states contributed initially to a reluctance to apply such an absolutist judgement as the term 'terrorism' implies to anti-system violence within such a state.

However, the wider existence of liberal-democratic forms of government in the Third World has to some degree overcome this reluctance, since no very obvious grounds of political principle exist for treating such states differently from liberal-democracies in Western societies. For some writers, therefore, applying the term 'terrorism' to anti-system violence of whatever kind in any country with a liberal-democratic form of government has been seen as a matter of being consistent in their use of language. For others, it has simply been a way of proclaiming their faith in liberal-democratic values.

But whatever justification is advanced for employing the concept in this context, applying the term 'terrorism' to anti-system violence in Third World liberal-democracies has far-reaching implications for the scope of the concept. In the case of Western liberal-democracies, it is possible to use the term *both* as a way of indicating the illegitimacy of political violence in circumstances where non-violent means of influencing the decision-makers are available to the ordinary citizen *and* as a way of describing a category of clandestine methods of violence, such as bombings and assassination. Indeed, there is a third dimension to the term in this context, the implication that one is talking about a low level of violence indicative of its lack of significant popular support. In practice, there is little conflict among these different meanings, as only in very exceptional cases, such as occurred in Northern Ireland, does organized political violence in a Western liberal-democracy enjoy anything but marginal support. This factor and the effectiveness of governmental measures to maintain law and order in such societies almost automatically dictate the employment of clandestine methods of violence and the low level of any campaign of violence.

This unity of meanings simply does not exist in the Third World. In reality, the capacity of a state to maintain law and order is more a function of the level of economic development in the society than it is a reflection of the type of political system. Liberal-democracy has proved little more successful than other forms of political system in overcoming the relative weakness of the state in many Third World societies. Widespread defiance of central government is not merely possible in a Third World liberal-democracy. It is commonplace.[24] Indeed, it may reasonably be argued that the norms of liberal-democracy make the state's task of establishing its authority more difficult since they impose restraints on the means that may be employed by the state to uphold its authority. These restraints stretch the capacity of government in an industrialized society to prevent disorder. The belief that liberal-democracy was an obstacle to both nation-building and the creation of effective authority was one reason why so many former colonies abandoned liberal-democratic forms after independence.

Where liberal-democratic forms have been retained or revived, whether in deference to Western opinion or because of an indigenous commitment to such a system of government, the state has frequently been afflicted by political violence. Both the nature of the violence and the level has varied considerably. The methods of violence have by no means been confined to clandestine operations, and in some cases 'civil war' is the only apposite description of its level. Yet that has not prevented Western journalists, politicians, and academics from characterizing political violence in these societies as terrorism, though there has been enough confusion within the West over the appropriateness of using the term in such alien contexts as to prevent the emergence of a clear consensus on when the concept should be used.

If the form of government matters above all else, then presumably the term 'terrorist' can be applied to any group engaged in fighting the system, even if it has the size and character of an army, and the role of clandestine violence in its operations is trivial. To add to the confusion, it is inevitably the case that civilians who perceive themselves to be on the opposite side to an army, whether it is a guerrilla army, the army of the state, or the army of a particular religious or ethnic community, as in the Lebanon, will feel themselves terrorized by such a force, lending verisimilitude to the use of the word 'terrorism'.

Thus, in a footnote to a chapter on the urban guerrilla in Latin America, Richard Gillespie makes the claim that 'the only important insurgent movement in Latin America which indisputably practises terrorism is the neo-Maoist Sendero Luminoso in Peru'.[25] The argument presented in the chapter itself is that urban guerrilla warfare as it was carried out by groups such as the Tupomaros is distinguishable from terrorism by virtue of being more discriminate and predictable.[26] Yet in terms of the methods employed, the Tupomaros and the other urban guerrillas bear a far closer resemblance to groups such as the Italian Red Brigades or the West German Red Army Faction than do the rural guerrillas of Sendero Luminoso. Further, it is difficult to escape the fact that the activities of the Latin American urban guerrillas themselves played a considerable role in shaping contemporary perceptions of the concept of terrorism.

However, the conflict among the different criteria for characterizing political violence allows considerable latitude to any writer to argue that a particular campaign of violence within the Third World should or should not be characterized as terrorism. The spread of liberal-democratic forms in the Third World has helped to strengthen the case of those arguing for an extensive interpretation of the concept, allowing, for example, rural guerrillas to be labelled as terrorists. The line of argument commonly advanced is that the illegitimacy of any kind of political violence within the context of a liberal-democracy provides a justication for using the label 'terrorism' regardless of the particular methods of violence employed. It has been applied not just to the Sendero Luminoso but to separatist groups such as the Liberation Tigers of Tamil Eelam (LTTE) in Sri Lanka. But if it is appropriate to apply the term in the context of debilitated liberal-democracies unable to establish their writ over large areas of the territory under their jurisdiction, it becomes a short step to apply it to any group employing any method of organized violence against what one considers to be a legitimate government, whatever the character of the political system in the country in question. In practice, this has allowed the labelling of violent movements to become a matter of name-calling, reflecting one's own particular political prejudices and preferences.

Name-calling

Thus, during the 1980s many on the left, broadly sympathetic to the Sandinistas in their confrontation with the United States, called the Contras operating in Nicaragua terrorists.[27] Similarly, UNITA (Uniao Nacional para a Independencia Total de Angola – National Union for the Total Independence of Angola) has been characterized as a 'pseudo-insurgency'[28] because of the support and arms it received from Pretoria. Admittedly, the Contras did not fit the classic stereotype of a guerrilla as a fish operating in a sea of peasant discontent, but at the same time they bore little resemblance to the stereotype of a terrorist as a masked gunman. A justification often given for the label is that the Contras carried out atrocities against the civilian population. If that criterion were to be widely used as a basis of calling organizations terrorist, many conventional armies involved in fighting insurgencies would also merit the description.

In contrast to the Contras, UNITA, with a strong base among the Ovimbundu people of Angola, clearly did (and does) fit the criteria of a rural guerrilla movement. Indeed, it is typical of a number of such movements in African states in which ethnicity rather than class has been the major determinant of the movement's popular support. These range across the ideological spectrum, though in the case of some of these movements, their ideological stance is largely a function of their external sources of support and will vary according to external circumstances. Thus, before the collapse of Portuguese colonial rule, the ideology of UNITA was Maoist,[29] but during the 1980s it consciously cultivated an image of being 'pro-Western' in its ideology and achieved a measure of success in persuading the media to describe it in these terms, despite the fact that the actual political behaviour of the movement in the zones it controlled included the burning alive of political opponents in the manner of witches.[30]

From the other end of the political spectrum, a number of reference works on terrorism have labelled both the South West Africa People's Organization (SWAPO) and the African National Congress of South Africa (ANC) as terrorist organizations.[31] An example is the inclusion of SWAPO and the ANC in a list of 'active terrorist groups' in *Terrorism as State-sponsored Covert Warfare* by Ray Cline and Yonah Alexander,[32] writers widely treated as experts in the field of terrorism. The listing of SWAPO among terrorist organizations is quite extraordinary at a number of levels. Not merely was South African rule in the territory of South West Africa unambiguously illegitimate in terms of the established international norm of self-determination, making it a clear-cut case of colonial rule; it had actually been declared to be illegal in 1971 in an Advisory Opinion of the International Court of Justice. This followed the decision of the United Nations General Assembly to withdraw the League of Nations mandate under which South Africa had ruled the territory since the end of the First World War.

The nature of SWAPO's campaign from the outset had been one of rural guerrilla warfare, and it had been evident at an early stage of the conflict that it enjoyed widespread popular support in the areas where it was fighting. In response the South African government had mounted large-scale military operations both within the territory and in Angola. Activities generally associated with terrorism such as urban bombings or attacks on foreigners played very little part in SWAPO's campaign. This is not to sanitize the nature of the conflict, which was marked on both sides by actions that ran clearly contrary to the Geneva Conventions on the conduct of war and by loss of life far exceeding the numbers of those killed globally in all acts of international terrorism since 1968. It is simply to underline the point that the labelling of SWAPO as a terrorist organization had little basis in the methods the organization used.[33]

It is also evident that the label was not based on any judgement as to the degree of popular support the organization enjoyed. In particular, it seems very unlikely that Cline and Alexander included SWAPO in their list out of a sincere but mistaken belief that the organization enjoyed only limited backing from the people of Namibia. In fact, SWAPO's victory in the elections in 1989 to the constituent assembly in Namibia, when it won 57 per cent of the vote, was not treated by the Western media as a surprising outcome.[34] The key issue for Cline and Alexander clearly was the fact that SWAPO received support from the Soviet Union and its allies. Given Western reluctance to support any movement that used violence of any kind against white rule, such links were hardly surprising.

At the same time, they presented elements on the right with a pretext for supporting the continuation of white rule in southern Africa in the name of anti-communism. The African nationalist movements in these countries were not called terrorist in the belief that they did not represent the majority of the population in these countries. Consequently, calling them terrorist, notwithstanding their strong claim to represent a majority of the population, carried the implication of approval of the continued denial of political rights to the majority of the population. The muted concern over that implication on the right can be seen as reflecting a measure of ambivalence over the ending of the colonial era, a reluctance to accept fully the legitimacy of the post-colonial order, and hostility to the additional demands of nationalists in the Third World for a greater share of the world's wealth.

However, the implication of support for white supremacy was one reason why the more liberal sections of opinion in South Africa were reluctant to call the ANC or even its military wing terrorist,[35] despite the fact that one component of its armed struggle had been urban bombings that clearly fitted most people's conception of acts of terrorism. And while the declared policy of the ANC was to avoid civilian casualties in such bombings, in practice, civilians were killed and injured in the attacks. The fact that white liberals recognized the ANC's political legitimacy did not prevent them from condemning these tactics. While urban bombings were relatively infrequent and were not a major or even particularly significant source of political violence in South Africa during the 1980s, they provided the American State Department with a pretext for including the ANC in its 'world-wide overview of organizations that engage in terrorism'.[36]

The emphasis the State Department's 1989 report, *Patterns of Global Terrorism*, gave to the ANC's links with the South African Communist Party and the support it received from the Soviet Union provided an indication of the American government's priorities in respect of the ANC, though the negative picture given of it was qualified by the observation that the organization had not attacked American interests.[37] The case of the PLO parallels in some respects that of the ANC. The insistence of the Israeli right and those sympathetic to them in the West on continuing to call the PLO a terrorist organization, even after Arafat's specific repudiation of the use of terrorist methods in December 1988, stemmed less from scepticism about his sincerity than a desire to deny all political legitimacy not just to the PLO but to the Palestinians as a people entitled to exercise the right of self-determination in some shape or form.

Precisely because the element of propaganda in the use of the terms 'terrorism' and 'terrorist' is so evident in cases like these, writers or newspapers seeking to present an objective analysis of the situation tend to avoid their use.[38] Another factor operating against the use of the terms in the context of the Third World is the fact that the Western media devote very little coverage to events in the Third World, and only situations that involve very high levels of political violence tend to be reported in any depth. But in situations of turmoil where there is a great deal of overt violence taking place, it becomes difficult to isolate particular incidents as acts of terrorism in the sense that the term is generally understood in the West and to distinguish its occurrence from other forms of violence. Even in the West, when clandestine violence exists alongside other forms of violence such as rioting, there is disinclination to use the term 'terrorism' as a generalized description of the clandestine violence because of its association with a larger problem of political violence that has to be addressed politically.

In the Third World, information about the circumstances in which people have died is often extremely scanty, and reports of serious incidents involving large loss of life may provide little more information than rough estimates of the numbers killed. An example is provided by the reporting of intercommunal violence in Burundi between Hutu and Tutsi in August 1988. News of the conflict was brought first by Tutsi refugees to neighbouring Rwanda, then by a much larger group of Hutu refugees with horrifying stories of a reprisal massacre by the Tutsi-dominated armed forces. Estimates of the numbers killed ranged from 5,000, a figure given by Burundi's foreign minister, to 24,000.[39] This was by no means the first episode of this type in Burundi.

The killings in Burundi in August 1988 also illustrate well a general problem of using the term 'terrorism' in a Third World context. The terror felt by those who fled to neighbouring states in fear of their lives would seem to provide excellent grounds for using the term 'terrorism' as a description of what they experienced, yet their experiences could hardly be further removed from the context in which the term is used in the West. The huge difference in living standards between First World and Third World, underlined at the beginning of this chapter, is also reflected in very large differences in life experiences.

Fear of the Third World

In comparison with the turmoil that affects the Third World, political violence in Western societies or attacks on Westerners outside their own societies remain a very trivial problem. Nevertheless, it remains far easier for most of the consumers of the Western mass media that dominate global communications to empathize with victims of the latter than with those of the former. This comes out very strongly in the literature on terrorism itself. Charles Kegley opens a study of international terrorism with the following fictional example:

> Picture yourself a passenger on an international flight from New York to London. Without warning, the pilot announces that gunmen claiming to represent the Third World Liberation Army have seized control of the aircraft and intend to hold you and the other passengers hostage until their demands are met by the governments of the North Atlantic Treaty Organization. Moreover, the pilot announces that the commandos have declared that the failure to receive compliance with their demands will result in the death of the entire crew and passengers.[40]

While Kegley invents the idea of a 'Third World Liberation Army', he makes no suggestions as to what the demands of such a group might be. It is perhaps unnecessary for him to do so, as the divide between the First and Third World provides such wide scope for the generation of demands. At the same time, there appears to be little possibility of a defusing of North–South tensions, since it is by no means clear how the gap between the rich and poor nations of the world can be prevented from growing, let alone reduced. Indeed, it can be argued that it is the very absence of any obvious political or economic solution to the problem of global inequality which generates fear within the affluent world of a violent reaction in the Third World that will cross into the First World itself.

The growth of the extreme right in Europe reflects, in part, receptivity to the argument that immigration from the Third World facilitates the spill-over into the West of the political problems of the poor nations, including that of political violence. The argument is frequently presented in terms of a medical metaphor of the spread of disease. It is an analogy that finds plenty of echoes in the literature on terrorism. Kegley is a striking example.

> Since the 1960s, acts of international terrorism have recurred with sufficient frequency for terrorism to rise steadily on the global agenda. Regarded as a chronic condition potentially of epidemic proportions, it has commanded increasing resources to combat. As the affliction has contagiously spread, it has changed from a problem once overwhelm-ingly identified with obscure insurrectionists in remote areas to one that today might strike anyone, any place.[41]

While such alarmism is hardly justified by the actual threat to life and limb that international terrorism poses to the citizens of the West, it does provide a relatively easy means of persuading readers of the significance of the subject. It derives credibility both from the high priority given to the need to fight the scourge of international terrorism by Western politicians and from the extensive coverage acts of international terrorism attract from the mass media. The attention that international terrorism receives is in striking contrast to its level. Compared to civil conflicts in the Third World, the numbers killed in international terrorism are minuscule. However, the issues are not entirely separate.

Part of the fear of international terrorism derives from concern that instability in the Third World will give rise to violence across national boundaries. There are sufficient examples of a connection between the two levels of violence to lend credibility to such concern. The Lebanese civil war between 1975 and 1991 provides the most clear-cut case of the link. This aspect of the Lebanese conflict is discussed further in the next chapter. But the existence of examples of such a link should not obscure the fact that in the vast majority of cases there has been relatively little spill-over from political violence within Third World states into the international arena.

9

The international dimensions
of terrorism

As we have already noted, most sets of statistics on global terrorism
are limited to international terrorism. The generally accepted definition of 'international' in this context is that the terrorism involves the
citizenry or territory of more than one country. On this interpretation,
the murder of an American soldier based in West Germany by Germans would count as an act of international terrorism, provided of
course the killers had an identifiable political motive.[1] The kidnapping
of an Italian businessman by urban guerrillas in Argentina would also
find its way into the statistics on international terrorism.[2] Another
example might be the killing of a South African exile in France by a
South African death squad,[3] though the issue of state involvement
complicates the issue in this case, as does the absence of a claim of
responsibility. The difficulty of getting information on domestic
terrorism in well over 200 different political entities, approximately
175 of which are sovereign independent states, is often given as a
justification for confining the figures to international terrorism. However, the reasons for the exclusion of domestic terrorism in truth go
much deeper than the problem of collecting the data.

Political context affects the judgement of whether an act of political
violence should be labelled one of terrorism. Simply to label acts of
violence directed against governments as terrorism would be to give a
blanket endorsement to the legitimacy of the political *status quo* in
every country, regardless of either the ideology of those in power or
the regime's durability. Even a restricted definition of what types of
violence to include in the category of terrorism provides only a partial
answer to the problem, since however such a list was constructed,
particular political contexts would suggest that the list was either too
broad or too narrow. While there is a wide consensus in the West on
the legitimacy of the liberal-democracies in the industrialized world,
which might permit cross-country comparison of domestic terrorism

in these states, such a consensus would be very difficult to achieve in respect of the diverse political systems of the Third World.

To admit that one's figures depend on the political judgements one makes about particular situations has quite naturally not been a course that commended itself to those working in the field of compiling statistics on terrorism. However, the difficulty of judging the legitimacy of different types of regime and the problem of collecting the data are not the only reasons for the exclusion of domestic terrorism. The presumption is that most cases of terrorism have international dimensions. Wilkinson has argued that terrorism is 'inherently international in character' and that it is 'very hard to find a pure case of internal terrorism'.[4] This is at least partly due to the disposition to attach the label of terrorism to political violence that crosses international boundaries and disturbs the peace of the stable liberal-democracies of the industrialized world.

International norms

The emphasis on compiling data on international terrorism also carries the implication that the illegitimacy of the violence in question partly derives from its international character. Involving foreigners or the territory of another country in a battle for control of the state is generally seen as a violation of the normative limits on such a struggle for power. It is a corollary of another norm, that states should not involve themselves in the domestic affairs of other countries.[5] This norm places foreigners in the position of innocent bystanders. By the same token, making use of another state's territory constitutes a violation of its neutrality. Of course, all this presupposes both that it is possible to draw a reasonably clear distinction between the domestic affairs of the state and its role in the international system, which is a legitimate concern of other states, and that the norm of non-involvement in the domestic affairs of other states is sufficiently generally adhered to, that foreigners or foreign territory do not appear to constitute legitimate targets.

Both these propositions have been strongly contested by groups that have justified attacking foreigners or extending their conflict with domestic counterparts to foreign soil. Indeed, if one were to assume that terrorism embodied some form of ideology, then the contention that foreign interests constitute an illegitimate prop of local power structures might be taken to be one of its key assumptions. As we saw in Chapter 5, a feature of many groups that have attracted the label of terrorist is the assertion that they are engaged in a struggle against imperialism. However, anti-imperialist groups which engage in political violence are far from being alone in their treatment of the distinction between the domestic and foreign affairs of the state as artificial. States, especially the most powerful states, have increasingly taken the view that they have a legitimate foreign-policy interest in the outcome of domestic conflicts which justifies their intervention in such conflicts. Further, the argument that the non-intervention norm should be overridden in cases of gross violations of human rights has attracted increasing support.[6] At its most extensive, intervention takes the form of overt military action, including the dispatch of troops to the territory in question. Below that level, intervention may take the form of covert action, involving forms of violence such as assassinations and bombings that are very commonly labelled terrorism when carried out by sub-state groups.

The overlapping of the methods of covert warfare and those of terrorism raises the question of whether a clear distinction can be drawn between them. If covert warfare is treated as a species of terrorism, then it becomes much more difficult to claim that terrorism at an international level is a novel development, since covert warfare has been a feature of international relations since time immemorial. At the beginning of the age of terrorism, two factors appeared to distinguish the new violence from covert warfare. Firstly, it was perpetrated by members of sub-state groups and not directly by the agents of any state. Secondly, while employing clandestine methods, the perpetrators were eager to secure publicity for their cause and even for their organization. By contrast, the covert warfare waged by states was rarely conducted with an eye for such notoriety.

Transnationalism

The involvement of sub-state groups in violence at an international level formed the main focus of analysis in the 1970s and was encapsulated in the description 'transnational terrorism'. 'Transnational' was used to describe activities that crossed the boundaries of states, but which did not involve the state as an institution. Thus, a contrast was drawn between 'international' relations and 'transnational' relations, with the former confined to inter-state relations. An example of the usage of the term that was common in the 1970s was the description of multi-national companies as transnational corporations, which was sometimes shortened to TNCs. The growing volume of social intercourse across national boundaries that was independent of the state attracted considerable attention, and the general significance of transnationalism as evidence of the increasing interdependence of states was a subject which was hotly debated within the academic discipline of international relations.[7]

ınce of transnationalism
...stinction between dom-
ᴄᵴᴛᴵᴄ ᴀᴎᴅ international politics. On the other hand, their critics stressed the continuing primacy of the state in relation to maintenance of security. On the whole, the critics got the better of the argument because interdependence did not have the dramatic political consequences that some of the proponents predicted. In particular, the nation-state has not become obsolete, nor has the political power of multi-national companies begun to match their size in economic terms. The failure of these predictions has tended to obscure the fact that the consequences of the growth of interdependence have, none the less, been profound.

Of these, perhaps the most significant has been the erosion of the autonomy of the state in economic matters. The political impact of this erosion has varied. In general, it has tended to strengthen rather than to weaken the political appeal of nationalism. This is despite the fact that interdependence has tended to make the pursuit of policies of economic nationalism both more difficult and much more costly. In the West this has resulted in greater emphasis on market-oriented economic policies, whatever the ideological complexion of the government in power in a particular country. But the greatest impact has been on the countries of Eastern Europe, where it has contributed to the shattering of the communist system.

Political violence at the international level can also be viewed as the product of the growth of interdependence among nations, as the term 'transnational terrorism' suggests. Indeed, one can trace the political evolution of violence from below as predominantly local in scope prior to the French Revolution; impinging more and more on national politics during the two hundred years following the revolution; and finally operating at an international level in the twentieth century, when sub-state groups acquired the capacity and, just as importantly, the motivation to intervene at this level. This evolution can itself be linked both to the increasing portability of the material instruments of violence and to the greatly enhanced mobility of its human agents. Powerful explosives such as Semtex that are difficult to detect, sophisticated electronic timing devices, and lightweight automatic weapons number among the instruments, while the ubiquity and ease of air travel mean that there are few major cities in the world that are more than a day apart in travelling time. If this seems to be no more than a statement of the obvious, something that people in the West have come to take for granted, it is worth reflecting that prior to the 1960s, travel beyond national borders was confined to a tiny minority of the population even within the affluent industrialized world, except in the special contexts of migration and war.

The picture that the concept of transnational terrorism presented was of a challenge to the international political system by sub-state groups, a challenge made possible by the shrinking of the world through the spread of modern communications. Palestinian groups such as the Popular Front for the Liberation of Palestine (PFLP) and Black September seemed to fit this picture well. The Palestinians themselves stood out as perhaps the leading example of a community that had missed out on the process of state formation that took place in the Third World as a result of decolonization. They had paid the price for the understandable desire of the industrialized world to accommodate Jewish demands for the creation of a Jewish state in the wake of the Holocaust. The resort of Palestinian groups to forms of violence such as hijacking and hostage-taking could be seen both as a response to the defeat of the Arab states during their 1967 war with Israel and as a protest against the existing international order.

The logic of directing violence at international targets was that the Palestinians' demand for self-determination depended on change in the international political system itself and that it was only through action at this level that the attention of the world was likely to be drawn to the plight of the Palestinians as a stateless nation. The weakness of this rationale for violence was that securing the attention of the world by no means guaranteed its sympathy. Indeed, the use of violence as a means of attracting attention is inherently risky, since, unless such violence appears to be linked to other, more legitimate ends, it is likely to repel rather than attract sympathy. In particular, as a means of generating support for the Palestinian cause, hijackings and hostage-taking soon became counter-productive, as the PLO itself recognized from the mid-1970s. However, the Palestinian cause continued to be identified with terrorism and that affected attitudes towards the PLO internationally prior to the Oslo accord between the PLO and the Israeli government. In December 1988 the PLO leader Yasser Arafat issued the unequivocal repudiation of terrorism sought by the United States as a condition for dialogue with the organization.[8] However, this breakthrough proved short-lived. In May 1990, Israeli forces foiled an attack on a Tel Aviv beachfront by members of the Palestinian Liberation Front (PLF), an organization affiliated to the PLO. When Arafat failed to take action against the PLF over the attack, the United States government suspended its dialogue with the PLO. A State Department report noted that the PLF's attack was carried out 'with substantial assistance from Libya'.[9]

State sponsorship

The emphasis placed on the role that states played in supporting violence by sub-state groups was one of the reasons why the concept of transnational terrorism became less and less used during the 1980s. Concern over state sponsorship of terrorism was reflected in the passage of legislation in the United States in 1979 requiring the Secretary of State to impose sanctions on countries which he considered had repeatedly provided support for acts of international terrorism.[10] Such states were named in a list sent annually to Congress. States could be added to or subtracted from the list at any time. They became known as the 'terrorist states'. In theory, a distinction could be made between states which sponsored sub-state groups and states which themselves directly participated in covert warfare, but in practice the distinction became somewhat blurred. Thus, North Korea was on the State Department's list, principally because of the involvement of its own agents in acts of international terrorism.[11]

The notion of a 'terrorist state' should not be confused with the notion of 'state terrorism', which is generally applied in the first instance to a regime's overt use of terror on a large scale within a domestic context. The State Department has at least been consistent in distinguishing between the two notions. Thus, violence within the state without an international dimension is not taken into consideration in the compiling of its list. For example, its reports concern themselves with the sanctuary that Saddam Hussein has given to the Kurdish Workers Party, which operates in Turkey, and not his treatment of the Kurds inside Iraq.

Nevertheless, the limitations of the State Department's list remain very considerable. On the basis of the types of support that the State Department uses to justify including particular countries on its list, such as providing safe havens to sub-state groups engaged in terrorism, it would be possible to make out a case for the inclusion of a very large number of countries, especially given its broad definition of terrorism as 'premeditated, politically motivated violence perpetrated against noncombatant targets by subnational or clandestine agents'.[12] Further, 'noncombatant' in this context includes unarmed or off-duty military personnel, and even armed personnel in some contexts. In practice, whether a country is listed as a 'terrorist state' is at least as much a reflection of that country's relations with the United States as it is of its actual behaviour. The 1989 report, *Patterns of Global Terrorism*, noted that 'the United States has maintained its formal designation of six countries as state supporters of terrorism – Cuba, Iran, Libya, North Korea, South Yemen, and Syria'.[13] While the report provided information to justify the inclusion of each of these countries on the list, its discussion of state-sponsored terrorism was not confined to these countries, and the report as a whole gave information that could readily have been used to include many more countries on the list.

A notable omission from the 1989 list was Iraq. It had been removed from the list in 1982. It was reinstated in September 1990, following the Iraqi invasion of Kuwait.[14] In the course of the 1988 presidential election campaign, the omission of South Africa from the list was raised by the Democratic candidate. After giving accounts of a number of attacks on members of the ANC outside South Africa in the course of the year, the 1988 report from the State Department on *Patterns of Global Terrorism* noted that 'the US Government has expressed serious and repeated concern to the South African Government about the incidents of cross-border violence'.[15] This criticism of the South African government was balanced by reference to the fact that the struggle against apartheid, 'although largely nonviolent', had also resulted in 'some acts of terrorism'. The report went on to criticize the failure of the ANC to take action against members who violated its policy of not targeting civilians, and it noted that 'the US Government has strongly counseled the ANC against further acts of violence of this nature'.[16]

Self-defence

The relatively small number of states designated as 'terrorist states' is in part due to a reluctance to extend the number of countries to which the United States would be obliged to apply trade sanctions. But it is also a reflection of the fact that states can plead self-defence as a justification for covert warfare by their agents. That theme runs through the State Department reports' description of operations carried out by Israel, including such action as the abduction of a prominent Hizbollah cleric, Sheikh Obeid, in 1989. During the Reagan administration, there was strong endorsement of the steps taken by Israel to fight terrorism in line with its own commitment to forceful action against terrorism directed at the United States or against American citizens.

A change of tone is evident in the 1991 State Department report, which is more critical of Israel's actions than any of the earlier reports. However, the theme of justified self-defence remains prominent. It notes:

Israeli counterterrorist efforts continue to target countries aiding, harboring, or failing to inhibit terrorists. Israeli military forces have launched preemptive and retaliatory airstrikes against suspected terrorist installations in neighboring Lebanon and have occasionally detained Lebanese nationals in an attempt to thwart attacks.[17]

The characterization of Israeli actions contrasts most sharply with the designation of similar sorts of cross-border operations carried out by the Soviet-backed Afghan government in the course of the 1980s as international terrorism, even when explicitly discussing the targeting of 'antiregime fighters'.[18]

But if state involvement makes it hard to draw a clear distinction in theory between terrorism and counter-terrorism, in practice the Reagan administration seemed to have little difficulty in deciding which governments were its enemies, particularly in the context of the 'Second Cold War'[19] of the early 1980s, and designating its actions accordingly. It met little resistance in defining the issue of international terrorism in terms that fitted in with its wider foreign policy objectives from a public whose prime concern quite naturally was terrorism that presented a threat to the West or to Westerners. The Reagan administration used the issue to reshape the priorities of American foreign policy. Thus, shortly after taking office as Secretary of State, Alexander Haig announced:

> International terrorism will take the place of human rights as our concern, because it is the ultimate abuse of human rights. And it's time it be addressed with greater clarity and greater effectiveness by Western nations and the United States as well.[20]

Clarity was provided by the emphasis placed on state sponsorship, while Haig's castigation of the Soviet Union for training, funding, and equipping terrorists elevated the issue to one of strategic concern.

It was a perspective echoed in a number of books on terrorism published during the 1980s.[21] Chalmers Johnson attributed the change in American perceptions of the nature of terrorism to the holding of American diplomats as hostages in Tehran between 1979 and 1981. He concluded: 'It became clear that much of the terrorism of the 1970's was not transnational but international, a form of surrogate warfare in an international system in which open warfare had become too dangerous.'[22] That international terrorism was an instrument of the foreign policy of certain states became the new orthodoxy. In 1986, the American Ambassador to the United Nations, Charles Lichtenstein, asserted simply that 'all terrorism is in fact state terrorism'.[23]

Western response

Lichtenstein's assertion coincided with one of the highpoints of Western concern over the issue of terrorism, prompted by a series of outrages. In June 1985 a Trans World Airlines (TWA) Boeing 727 was hijacked by members of Islamic Jihad on a flight from Athens to Rome. They diverted the flight to Beirut. It took protracted negotiations through intermediaries to secure the release of the passengers and crew, some of whom were held hostage for two weeks. Their ordeal attracted huge media attention. One passenger, a diver in the US Navy, was murdered by the hijackers at an early stage. In the same month, an Air India Boeing 747 exploded in mid-air over the Atlantic, with the loss of 329 lives. Suspicion immediately fell on Sikh separatists.

In August, a car-bomb killed two Americans in a US Air Force base in West Germany, an attack carried out by the Red Army Faction. In September, members of a Palestinian organization, Force 17, murdered three Israelis on a yacht in Larnaca marina, Cyprus. Their claim that the three were Mossad agents was denied by Israel. That was followed in October by the hijacking of an Italian cruise ship, *Achille Lauro*, during which an American in a wheelchair was murdered. In December, 19 people died in co-ordinated attacks on El Al check-in desks at airports in Rome and Vienna. In April 1986, four passengers died when a bomb blew a hole in the side of a TWA Boeing 727 on a flight from Rome to Athens. Three days later an American soldier and a Turkish woman died and 204 people were injured in a bomb attack on a West Berlin discotheque.

This attack was followed by American military action against Libya. In justifying the bombing of Tripoli and Benghazi, President Reagan disclosed the contents of communications between Tripoli and the Libyan People's Bureau in East Berlin which, he argued, suggested that agents of the Libyan state had been involved in the discotheque bombing. Later in the same month, April 1986, El Al security staff at Heathrow airport thwarted an attempt to smuggle a bomb on board a flight to Israel. Police arrested a Jordanian, Nezar Hindawi, who implicated diplomats in the Syrian embassy in London in the attempt.[24]

The subject of international terrorism was discussed at a summit of the leading industrial nations of the world in May 1986. A declaration was issued, reflecting current opinion on the issue. Not surprisingly, it placed a lot of emphasis on the question of state sponsorship. It began:

We, the heads of state or government of seven major democracies and the representatives of the European Community, assembled here in Tokyo, strongly reaffirm our condemnation of international terrorism in all its forms, of its accomplices and of those, including governments, who sponsor and support it. We abhor the increase in the level of such terrorism since our last meeting [in May 1985 in Bonn], and in particular its blatant and cynical use as an instrument of government policy. Terrorism has no justification. It spreads only by the use of contemptible means, ignoring the values of human life, freedom, and dignity. It must be fought relentlessly and without compromise.[25]

The statement went on to name Libya as a sponsor of international terrorism, providing retrospective justification for the American raid on Tripoli and Benghazi.

Even at the time it was issued, the limitations of this perspective on the problem of terrorism were apparent. In a piece published in 1986, Adam Roberts used the paragraph quoted above as the basis for a wide-ranging critique of Western policy. In particular, he questioned whether isolating 'terrorist states', the course of action urged by the summit, was as easy a solution to the problem as it appeared, pointing out that 'the state which engages in support for one terrorist cause may itself be a valued partner in some other activities – not just in trade, but also in matters relating to international security, even in the control of some forms of terrorism'.[26] Further, he argued that 'preoccupation with the idea of the "terrorist state" as the *fons et origo* of terrorism may serve to obscure the other causes of this phenomenon'.[27] In fact, events themselves underlined the difficulty of trying to make states accountable for the violent actions of sub-state groups.

Western impotence when the TWA airliner had been hijacked to Beirut in June 1985 was not the result of the relationship of the hijackers to any terrorist state, but rather a consequence of the weakness of the Lebanese authorities. The incapacity of the Lebanese state meant that it could not reasonably be held responsible for most of the acts of political violence that occurred within its boundaries. By the time of the Tokyo summit, a number of foreigners had been kidnapped in West Beirut, including, among others, an American journalist, Terry Anderson; an American academic, Thomas Sutherland; and a British journalist, John McCarthy. They were to become household names before their release in 1991, as the fate of Western hostages in Lebanon increasingly came to preoccupy Western governments, media, and public.

Hostages in Lebanon

The issue of foreign political hostages in Lebanon underlined the complexity of the relationship between states and sub-state groups engaged in violence. Lebanese society was deeply divided among a number of different religious communities. When the country became independent in 1943, the leaders of the different communities agreed on a complex formula for the representation of the communities within the political system. Modernization and demographic change slowly undermined the basis of accommodation among the communities. The first breakdown occurred in 1958, when an attempt by the Christian Maronite president to align the country with the West, contrary to the National Pact agreed in 1943, provoked a revolt by Muslims. Equilibrium was restored by the commander of the armed forces, General Chehab, who refused to allow the army to be used on the side of the Maronites.

After he was elected president himself, Chehab sought to strengthen the state as a force that could stand above the society's divisions. However, in 1970 a regional clan leader was elected president and he destroyed the system that Chehab had created. Lebanon never recovered. The start of Lebanon's second civil war is generally dated from April 1975 and a massacre of 27 Palestinians on a bus ambushed by Maronite gunmen. The episode reflected the importance of the Palestinian presence in Lebanon and Maronite reaction to it as a cause of the country's slide into civil war. After the first Arab–Israeli war in 1948–49, 100,000 Palestinian refugees settled in Lebanon. Their numbers grew further after the 1967 Arab–Israeli war and the 1970 expulsion of the PLO from Jordan. By 1975, there were 350,000 Palestinians in Lebanon, constituting about 10 per cent of the country's population. The Maronites regarded their presence as a destabilizing force within the country that disturbed the balance of power among the different communities. At the same time, the PLO's use of Lebanese territory as a launching pad for attacks on northern Israel was turning Lebanon into a target for Israeli retaliation. The hands of the Lebanese state were tied by the 1969 Cairo agreement, which obliged Lebanon to support the Palestinian cause.

But there were also other factors fuelling conflict within Lebanon. Muslims now constituted a clear majority of the population, but had fewer representatives within the political system than Christians under the rigid and outdated formula used to determine political representation of the communities. The enormous gulf between rich and poor was a further source of conflict. The main contestants in the first phase of civil war were a right-wing Maronite-led grouping, the

Lebanese Front, and a left-wing, mainly Muslim grouping, the National Movement. In April 1976 Syrian troops intervened at the request of Lebanon's Maronite president. In 1975 and 1976 50,000 people died in the civil war. Syrian intervention had failed to end the conflict, but at the same time Israel became increasingly disturbed by the extension of Syrian influence.

In 1978 the Israelis moved into southern Lebanon, withdrawing after the establishment of the United Nations Interim Force in Lebanon (UNIFIL) to stop Palestinian incursions into Israel from Lebanon. In 1982 Israel mounted a full-scale invasion on the assumption that ending the PLO's military presence in Lebanon would destroy the organization's political influence in the occupied territories.[28] After Israeli troops besieged Beirut, a multi-national force composed principally of American and French troops was established to supervise the withdrawal of the PLO from Beirut. Adding to the catalogue of external interventions was the presence of revolutionary guards from Iran, reflecting the influence of Iran's Islamic revolution on the Shia Muslim population of Lebanon, the largest and poorest of the country's confessional communities.

The impact of the arrival of all these foreign forces on Lebanon's civil war inevitably made them targets of violence from those who felt disadvantaged by their presence. In this context the high-minded motives that outside powers put forward to justify their intervention in Lebanon unsurprisingly counted for very little. Violence against foreigners took a variety of forms. One was bombings. In April 1983, the American embassy in Beirut was bombed, killing 60 people, while in October simultaneous attacks by suicide truck-bombers on the headquarters of the American marines and the barracks of French paratroopers killed 241 American and 58 French servicemen. In November, the Israeli military headquarters in Tyre were struck by the suicide bombers. Sixty died in that attack. In September 1984, nine died when the American embassy in Beirut was attacked once again.

However, the foreign powers were not simply the victims of bomb attacks. In a number of cases they were directly or indirectly responsible for such outrages themselves. In March 1985, a massive car-bomb outside the offices of a Hizbollah leader, Sheikh Fadlallah, killed 80 people and injured another 256, many of them women and children who had been worshipping at a nearby mosque. Sheikh Fadlallah escaped unharmed. He was the target of the bombing, which the *Washington Post* reported had been carried out at the behest of the Central Intelligence Agency (CIA), apparently in revenge for the October 1983 attack on the American marines.[29] Hizbollah (the Party of God) draped a banner reading 'The work of the United States' over the ruined buildings.[30]

Another form that violence against foreigners took was hostage-taking. Its first victims, excluding local Palestinians and Syrians, were three Iranians, two of whom were diplomats. They were kidnapped by a Maronite militia, the Lebanese Forces, in July 1982. In 1991 an Israeli intelligence report concluded that they had been murdered shortly after their capture. The abduction of the Iranians was followed in the same month by that of David Dodge, the acting president of the American University of Beirut. His abduction was linked to that of the Iranians. He was released a year later without explanation, though it did emerge that he had been held in Iran for part of his captivity. Responsibility for his abduction was claimed by Islamic Jihad, which turned out simply to be one of Hizbollah's many *noms de guerre*. The next abductions were in 1984. In the course of the year an American academic, a French construction engineer, the CIA's station chief in Beirut, an American pastor, a British reporter, and an American reporter were taken hostage.

A wave of kidnapping followed the attempt on Sheikh Fadlallah; another the American bombing of Libya. When the last of the Western hostages, two German aid workers who had originally been abducted in May 1989, were released in June 1992, some 80 foreigners had been kidnapped. Some were held only briefly. A small number even managed to escape from their captors. Others died or were murdered in captivity, though the proportion of foreign captives who met this fate was very much smaller than the fatalities among the thousands of Lebanese and Palestinians abducted during the civil war; many of them were murdered soon after their capture. The foreigners who remained in captivity for a period of years, such as the American reporter Terry Anderson, who was abducted in March 1985 and only released in December 1991, attracted the most publicity. The appalling conditions in which hostages were held added to public concern over their plight.

Negotiations

The hostage crisis presented Western governments with a dilemma. Doing nothing conveyed an impression of impotence, an appearance of weakness which enhanced the vulnerability of their interests to attack. Since Western military forces had been driven out of Lebanon in 1984 by the suicide truck-bombers, military intervention to rescue the hostages was not a realistic option. Public policy that no concessions should be made to terrorism ruled out direct deals. That left as the only option seeking the assistance of third parties in a position to influence the behaviour of the kidnappers. However, the legitimacy of this option depended on governments' being able to maintain that there was a clear distinction between such third parties and the kidnappers themselves. Otherwise, any rewards for the third parties would look like just another form of surrender to terrorism.

The emphasis that Western policy-makers had put on state sponsorship of terrorism, and particularly, in the case of the United States, on the role played by Iran and Syria, made their position more difficult. When the Iran-Contra scandal, involving the sale of American arms to Iran and the siphoning of the proceeds to rebels in Nicaragua, broke in November 1986, the Reagan administration was widely condemned for breaching its own precepts on international terrorism, because Iran's use of its influence with Hizbollah to secure the release of three Americans formed part of the deal. France also dealt with Iran to secure release of hostages.[31]

In the light of the rhetoric of Western governments on the subject of terrorism, such dealings understandably gave rise to considerable public cynicism. And Western governments themselves were largely to blame for public misperception of Hizbollah as simply a surrogate of the Iranian government. In fact, the failure of Iran's President Rafsanjani to achieve his objective of ending the hostage crisis by the close of 1990 underlined the independence of the Lebanese paramilitaries, notwithstanding the close ideological and other ties between Hizbollah and Iran, in particular. The catastrophe that befell Lebanon as a result of foreign intervention in its civil war provided the various Lebanese factions with ample reasons of their own for hostility towards foreigners. Whereas in most civil conflicts the fear of provoking foreign intervention constitutes a reason for restraint by contending factions, that consideration hardly applied in Lebanon. The extent of foreign involvement in Lebanon was the reflection of a number of factors: the strategic importance of the Middle East, the intensity of competition among different powers for influence in the region, and the extreme weakness of the Lebanese state itself. By internationalizing the conflict, these larger factors contributed indirectly to the creation of the hostage crisis. By the same token, changes in international alignments in the region as a result of the end of the Cold War and of the 1991 Gulf War were factors contributing indirectly to its resolution.

The piracy analogy

While the case of the Lebanese hostages demonstrated all too clearly the superficiality of treating international terrorism as an aspect of the foreign policy of hostile states, the way in which the issue was interwoven with relations between states underscored the limitations of the notion of transnational terrorism. Further, the concept was almost an oxymoron in the context of the perspective on international relations with which the term 'transnational' was associated. That perspective emphasized the benign effects of interdependence in reducing the barriers between peoples and in encouraging a process of harmonization. An analogy adopted at the beginning of the age of terrorism in relation to hijacking provided a less discordant description. When it was first proposed, in October 1969, that the issue of hijacking be put on the agenda of the United Nations General Assembly, it was under the title 'Piracy in the Air'.[32]

In fact, the term 'air piracy' became a synonym for hijacking. It seemed an apt analogy. Both hijackers and pirates made use of spaces that lay outside the jurisdiction and control of states. They also both exploited political differences between states to escape capture and punishment. One could even point to instances of state sponsorship of piracy analogous to the links that sometimes existed between states and hijackers. Elizabeth I's encouragement of piracy against Spanish fleets and colonies in the late sixteenth century provided the best-known example.[33] Both hijackers and pirates frequently took hostages.

The main difference between hijackers and pirates was that the former generally had a political motive for their actions, while the motive for piracy was commonly personal enrichment. However, the distinction between the political nature of international terrorism and the criminal nature of piracy can be overdrawn. Increasingly, the term 'terrorism' is being applied to the violent activities of criminal organizations such as the Mafia, as well as to personally motivated acts of hijacking, while the label of 'pirates', or, even more commonly, 'bandits', was applied in the past to groups pursuing political as well as simply criminal aims.

Take, for example, the case of the Chinese pirates who kidnapped four officers of the British merchant navy from a ship anchored off a port in Japanese-occupied Manchuria in 1933.[34] The first of their ransom letters demanded arms: 100 light machine guns, 3,000 Japanese rifles, 120 German rifles, and 20 heavy trench mortars, and supplies of ammunition for these items. It explained why as follows:

> The reason why we want these things is solely because Japan has occupied the territory of the Three Eastern Provinces, so that the people have been driven out. Koreans also own and cultivate the region of Ying-K'ou and Tien-chuangt'ai in the Three Eastern Provinces. We Chinese cannot endure this and burn with resentment. the people are

forced to become bandits. The Chinese do not willingly become bandits: it is solely because your League of Nations speaks not of right principles.[35]

Eventually, after protracted negotiations, drawing in the Japanese and their Chinese clients, and the payment of a relatively small monetary ransom, which British officials rationalized as 'a grant in aid of expenses incurred',[36] the officers were released. In the same way, France and Germany paid 'expenses', though these were measured in millions of dollars, to secure the release of nationals held as hostages in Lebanon.[37]

The analogy between piracy and international terrorism can be developed further. Piracy flourished in conditions of international disorder, whether at a local, regional, or global level. For example, the period from 1400 to 1700, coinciding with the seaborne expansion of Europe, was a heyday of piracy. After building overseas empires, Portugal and Spain faced challenges to their position from other European maritime powers, in particular France, England, and the Netherlands. Pirates both exploited the enmities among the maritime powers and were exploited by the powers themselves. Competition for influence among the powers was particularly intense in Central America and the Caribbean. The island colony of Jamaica was one of the main centres of the buccaneers, as the pirates in this area were known, and even after the 1670 Treaty of Madrid between England and Spain, Jamaica continued to provide a safe haven for buccaneers. However, the spread of piracy to other areas, particularly the establishment of pirate settlements in the Indian Ocean, where they had access to the Asian shipping routes, threatened the commercial interests of the powers. At the same time, the global reach of piracy made it 'too dangerous to be supported by any nation as a policy against its rivals'.[38] The tolerance that states showed towards piracy during the period of seaborne expansion ceased, a change symbolized by the passage in England in 1700 of an 'Act for the More Effectual Suppression of Piracy'.[39]

A somewhat similar case can be made in respect of international terrorism. The first international conventions on terrorism were drafted against the backdrop of the unstable international conditions in Europe during the 1930s. The present age of terrorism is usually dated from the late 1960s. It coincided more or less with the start of the post-colonial age. But just as importantly its onset came at a time when it was evident that the Cold War structures that had given the world a decade of almost unparalleled peace and prosperity were breaking down. In particular, the bipolar structure of the international political system was beginning to fracture. The war in Vietnam emphasized the limits of the Pax Americana, while the Sino-Soviet split underlined the limits of communism as a monolithic force. The waning power of the super-powers was a stimulus to all manner of challenges to the *status quo*. Where political movements arose that challenged the interests of one or other of the super-powers, it was hardly surprising that they attracted support from the rival super-power or from other states seeking to break the super-powers' duopoly. The relationship between opposition movements and foreign powers took a number of forms, and the closeness of such relationships also, of course, varied very considerably.

Terror networks

During the late 1960s and through much of the decade of the 1970s, the reasons for the rise of opposition movements tended to be the focus of political analysis. Inevitably, those instances where opposition to the *status quo* resulted in political violence which spilled across international boundaries tended to attract most attention. In the 1980s with the demise of détente, conservative political analysts and the Reagan administration latched on to the issue of state sponsorship of violence, treating the relationship which existed between a number of violent sub-state groups and the Soviet Union (or countries allied to it) as evidence of a co-ordinated terrorist assault on Western interests.

The weakness of such analysis was that it failed to explain the existence of numerous violent groups that quite obviously could not be fitted into such a framework. And, in fact, by focusing on right-wing groups, left-wing critics of Sterling and of the Reagan administration were able to construct a picture of an alternative terror network that emanated from Washington rather than Moscow.[40] But even two terror networks rather than one left much unexplained. In reality, the implication that either Washington or Moscow could control events in this way was implausible. For years Western governments gave extensive support to the Mujahedin in Afghanistan, but that has not enabled them to exercise much influence over the conflict among the Afghan resistance groups that has arisen since the fall of the old regime.

Indeed, state support for violent movements in other countries or operating internationally is more commonly a sign of weakness than of strength, given the difficulty of exercising influence through such means. Further, as, generally speaking, such support is a violation of the international norms, such as the norm on non-intervention in the domestic affairs of other states, its prevalence may be taken as a sign

of disorder within the international political system. But that is perhaps too state-centric a perspective. The source of the instability is
provided by the activities of the violent sub-state groups themselves,
which for the most part were not created by states, even if they derive
some support from some states.

In particular, the notion that most, let alone all, international
terrorism is state terrorism, is very wide of the mark. It is also easy
to exaggerate the problem of international terrorism, while under-
estimating the difficulty of getting agreement on what it encompasses.
For all the attention that Western governments have lavished on the
issue, on their own calculations, the numbers killed in international
terrorist incidents are minuscule.[41] The fears that international terrorism aroused in the late 1960s and early 1970s must be seen at least in
part against the backdrop of the stability that prevailed within most
Western liberal-democracies during the 1950s.

New World Disorder

Despite the representation of international terrorism as a form of
covert warfare against the West, the demise of the communist system
in Eastern Europe and the Soviet Union has prompted few predictions
of the ending of the age of terrorism. This is not because the demise
of the Soviet Union is perceived as making no difference to violent
sub-groups that previously had ideological or other ties with Moscow,
but rather because it is recognized that, while the ending of bipolarity
may contribute to the resolution of some conflicts and lead to a de-
escalation in others, it has created new sources of instability in the
world which are likely to generate violence across national frontiers.
This has led some to fear a growth of terrorism in the wake of the
collapse of communism.[42]

Indeed, it is already apparent that the New World Order seems
likely to be an era of instability. The break-up of the Soviet Union
and of Yugoslavia have destroyed the international anathema against
secessionism, raising a question-mark over the survival of a number
of states as single entities within the international political system. At
the same time, questions of human rights and minority rights have
tended to erode the norm of non-intervention in the domestic affairs
of states, making it more difficult to maintain the distinction between
domestic and international affairs in the context of violent conflict. If,
on occasion, competition between the super-powers was a spur to
their intervention, more commonly bipolarity acted as a restraint
against intervention, whether by individual states or collectively
through the United Nations.

The more prevalent intervention becomes, the greater must be the danger of another situation like that in Lebanon during the 1980s. But the end of the Cold War also holds out the hope that global accord on issues such as terrorism may be easier to achieve, permitting effective action against some of the forms of violence most closely associated with the concept. This is one of the issues addressed in the next chapter on the stopping of terrorism, but this chapter also emphasizes the primacy of political factors in the ending of campaigns of clandestine violence by small groups.

10

Stopping terrorism

Much of the literature on terrorism is taken up with the issue of the adoption of effective steps against it. At the start of the age of terrorism, there was a measure of justification for this emphasis. In particular, there were few provisions in international law governing clandestine violence by small groups across national boundaries. Further, states themselves were ill-equipped to prevent the hijacking of planes or to handle situations where this led to the threatening of passengers as hostages, to take two examples. These shortcomings have largely been made good. International law has been developed to cover the methods associated with transnational terrorism, as will be described below. Every air-traveller is aware of the enhanced security at airports. At the same time, most governments have trained special units for the forcible ending of hostage situations. With the adoption by criminals of methods previously associated with politically motivated small groups, such precautions have increasingly become a matter of routine and are likely to remain so. However, it will be argued in this chapter that the primary factors that have stopped terrorism, at least as the concept was understood at the beginning of the age of terrorism, have been political. In particular, the failure of clandestine violence to achieve the objectives for which it has been employed has frequently led to its abandonment. In other cases it has been ended by political change, usually involving the initiation of negotiations. Both types of ending are illustrated below.

Evolution of international law

Initially, the main concern of governments in respect of violence by sub-state groups outside their own jurisdiction was to shore up the distinction between the domestic and international realms. This was reflected in the gradual evolution of a general principle of non-intervention in the domestic conflicts of other countries. The advantage to states of such a posture was that it gave the contending parties in domestic disputes an incentive not to extend their conflict to the international realm. When international co-operation to combat crime was formalized through extradition treaties, the principle of non-intervention in domestic conflicts was enshrined through the inclusion in the treaties of a clause excluding political offenders from the scope of extradition. The Franco-Belgian extradition agreement of 1834 established the precedent, which others followed. However, an attempt on the life of Napoleon III in 1855 led to a modification of the terms of the political exception clause so as to make the murder or attempted murder of a head of state or that person's immediate family an extraditable crime.[1]

British legislation of 1870 simply provided that 'no person is to be surrendered if his offence is of a political character',[2] which was enshrined as the basis of the political offence exception clause in numerous extradition treaties between Britain and other countries. The meaning of 'offence of a political character' was clarified by the High Court in London in 1891. The case involved the murder of a member of the local government during a rebellion in a Swiss canton. The judges laid down two simple rules: the existence of serious disturbances in the polity in question and a clear connection between the offence for which extradition was being sought and the disturbances. On this basis, the extradition of Angelo Castioni from Britain to the canton of Ticino was refused.

Three years later the High Court added a gloss to its judgement in the Castioni case by allowing the extradition of a French anarchist, Theodor Meunier, who was wanted for the bombing of a Paris café which had killed two civilians. The central argument of the judgement was that anarchists were the enemies of all governments and thus did not meet the requirement of being contenders for political power within the state.[3] One could perhaps regard the attempts to limit the scope of political asylum by the authorities, judicial and executive, as an early form of international co-operation on terrorism, since assassinations of heads of state and anarchist violence formed a large part of nineteenth-century conceptions of what constituted terrorism.

The issue of terrorism as such was considered by a series of international conferences on the unification of penal law during the early 1930s. A definition of terrorism was proposed and it was recommended that acts that fell within the scope of the definition should be excluded from the protection of political offence exception clauses in extradition treaties. However, nothing came of this recommendation. Following the assassination of the King of Yugoslavia and the French foreign minister by Croatian nationalists in Marseilles in 1934, the League of Nations took up the issue, prompted particularly by the transnational dimensions of the killings. The Council of the League established a committee of experts to study the problem. The result of the committee's work was an international conference in 1937 to approve the texts of two conventions on the subject, one on the prevention and punishment of terrorism and the other on the establishment of an international criminal court.[4] Neither convention came into force. In the context of the times, the issue of transnational terrorism by substate groups was a low priority for most countries. Indeed, only one country, India, actually completed the process of ratifying the two conventions.

However, the two conventions are not quite forgotten. In particular, the idea of an international criminal court to try hijackers and others whose crimes take place in the international arena has had many supporters over the years since the end of the Second World War.[5] But the central emphasis placed in the first of the 1937 conventions on attacks on heads of state strikes a slightly odd chord today in the light of the post-war debate on the morality of assassinating Hitler, even though outlawing such attacks has been a persistent feature of state endeavour in this field.

Responses to hijacking and hostage-taking

In the first two post-war decades, the issue of terrorism had a low priority. Indeed, use of the term 'terrorism' was relatively uncommon in this period. It cropped up in a 1954 Draft Code of Offences against the Peace and Security of Mankind prepared by the International Law Commission for the United Nations General Assembly, though not acted on.[6] It is noteworthy that the context of its references to terrorism was state involvement in the domestic subversion of the government of another country. While a considerable number of hijackings of commercial aircraft took place in the course of the two decades, particularly in the early 1960s between Cuba and Florida, there was little inclination to label these as terrorism.

The change in attitudes towards hijacking came when hijackers started to threaten the lives of the crew and passengers for purposes other than diverting the aircraft to a different destination. However, there was a tightening of the law in respect of air transport in advance of the onset of the age of terrorism. The 1963 Tokyo Convention on Offences and Certain Other Acts Committed on Board Aircraft provided that the jurisdiction over a plane in flight lay with the country where the aircraft was registered and laid down rules for dealing with offenders, including hijackers. It was followed by further measures in this sphere during the age of terrorism: the 1970 Hague Convention for the Unlawful Seizure of Aircraft; the 1971 Montreal Convention for the Suppression of Unlawful Acts Against the Safety of Civil Aviation; an addendum to the Montreal Convention in February 1988 to include attacks on passengers at airports as well as on board aircraft; and the 1991 Convention of the Marking of Plastic Explosives for Detection.[7]

In a similar way, the 1961 Vienna Convention on Diplomatic Relations and the 1963 Convention on Consular Relations, which insisted not merely on the inviolability of diplomatic agents, but also their families and supporting staff, and reaffirmed the responsiblity of the receiving states to protect them, were followed by the 1969 New York Convention on Special Missions and the 1973 Convention on the Prevention and Punishment of Crimes against Internationally Protected Persons, including Diplomatic Agents. This included heads of state, heads of government, and foreign ministers in the category of protected persons. However, there was not quite such an obvious precedent from before the late 1960s for the 1979 International Convention against the Taking of Hostages, though Article 3 of the Third Geneva Convention for the Protection of Civilian Persons in Time of War forbade the taking of hostages in any armed conflict. The 1979 convention was arguably the most important of all the conventions dealing with a particular category of actions within the broad area of international terrorism, since it went furthest in establishing a generalizable normative principle.

The convention defined the offence of hostage-taking as the taking of a person in order to compel a third party, such as a foreign state, to do or omit doing something by threatening physical harm to the hostage.[8] It obliged states ratifying the convention to penalize any person committing such an offence in an international context. Hostage-taking without an international element by reason of the nationality of the perpetrator or victim or the party to whom demands were directed lay outside the scope of the convention. West Germany had proposed the drawing up of such a convention in 1976, and the issue was referred to a special committee. The actual approval of the convention by the UN General Assembly followed in the wake of the seizure of the American embassy in Iran.

Responses to terrorism in general

The advantage of conventions which dealt with a particular category of actions was that they obviated the need for an agreement on a general definition of terrorism. Further, states were not obliged to accept that this or that action outlawed in a convention was an act of terrorism, merely that it should be prohibited. This was an important consideration for states fearful that the labelling of particular actions as terrorism would be used to legitimize intervention in the name of counter-terrorism. Nevertheless, there have been attempts within the framework of the United Nations to establish a general consensus on the issue of terrorism. In 1972, following the attack on Israeli athletes at the Munich Olympics, the Secretary-General of the United Nations, Kurt Waldheim, asked the General Assembly to consider the issue of terrorism.

At the outset of the debate, the United States put forward a draft Convention for the Prevention and Punishment of Certain Acts of International Terrorism.[9] The American proposal was opposed by Third World states, who were concerned that part of the purpose of the draft was to detract from the legitimacy of the use of violence by groups fighting for self-determination in the context of colonial or minority rule, which had recently been affirmed by the United Nations. The resolution that the General Assembly adopted in December 1972 reflected their concern. It placed a strong emphasis on the legitimacy of the struggle of national liberation movements, while agreeing to the establishment of an Ad Hoc Committee on International Terrorism to make recommendations to tackle the problem, including its underlying causes.[10] Many Third World states were particularly concerned that no action should be taken by the international community that could be interpreted as detracting from Palestinian demands for self-determination, at the very least within the territories Israel had occupied following the 1967 war. However, Third World states did recognize the need to criminalize certain types of violence. At the 1985 General Assembly session this was reflected in the passage, with Third World support, of resolutions strongly condemning particular forms of terrorism and urging states to ratify the relevant conventions.[11]

In seeking support for measures to combat international terrorism, Western states have generally emphasized the illegitimacy of certain kinds of actions, regardless of their political motive. That approach is reflected in such collective agreements among Western states as the 1977 European Convention on the Suppression of Terrorism, an initiative of the Council of Europe. Article 1 of the European Convention provides that for the purposes of extradition none of the offences it lists should be regarded as political offences. The list includes offences within the scope of the Hague and Montreal Conventions, a serious offence involving an attack on internationally protected persons, kidnapping, hostage-taking, and any offence 'involving the use of a bomb, grenade, rocket, automatic firearm or letter or

parcel bomb if this use endangers persons'.[12] Attempting to carry out
such offences or acting as an accomplice was also listed. Article 2
provided that governments might permit extradition in serious cases
of violence not listed under Article 1, but in the light of other provisions of the convention, Noemi Gal-Or argues that 'a practical use
of Article 2 seems rather unlikely'.[13]

However, even in relations with other Western states, governments
have found some of the implications of such a strategy of criminalization not to their liking and have favoured a more political approach,
one of the advantages of which from a governmental perspective has
been to reduce the influence of the courts on the process. Critics of
the 1977 European Convention argued that the list of offences outlined
in Article 1 had not been defined with sufficient rigour and that the
standard it set was applicable only within the context of a liberal-
democracy, and, they might have added, a *stable* liberal-democracy,
since one of the concerns of the critics was that it did not draw a
sufficiently clear distinction between guerrilla warfare and terrorism.[14]
Yet in comparison with domestic legislation, such as the British Prevention of Terrorism Act, which treats all violence for political ends
as terrorism,[15] the scope of the convention was limited. The result has
been that a number of applications that Britain has made to European
countries for the extradition of individuals accused of terrorist offences
under British law have been rejected on the grounds that the offence,
for example possession of weaponry, lay outside the scope of the
convention.

At the same time, the approach of the convention to the definition
of terrorism, with its emphasis on forms of violence that threaten the
lives of innocent bystanders, whether intentionally or as the predictable
consequence of the use of a particular weapon, is broadly in line with
the evolution of judicial interpretations of the political offence exception. As a result of concern over terrorism, judges in many Western
countries have tended to take a much narrower view of the political
offence exception in extradition cases than they did before the issue
of terrorism came to the fore. However, the fact that extradition has
become easier between Western countries, because of the trend in
judicial interpretation of what constitutes a political offence, has attracted far less attention than cases where for one reason or another
extradition has been refused.

The Doherty case

A good example is the outrage in Britain that greeted United States
District Judge John Sprizzo's decision not to allow the extradition in

1984 of a member of the Provisional IRA, Joe Doherty. Doherty had
fled to the United States following his escape from prison in Northern
Ireland, where he had been convicted of the murder of a captain in
the Special Air Services (SAS) and was serving a life sentence.
Doherty was a member of a Provisional IRA Active Service Unit
(ASU) that had set out to ambush a military convoy. The authorities
had gained advance knowledge of the attempt and had sent in a unit
of the SAS to take the Provisional ASU by surprise. The SAS operation went awry because of a failure to identify the correct entrance to
the house in which the ASU was ensconced. In the ensuing shoot-out
between the SAS unit and the ASU, the officer in charge of the SAS
unit was killed. Sprizzo argued that the existence of a political conflict
in Northern Ireland and the fact that the offence was committed in
the course of the conflict did not in themselves constitute sufficient
grounds for refusing extradition as 'not every act committed for a
political purpose or during a political disturbance may or should
properly be regarded as a political offense'.[16]

In particular, he asserted that the law required that 'no act be
regarded as political where the nature of the act is such as to be
violative of international law, and inconsistent with international
standards of civilised conduct'.[17] As an example, he gave the placing
of a bomb in a public place. But he concluded that Doherty's actions
did not fall into this category and refused the application for his
extradition. In response to the Sprizzo judgement, the British and
American governments drew up a new Extradition Treaty in 1985. It
eventually secured passage through the United States Senate in July
1986, after President Reagan appealed to senators to reciprocate
British support for the bombing of Libya in April that year.

The Treaty's extensive list of offences for which the plea of political
offence would no longer provide a defence against extradition was
intended to cut the courts out of the process of determining what
constituted terrorism and to prevent the possibility of a repetition of
the Doherty case. The governments' pursuit of Doherty continued,
and in 1992 he was returned to Northern Ireland to serve his sentence,
not as a result of a process of extradition, but after deportation on the
grounds of illegal entry to the United States. By this time, Doherty's
case had become a *cause célèbre* and his plea to be granted asylum had
attracted widespread political support within the United States.[18] The
Doherty saga is reflective of a much more general tendency for Western governments to seek control over the handling of the problem of
terrorism, so that the battle against terrorism accords with their own
political priorities. Governments that feel themselves threatened by
particular campaigns of political violence are especially prone to this

tendency. The effect has been to undercut the efforts being made by a number of organizations to establish the basis for a universal consensus on what constitutes terrorism, and is unacceptable in the context of any conflict.

International humanitarian law

In 1977, under the aegis of the International Committee of the Red Cross (ICRC), two protocols were added to the 1949 Geneva Conventions on the laws of war to extend the scope of international humanitarian law to cover guerrilla warfare. The first protocol expands the laws governing international wars and colonial conflicts. The second protocol applies to non-international armed conflicts between a state's armed forces and dissident forces operating under responsible command and exercising control of part of the state's territory.[19] Situations of 'internal disturbances and tensions'[20] are specifically excluded from the scope of the protocol.

This limitation in the applicability of international humanitarian law to violent conflicts prompted Hans-Peter Gasser, a legal adviser to the ICRC, to draft a code of conduct, with the aim of promoting greater respect for human values in such situations.[21] At the same time, human rights organizations, such as Amnesty International and Helsinki Watch, increasingly came to recognize during the course of the 1980s that bodies other than governments and states were frequently responsible for serious violations of human rights, and they now include criticism of the conduct of paramilitary bodies outside the control of states and governments in their reports. A further initiative in this field was the 1990 Declaration of Minimum Humanitarian Standards, put forward by a group of experts working under the auspices of the Institute of Human Rights in Turku/Abu in Finland. It is intended that the standards should bind governments as well as other bodies.

For example, Article 6 of the declaration outlaws 'acts or threats of violence the primary purpose or foreseeable effect of which is to spread terror among the population'.[22] A reason why interest in these initiatives has been limited may simply be the problem of enforcing such a standard even if it became an accepted part of international law. In fact, this is a general difficulty of international law in a world of sovereign states. Compliance depends on the states themselves. That applies to all the conventions dealing with particular types of violence and even to the European Convention on the Suppression of Terrorism. It also provides states with the justification for taking unilateral action of their own against sub-state groups or even other states they hold responsible for acts of terrorism against their citizens.

However, the resort from time to time of the Western powers to the use of force to counter terrorism can only partly be explained by the difficulties of enforcing international law. This may be illustrated by the case of Libya. As a result of the investigation into the destruction of Pan Am Flight 103 over Lockerbie, Scotland, two Libyan intelligence agents were indicted by the American and British authorities. The bombing killed 270 people, of whom 189 were Americans. A French magistrate accused four Libyans of responsibility for another atrocity, the destruction of UTA Flight 772 over the Chad-Niger border in September 1989, in which 170 people died. The American, British, and French governments demanded that the accused Libyans be handed over for trial in the West. Their demands were backed up by the threat of economic sanctions, which were imposed through the United Nations Security Council when Libya failed to comply.

In the process, Libya's readiness to prosecute the agents itself in accordance with the Montreal Convention, which it had ratified, was simply disregarded. This prompted some criticism of the action of the Western governments as itself contrary to international law.[23] Admittedly, the scale of the two atrocities for which the Western powers are seeking redress might make a concern with legal technicalities appear pedantic. None the less, the fact that the Western powers have chosen to use their new-found influence over the decisions of the Security Council, not to create a mechanism for the enforcement of the conventions, but to pursue an agenda outside the conventions, does not augur well for reliance on legal remedies. In defence of the West's actions, it can be argued that the objective remains the completion of a legal process, in the face of greater provocation than existed when President Reagan ordered the bombing of Tripoli and Benghazi in April 1986, in which 63 people died.[24] However, the suspicion has not entirely been dispelled that the manner in which the Western governments have pursued the case against Libya has been dictated by political considerations.

Question of proportionality

One reason why in general there may be a reluctance on the part of the Western powers to pursue a course based on law in dealing with the problem of clandestine violence across national boundaries is the limitations that the principle of proportionality would place on their actions. One of the most extraordinary aspects of the age of terrorism has been the extent to which the threat of international terrorism has been exaggerated, to the point where the fear of terrorism has had a significant impact on global patterns of tourism, most particularly on the numbers of Americans crossing the Atlantic to visit Europe in any one year. It is worth focusing on the American case, since it provides the most striking example of disproportion between the perception of threat and its actuality and between challenge and response.

In 1987 the State Department published a document giving details of all lethal terrorist actions against Americans in the period 1973 to 1986.[25] The report interprets 'lethal terrorist action' loosely to include the death of any American abroad as a result of political or group violence outside of actual war. For example, Latin American drug traffickers number among 'the most prominent terrorist groups involved in lethal anti-American attacks'.[26] In the period as a whole, according to the report, 440 Americans were killed in lethal terrorist actions. Over half the total died in a single incident, 241 marines killed in the suicide bombing of their barracks in Beirut in October 1983.

The report breaks down the figures into private, diplomatic, military, and other government. Fatalities among private citizens numbered just 138. In the period covered by the report, the most lethal incident involving American private citizens was the destruction of an Air India jet over the Atlantic in June 1985, in which 19 Americans died. Responsibility for the bomb attack was attributed to Sikh separatists. From the perspective of the perpetrators, the Americans were almost certainly incidental victims of an atrocity directed at the Indian government. But even where Americans were deliberately targeted, there was a very wide ideological diversity in the organizations responsible, from the El Salvador National Guard to the Abu Nidal Organization, the Palestinian group which heads State Department lists of terrorist organizations that threaten Americans. However, the role that right-wing groups have played in the death toll of Americans abroad has rarely been acknowledged in reports dealing with terrorism. Thus, following the abduction of an American missionary nurse in Mozambique by the anti-communist Mozambique National Resistance (RENAMO), the State Department report, *Patterns of Global Terrorism: 1987*, noted: 'RENAMO has not directly attacked US interests, but Americans who travel in Mozambique could become inadvertent victims'.[27] The main focus of the reports has overwhelmingly been on groups seen as America's ideological enemies.

State perspectives

Indeed, from the perspective of individual states, the labelling of political enemies as terrorists may be of far greater importance than the regulation of conflict so as to outlaw particular forms of political violence. In particular, until relatively recently, both the Israeli and the South African governments were as much concerned to de-legiti-mize the objectives of Palestinian and African nationalists as they were to combat their violent manifestations. Thus, Israel and South Africa adopted draconian measures against peaceful expressions of support for, respectively, a Palestinian state and majority rule. Similar-ly, during the period of Unionist rule in Northern Ireland, little tolerance was shown for Catholic aspirations for a united Ireland. In such siege societies a common assumption within the dominant com-munity is of a never-ending struggle with the forces of evil in a hostile environment.[28] Peace in this context is regarded as a temporary lull before the state's enemies launch a fresh assault. Here eternal vigilance is seen as a requirement of survival. That makes more remarkable the changes that have recently occurred in the three societies and they will be examined further below.

Even in societies where terrorism is not seen as an eternal political threat, a demonic picture of terrorism and terrorists may prevail, since people's image of terrorism naturally tends to be based on the most outrageous of atrocities. Since demons can be stopped only by being destroyed, the consequence is a reinforcement of the assumption that campaigns of terrorism can be ended only by effective counter-terrorism or even 'terrorizing the terrorists'.[29] Of course, very high levels of state coercion may be successful in suppressing violence by small groups. Examples are the suppression in the 1970s of the Montoneros in Argentina and the Tupomaros in Uruguay. But these examples also show how high the cost of the strategy of suppression can be. In these two cases of military rule and massive human rights violations, the cure was clearly worse than the disease.[30]

In her seminal essay 'On Violence', Hannah Arendt argued that 'violence, being instrumental by nature, is rational to the extent that it is effective in reaching the end that must justify it'.[31] To put the point another way, success or, at any rate, the prospect of success is crucial to the legitimization of violence. In the case of political violence this means that the assumptions justifying the political goal itself and providing the analysis of how that goal is to be achieved are of vital significance in its legitimization. It is by no means coincidental that terrorism tends to be viewed both as one of the least legitimate forms of political violence and as one of the least successful.[32] The end justifying the means is a necessary condition for the legitimization of violence, but that leaves plenty of room for argument about the value of the end being pursued and the proportionality of the means. Of course, it is very much easier to apply such judgements to particular situations with the benefit of hindsight than it is to arrive at such conclusions in the midst of a conflict. And, as von Clausewitz put it, 'the state of circumstances from which an event proceeded can never be placed before the eye of the critic exactly as it lay before the eye of the person acting'.[33] Nevertheless, Arendt's conception of violence as instrumental provides a useful yardstick for examining the evolution of campaigns of violence, with these strictures in mind.

The case of South Africa

The two main African nationalist movements in South Africa, the African National Congress (ANC) and the Pan-Africanist Congress (PAC), were banned in 1960. Even after it was banned, the ANC attempted to sustain a mass civil disobedience campaign. To buttress the demand for the holding of a representative national convention, a stay-away from work was organized to coincide with the establishment of South Africa as a republic on 31 May 1961. It was only after the failure of the stay-away, following strong security force action against it, that ANC leaders made the decision to resort to violence. To this end, they established Umkhonto we Sizwe (Zulu for 'The Spear of the Nation'), also known as MK. Members of MK were recruited from the ANC and from the South African Communist Party (SACP). This was largely a legacy of the involvement of communists in the multi-racial Congress Alliance in the 1950s. MK, unlike the ANC itself at this time, was multi-racial in composition.

At his trial in 1964, Nelson Mandela gave a very full account of MK's formation in November 1961 and the reasons for the adoption of the strategy of violence. He argued that the fact that the government had met non-violence by force and had barred all channels of peaceful protest left African nationalists with no choice but to embark on violent forms of political struggle. The other main reason Mandela gave for the adoption of political violence was that 'unless responsible leadership was given to canalise and control the feelings of our people, there would be outbreaks of terrorism which would produce an intensity of bitterness and hostility between the various races of this country'.[34] He identified four possible forms of violence:

> There is sabotage, there is guerrilla warfare, there is terrorism and there is open revolution. We chose to adopt the first method and to exhaust it before taking any other decision. In the light of our background the choice was a logical one. Sabotage did not involve loss of life, and it offered the best hope for future race relations.[35]

The first series of MK attacks took place on 16 December 1961, the Day of the Vow, a national holiday celebrating the victory of the Voortrekkers over the Zulus at the battle of Blood River in 1838. They resulted in damage to a number of government offices in various parts of the country and to an electrical transformer in Port Elizabeth. The bombings were accompanied by the distribution of a flyer which expressed the hope that the actions would 'bring the Government and its supporters to their senses'.[36] There were some 200 MK attacks in the next 18 months. In the main, these adhered to the policy of the national high command to avoid any action that might result in the loss of life, though there were a significant number of exceptions.

The political impact of MK's sabotage campaign was relatively slight. Much of the campaign was directed from a headquarters on a farm outside Johannesburg, and MK suffered a crippling blow when police raided the farm at Rivonia in July 1963 and arrested 17 people under provisions that enabled the police to detain suspects for 90 days without charge. In retrospect, critics have viewed MK's resort to sabotage as a suicidal policy that was bound to end in defeat, and the aim of MK of putting pressure on the government to change course through acts of violence has appeared to many writers on this period as naive or disingenuous and sometimes both.[37] MK's strategy was based on the assumptions that sabotage and the political message that went with it of continuing African resistance to apartheid would lead to a collapse of foreign confidence in South Africa and that the economic consequences of the country's isolation would persuade the white electorate to turn against the government. In the light of the flight of capital from South Africa after the Sharpeville massacre in 1960, it seemed a plausible scenario.

With the benefit of hindsight, it is evident that Mandela and the other leaders of the ANC, including those like Luthuli who called for economic sanctions against South Africa, overestimated the strength of liberal anti-apartheid opinion in the West and both the willingness of the international community to go beyond rhetorical criticism of apartheid and its actual capacity to effect change within the Republic. The leaders of MK themselves were by no means entirely blind to the possibility that a campaign of sabotage might not have the desired political result. Indeed, the initial white response to the launch of the campaign was viewed by MK 'with anxiety', according to Mandela.[38] Preparations began as early as 1962 for training for guerrilla warfare as the next phase of the campaign. One of the documents seized by the police at Rivonia outlined a plan for the infiltration of guerrilla bands into a number of rural areas considered suitable for this purpose. The first attempts to infiltrate guerrillas into South Africa were made through Botswana and Rhodesia in 1967 and 1968. None of the guerrillas reached South Africa.[39] The heading of the brief account of the period in the *Facts on File* volume on *Political Terrorism* was 'Stern action curbs terrorism'.[40]

MK was not the only organization that engaged in violence against the government in South Africa during the 1960s. An organization of liberal intellectuals, the African Resistance Movement (ARM), also adopted the strategy of sabotage. Formed round a commitment to use violence rather than a set of political aims or a particular political philosophy, the ARM failed to institutionalize itself. It disappeared without trace, having no appeal to new generations of radical students who saw no prospect of the government being moved from existing policy by symbolic acts of violence. However, MK did survive in exile. The key to its survival was its links with a larger political movement with widespread international support. It could wait for the political environment to change.

Change came in 1976 after violent action by the police against a protest by schoolchildren in Soweto prompted nation-wide unrest inside South Africa. These events resulted in a crisis of governability that the South African government was unable to solve. The social and economic reforms it introduced in an attempt to defuse the crisis simply helped to fuel the political demands of strengthened opposition movements inside and outside the country. There was a revival of MK activity, though without the restraint that had characterized MK's campaign of sabotage in the 1960s. For example, in May 1983, a car-bomb placed by members of MK outside an air force and military intelligence office in Pretoria killed 19 people, while more than two hundred people were injured. In his autobiography, Mandela described the killing of civilians in such episodes as a tragic accident, but inevitable in the context of the 'armed struggle'.[41]

The violence of MK was a small component in the pressures on the South African government to negotiate with the ANC, though it undoubtedly strengthened the organization politically in the townships. President de Klerk unbanned the ANC and released Mandela from jail in February 1990. The MK's armed struggle was suspended in August that year. However, that did not end political violence. That continued at a high level largely as a result of rivalry in particular areas between the ANC and the Inkatha Freedom Party of Chief Buthelezi. A much more minor component of the violence was due to opposition to the transition from white supremacists on the extreme right. In particular, the extreme right carried out a series of bombings on the eve of the country's first non-racial, democratic elections in April 1994, which killed 21 people. However, in general, the scale of extreme right-wing violence through South Africa's transition was much lower than most observers had expected. Part of the explanation for the quiescence of the extreme right was its recognition of the new power realities, but another important factor in discouraging extreme right-wing violence was the readiness of the ANC to create constitutional avenues for the extreme right to pursue its aspiration of an Afrikaner homeland.

Israel and the PLO

The PLO never attracted the same level of international support as the ANC was able to muster. Indeed, the PLO was routinely referred to as a terrorist organization in the Western press. This was partly because the state of Israel enjoyed far greater legitimacy in the West than white minority rule in South Africa. It was partly also because of the international nature of the campaign of violence with which the PLO was associated. MK's campaign of violence was confined to southern Africa. While the actions of the PLO and other fringe Palestinian groups attracted far more publicity than any action carried out by opposition groups in South Africa, their political impact was scarcely any greater. What changed the political environment in relation to Israel was the *intifada*, a revolt by Palestinians in the occupied territories from December 1987 that created a crisis of governability for the Israeli state. Just as the unrest in South Africa in 1976 owed little to any action by the ANC, so the onset of the *intifada* owed little to the PLO.

The defeat of Saddam Hussein in the 1991 Gulf War paved the way to negotiations between Israel and Palestinian representatives. Formal talks were held under the sponsorship of the United States and the Soviet Union in Madrid in October and November 1991. Initially, the PLO, which had been damaged by its stance of support for Iraq during the Gulf War, was on the sidelines of the talks. However, it quickly became apparent that the Palestinian representatives at the talks lacked the political authority to conclude any agreement that did not have the explicit political approval of the PLO. That reality prompted the creation of the Norwegian channel through which the Israeli government and the PLO were able to negotiate directly. The process culminated in the signature by the Israeli government and the PLO of the Declaration of Principles in Washington, DC, on 13 September 1993.

The Declaration of Principles provided no more than the outlines of a political settlement, yet in the context of previous rhetoric on both sides it was a remarkable development. Partly for this reason, the peace process faced considerable opposition among both Palestinians and Israelis. International encouragement was given to these efforts by the award of the Nobel Peace Prize to the Israel prime minister, Yitzhak Rabin, to his foreign minister, Shimon Peres, and to the chairman of the PLO, Yasser Arafat. The award to Arafat was especially controversial, though he was by no means the first recipient of the Noble Peace Prize with a previous reputation in the eyes of adversaries as a terrorist. In an interview at the time of his receipt of the award, Shimon Peres stressed that the change in the international environment as a result of the end of the Cold War had been an important factor in facilitating the peace process, a change he characterized as a shift from a world of enemies to one of problems.[42]

Peace in Northern Ireland

The political actors in Northern Ireland, and most particularly the Republican movement, were profoundly affected by events in South Africa and in the Middle East. However, whereas the political frame of reference for the peace processes there was clearly, in the case of South Africa, the extension of the franchise to all South Africans and, in the case of Israel, the granting of some degree of Palestinian self-government, it is much less clear what the basis of a political settlement might be in Northern Ireland. In particular, Sinn Fein, the political wing of the Provisional IRA, has not accepted the principles for a settlement agreed between the British and Irish governments in the Downing Street Declaration of December 1993. The Republican ceasefire was the product of a number of different factors: the pressure of public opinion in nationalist areas was one; another was Sinn Fein's fear of marginalization as a result of negotiations taking place between nationalists and Unionists. A further factor was a desire to test what might be achieved through inclusion in the negotiating process.

But what remains particularly hard to gauge is how Sinn Fein perceives the balance of forces in Northern Ireland. Its public statements stress the strength of the nationalist position, both in terms of its increasing share of the vote in Northern Ireland and its capacity to mobilize international support, particularly from the United States. However, since there has been no shift in the British government's insistence on the need for the consent of a majority of people in Northern Ireland for any constitutional change, there seems little basis for expecting much tangible progress towards a united Ireland as the result of the negotiations. Indeed, British government assurances to the Unionists have been sufficiently unambiguous to have secured the support of the main Unionist party, the Ulster Unionists, for the process and to bring about a reciprocal Loyalist ceasefire.

Whether the current ceasefires turn out to be permanent or merely a temporary truce in an ongoing conflict is likely to depend on how far the process of negotiations itself succeeds in modifying the political aspirations of the parties. However, as in the cases of South Africa and Israel, the existence of a peace process has thrown a different light on past violence. Further, because both governments have a stake in presenting any settlement as satisfactory to all interests, the notion that it represents a defeat for anyone, even those who resorted to violence, is likely to be played down.

The Basque case

Just as the Republican movement split into Provisionals and Officials at the start of Northern Ireland's present troubles, so the Basque nationalist group ETA divided into ETA (Militar) and ETA (Politico-Militar) on the eve of Spain's transition to democracy. ETA (PM) accepted the proposition that the new political dispensation in Spain required the organization to modify the strategy it was pursuing to achieve the goal of Basque independence, so as to take advantage of the opportunities democracy presented for political mobilization. Following this logic, ETA (PM) eventually ended its campaign of violence in 1981 after the attempted right-wing coup against the elected Spanish government in February of that year. Negotiations between the Spanish government and ETA (PM) followed. The result was the policy of *reinsercion* (re-integration). Under this policy, imprisoned members of ETA (PM), provided they had not been convicted of *delito de sangre* (crimes of blood), were released on promising not to resort to political violence in future.

Under a second phase of the policy of *reinsercion*, members of both wings of ETA who had fled Spain were given pardons and allowed to return to the country on the same promise not to resort to political violence in future. About 300 members of the two wings of ETA have been re-integrated into society in this way.[43] While violence has not come to an end in the Basque region of Spain, it has declined. The policy of *reinsercion* has enjoyed the support of all of Spain's political parties with the exception of Herri Batasuna, the party allied to ETA (Militar). In contrast to the Italian policy of leniency to repentant terrorists, the Spanish policy did not require those seeking re-integration to repudiate their past involvement in, or support for, violence. This put the emphasis for changed behaviour on changed political circumstances. In short, the Spanish state based its policy on a recognition of the instrumental character of the violence of its opponents. A merit of both the Spanish and the Italian policies was that they provided a way out for those who had been drawn into involvement in violence in the expectation of effecting political change and had realized their mistake.

The United States and Canada

In their 1989 article on why terrorism subsides, Ross and Gurr provide evidence that oppositional terrorism in both the United States and Canada reached a peak in the late 1960s and early 1970s. Their broad definition of oppositional terrorism includes attacks on property. In justification they point out:

> In the U.S., all of the nineteen bombings claimed by the Weather Underground were targeted against property. In Canada, less than a tenth of the 166 violent attacks known to have been carried out by Quebec separatists had human targets or victims.[44]

A graph of domestic terrorist events in Canada between 1960 and 1985 shows two peaks. The first was in 1961 and arose out of a conflict in a tiny Russian religious sect, the Doukhobors. The activities of the Doukhobor Sons of Freedom included the dynamiting of an electrical power pylon in British Columbia in 1962, but were not of lasting significance. The second peak was over the period 1968 to 1971 and arose out of organizations supporting Quebec separatism. The most important of the violent separatist groups was the FLQ. A brief history of its campaign was given in Chapter 4 and there is no need to repeat that here.

Ross and Gurr analyse the decline of the organization in terms of four factors: pre-emption, deterrence, burn-out, and backlash. While they accept that security measures, such as the invoking of the War Measures Act in October 1970, made a contribution to the ending of the campaign, they argue that political factors played a more important role in the FLQ's decline, particularly the backlash after the murder of Pierre Laporte in 1970.[45]

In contrast to Canada, political terrorism in the United States in the same period was inspired by a very diverse range of causes, including the status of blacks, Puerto Rican nationalism, white supremacy, and left-wing revolution. Despite the diversity, Ross and Gurr find a similar pattern of subsidence. They give figures showing that the number of fatalities from political terrorism reached a peak of 24 a year in the late 1960s, falling to three a year in the 1980s. While again acknowledging the contribution of pre-emption and deterrence, they argue that political factors were more important, with backlash the principal factor, reflecting a change in the climate of public opinion.

The 'me decade' of the 1970s was a period of political consolidation and retrenchment, accompanied by widespread public opposition to the advocacy of radical social change and sharp resentment against groups making extreme demands and using disruptive or violent tactics.[46]

As evidence of the greater importance of political factors, they cite the history of the Weather Underground. The end of its campaign was the result of a decision in 1975 by a majority of its members to abandon terrorism. The decision can hardly be attributed to the effectiveness of security measures against the organization, since none of its activists had been arrested during its campaign of bombing between 1970 and and 1974.[47]

Conclusion

From the cases examined briefly in this chapter, it is possible to suggest a few generalizations about the ending of campaigns of violence, including terrorism. Firstly, a negative conclusion can be drawn. The examples examined do not bear out the common assumption that terrorism can be rooted out only by the state's adoption of draconian measures. In fact, state coercion may actually be counter-productive, even in a domestic context, where such a strategy faces fewer obstacles than it does in an international context. In particular, from the perspective of those engaged in violence, harsh repression may be seen as evidence of the effectiveness of their campaign and therefore a reason to persist. Of course, the impact of any set of repressive measures will depend on the precise circumstances in the society in question. The case of Northern Ireland, where the introduction of internment resulted not merely in a sharp increase in the level of violence, but in a much higher level of support in both communities for those resorting to violence, is by no means unique.

Secondly, although there is obvious difficulty in isolating this factor from others, the assumptions that violent groups make about the likely consequences of their campaigns do seem to have an important bearing on whether and in what form any campaign will continue. If events falsify a group's theory of change, there is a real prospect that the group will stop engaging in violence, disintegrate, or modify its behaviour to accord with a changed view of the world. In Arendt's terms, terrorist organizations by and large do behave rationally, using violence instrumentally. This may seem a paradox, given the association of terrorism with failure. However, in times of uncertainty or in politically unstable societies, calculations about the consequences of violence are sufficiently difficult that members of small groups can be persuaded of the potential utility of violence.[48] Times of uncertainty will tend to arise at different times in different societies as a result of domestic developments. But times of uncertainty are likely to arise at the same time in different societies when their source lies in developments within the international political system. This point will be taken up in the conclusion.

Thirdly, an important factor in the durability of any campaign of violence is whether a group using violence is able to institutionalize itself politically. This is more likely to be achieved by securing the commitment of followers to particular political objectives rather than simply their support for the use of violence. In the case of groups that are not politically institutionalized, the arrest of members of the group may simply end the campaign at a stroke. However, where any group has become institutionalized and is able to draw in fresh recruits from new generations, security measures (unless extreme) may be able only to limit rather than stop violence. The context in which a campaign of terrorism is most likely to end is if it proves impossible even for the participants to establish its relevance to the political ends used to justify it.

Fourthly, what the cases discussed in this chapter underline is that whatever criteria one might use to distinguish terrorism from other forms of violence, there is little reason for supposing that terrorism, uniquely among forms of violence, can be understood without reference to the users' perceptions of its utility. But once calculations of utility form part of the analysis, they tend to undermine the absolutist judgement implied when the term 'terrorism' is employed. Since negotiations, whether conditional on the abandonment of violence or not, presuppose that violence is used only as a means to an end, their very occurrence also tends to undercut absolutism, suggesting the existence of a world of problems rather than of enemies.

11

Conclusion: the end of terrorism?

The term 'terrorism' continued to be widely used in the early 1990s. Indeed, it was appropriated by all manner of causes to apply to many different types of violence, some of which, such as domestic violence within the home, had no claim to a political purpose. But the very permissiveness with which the term was used can be seen as a sign of the concept's disintegration, a loss of coherence that in the long run is likely to rob the notion of an age of terrorism of continuing meaning. At the same time, this incoherence is also an obstacle to speculation about an end to the age of terrorism. In any event, it would seem distinctly odd to speak in these terms when the sources of violence, particularly political violence, in the world seem to have multiplied so dramatically in the wake of the collapse of communism in Eastern Europe and the Soviet Union. Yet this multiplication of the sources of violence itself poses a problem for the concept of terrorism. On the one hand, the concept appears well suited to evoking the horror represented by ethnic cleansing, for example. On the other hand, it is difficult to deny the utility of violence or its instrumental justification in many of the conflicts that have erupted since the Berlin wall came down.

This duality is reflected in what might be seen as contradictory responses of the international community to the civil war in the former Yugoslavia: the intention to try those responsible for atrocities for war crimes and a preparedness to negotiate and bargain with political leaders on whose behalf the atrocities were being committed. Justification can readily be advanced for both responses, with justice for the victims demanding the first and both the realities of power on the ground and the nature of a deeply divided society compelling the second. The first accords with the principles that evolved for dealing with terrorism. The second does not, clearly running counter to one of the most clearly enunciated prescriptions of the age of terrorism, that there should be no negotiations with terrorists and no deals done that would reward their criminal acts.[1]

What gave this precept credibility was the comparison of terrorism with blackmail, with the same lesson that surrender in one instance encouraged the commission of more such crimes. So strongly did this notion become established that politicians would volunteer on television that they had signed declarations requesting that no negotiations be conducted with the perpetrators in the event of their being taken hostage. Conservatives particularly came to see this as the morally and politically correct response to the threat of terrorism. Both Margaret Thatcher and Ronald Reagan were associated with the notion of unyielding resistance to the demands of terrorists, with their stance on this issue being favourably compared with their political predecessors on both the left and right. This was one reason why the Iran-Contra scandal posed such a threat to President Reagan's reputation.[2]

While it may reasonably be argued that the concept of terrorism was losing its coherence even before the collapse of the communist system in Eastern Europe and the Soviet Union, the end of the bipolar system that existed between 1945 and 1989 represented a qualitative change in the nature of the international political system, with important implications for the concept of terrorism. In retrospect, it seems that the bipolar era was a period of remarkable stability, particularly for the affluent liberal-democracies of the West, though disorder increased in the latter part of the era, with the weakening of the relative power of the super-powers. Because the dominant feature of the period was the rivalry between the system's two super-powers, the United States and the Soviet Union, the whole era now tends to be referred to as one of Cold War, though this description is not entirely accurate, since relations between the two super-powers fluctuated between periods of antagonism and of détente.

This qualification is particularly important in relation to the age of terrorism, since its onset more or less coincided with that of détente in the late 1960s. Some writers on terrorism posited a more or less direct link between the two.[3] The crudest form of this argument was that détente represented a period of appeasement of Soviet communism by the West and that by demonstrating Western weakness it encouraged the launch of a terrorist offensive against the West to extract further concessions.[4] An obvious difficulty with this view, among very many others, is that the onset of the age of terrorism slightly preceded the era of détente, not the other way round, as this view would seem to require.

However, it is possible to posit a more subtle connection between the two. In Chapter 5 it was argued that the beginning of the age of terrorism was linked to the start of the post-colonial era. Resort to violence by small groups was explained, in part, in terms of the transitional character of the period. At the same time, it was argued that the construction of the notion of terrorism by opponents of this violence in its various manifestations was an attempt to draw a line between this violence and the violence of successful nationalist movements during the colonial era. But a further motivation for the construction of the notion of terrorism was the weakening of the anti-communist consensus that had prevailed in Western societies during the 1950s. This can be dated to the resolution of the Cuban missile crisis in 1962, which, because the Soviet Union backed down, greatly reduced fear within the West of Soviet aggression. From a conservative perspective the waning of the fear of Soviet communism had negative implications for the maintenance of social discipline within Western society. The notion of terrorism offered the prospect that a new consensus might be established round the threat of terrorism and that it might offer a fresh basis for demanding conformity of thought, whether in the media or in the universities.[5]

The writings of Paul Wilkinson provide a particularly striking example of such authoritarian impulses, as illustrated by the following extract, quoted by Stohl:

> In democracies our government and intelligence agencies should make a priority of examining the development of university bases of recruitment by the terrorist organizations operating in their region. And they should have close liaison with the academic authorities known to be sympathetic to the task of protecting free societies in order to elicit their co-operation in avoiding recruiting to university staff people who are likely to act as terrorist agents and propagandists. It's an ongoing business. As one man or woman is not given tenure, another one comes along who looks all right, who has been fitted out with all the appropriate qualifications, but really is primarily working for a terrorist organization. Thus, part of the war against terrorism has to be fought out in the seminar and lecture rooms of the universities of the Western world: it is literally a struggle for the souls of the young.[6]

Negotiating with terrorists

The link between the waning of the communist threat and the waxing of the terrorist threat is further underscored by the issue of negoti-ation. The belief that it was a mistake to negotiate with the leaders of the Soviet Union because they could not be trusted to keep their word was a central precept of American foreign policy through much of the Cold War, an aspect of the policy of containment strongly criticized by Henry Kissinger in his account of the first term of the Nixon presidency.[7] The context is appropriate since the precept was overturned from the outset of Nixon's presidency by his commitment to an era of negotiations. But if the precept had lost its credibility in the field of relations between the super-powers, terrorism provided a new field for its application.

This did not happen instantly. The initial impulse of Western governments faced by the kidnapping of diplomats or the taking hostage of civilians was to negotiate with the perpetrators and to make concessions to secure the release of the victims. There was criticism of this response, but it was muted in the absence of alternative courses of action. It took the creation of specialist forces or the training of existing forces in a new role to provide Western governments with the option of attempting to rescue hostages by force. Once this was in place, the previous response became anathematized much in the way that during the Cold War the conduct of negotiations with the Soviet Union or with the Chinese communist leaders during the Second World War came to be anathematized.

However, the terrorist threat was never quite able to work the same magic on Western society as the communist threat had done. At the heart of the Cold War system was the fact that the perception of Soviet communism as a threat functioned as a source of stability within Western society by placing limits on the scope of political discourse and protest.[8] While the onset of the age of terrorism was symptomatic of increased disorder within the international political system, its limits were a significant influence on perceptions of the violence. An important factor in the characterization of political violence as terrorism was the existence of a large distance between means and ends. The resort to covert violence in the cause of anti-imperialism by small groups on the political fringe of Western society epitomized this situation. The means at their disposal appeared utterly out of proportion to what seemed, in so far as they could be understood at all, to be utopian goals. Even the reduced stability of Western society and of the structure of international relations made a mockery of the revolutionary rhetoric in which they engaged.

In fact, marginality was practically written into the notion of terrorism itself. The consequence was that while the violence of terrorists appeared grotesque and evoked horror in much the same way that mass murderers or serial killers did, it did not lend itself to the creation of an anti-terrorist ideological consensus, despite the efforts of a number of writers to create one. While Western societies took steps to deal with the physical threat posed by terrorist violence, such as the searching of luggage and passengers at airports, the goals of terrorists were perceived as too diffuse, too varied, and simply too irrational to provide the basis for an ideological response akin to anti-communism.

Marginality did not reduce the inconvenience created by the threat of terrorism, nor did it prevent the creation of climates of fear at particular junctures in particular societies, but it did limit its political salience. Even raising the spectre of terrorists armed with a nuclear device could not infuse counter-terrorism with a political mission going beyond the taking of technical precautions to reduce the risk of such an eventuality. There were and are some societies where the fight against terrorism, invariably from a particular source rather than in general, became imbued with such a sense of mission.

Israel is an example. South Africa another. In Israel's case, the PLO was anathematized as a terrorist organization. In South Africa's the ANC. But in both cases, the search for a political settlement through negotiation necessitated the unwinding of these positions. Mandela's inauguration as president marked the successful completion of a difficult transition in South Africa. Israel is still at an early stage in the process. The legacy of past rhetoric and the political strength of those opposed in any case to a settlement constitute powerful obstacles to the peace process in the Middle East, and success is by no means assured. In many of the new ethnic conflicts in Eastern Europe and the former Soviet Union, the notion of terrorism with its overtones of absolute illegitimacy has helped to underscore the portrayal of the enemy in demonic terms, making still more difficult the achievement of any accommodation between communities.

However, outside of the actual societies in the grip of conflict, the credibility of the notion of terrorism has been undermined by the scale of instability that has characterized the post-bipolar world. This is because it has brought to the fore the instrumental value of violence. Atrocities carried out by Serbs in the former Yugoslavia have attracted world-wide condemnation, but at the same time the connection between the atrocities and the political goals of the Serbs has been quite obvious. Indeed, there has been almost as much emphasis on the illegitimacy of the goal of the creation of a Greater Serbia as there has been on the violent means being used to achieve it. In general the closer the relationship between means and goals, the more likely debate will revolve round the legitimacy of the goals. Only the most objectionable of goals are capable of evoking as negative a reaction as the means employed.

Consequently, where the instrumental purpose of violence is clear and the violence is perceived as having a reasonable prospect of achieving its aim, there may be a relatively muted reaction to the most horrific events. This in part explains why public reaction to incidents in which small numbers of people are killed in covert violence carried out by fringe groups may be more intense than it is to the carnage wrought by civil war. A further reason is that, whereas a bombing can take place anywhere, a civil war, involving the complete breakdown of a country's political system, is specific to the country where it occurs. Thus, it may be easier for an American to empathize with the victims of a bombing in, for example, London than with the victims of civil war in the former Yugoslavia.

The crumbling of international norms

Further, absolutist judgements in respect of goals have become more difficult with the crumbling of global consensus on the interpretation of international norms such as self-determination and non-intervention. Ironically, there was a larger measure of agreement in the international community on, for example, the illegitimacy of secession in an ideologically divided world than there presently exists in the post-bipolar world. The crucial role that such past agreement played in underpinning stability in the international political system is only now becoming apparent. The absence of a consensus on the interpretation of norms such as self-determination makes it still more difficult to make judgements on political violence, because of the link that has been forged internationally between the question of the legitimacy of violence and the issue of self-determination. How that link colours people's perceptions is encapsulated by the much-quoted aphorism: 'one man's terrorist is another man's freedom fighter'. The current uncertainty over how the principle of self-determination ought to be interpreted and what its limits are gives the aphorism's relativism added justification.

The recognition of Croatia and Slovenia by the international community marked the end of the anathema against secession so painfully upheld in Africa in the cases of Katanga and Biafra. It also meant the end of the post-colonial interpretation of the norm of self-determination, so central an aspect of that interpretation was the rejection of the legitimacy of secession. The pronouncements of the major powers provide some clues as to what in broad outline the content of a new norm might be. They suggest the right of secession will in general be limited to pre-existing sub-units of states, with the further conditions that the right is exercised through the ballot box and that provision is made by the seceding entity to protect the rights of minorities, particularly any minority that is produced by the process of secession itself. Rejected, at least in principle, will be the carving out of new political entities through the use of force.

But whether such a new norm will attain the credibility of the old norm is open to doubt. In practice, it is hard to see many states, except those weakened by political revolution or war, giving voters the opportunity to opt for the secession of their region; and in such cases limiting the right of secession is likely to prove extraordinarily difficult without extensive and costly intervention by the international community. Further, few minorities are likely to be reassured by the promise of protection for their rights in the context of the ethnic mobilization that secessionist movements engage in. These considerations mean that secession, even if initially it is rooted in the electoral process, will have a high propensity to give rise to violence. The weaker the credibility of international norms on these issues, the more likely it is that the outcome will be determined by the balance of forces within states and that the international community will be compelled to recognize (and thereby ultimately legitimize) whatever has been created on the ground, even if violence has played a large role in its determination.

Present instability and uncertainty about the future make it difficult to predict the outcome of the use of political violence in civil conflicts. The fact that the international community may in the end be compelled to accept the political results of the successful use of violence militates against the application of the term 'terrorism' in such situations, as does the fact that most of this violence is taking place within a domestic or at least narrowly regional context. The association of terrorism with a low level of violence, one of the three meanings of the term explored in Chapter 2, is in part simply a reflection of the simple fact that the lower the level of conflict, the greater the certainty that the use of political violence will fail to achieve its goals.

Similarly, the meaning of terrorism as violence against the West was partly buttressed by confidence that such violence did not pose a threat to the very existence of the West. In theory, a normative approach to the definition of terrorism is less dependent on the perceived durability of political institutions. In practice, establishing prohibitions on certain forms of violence as being without humanitarian constraints is likely to be more difficult against a backdrop of a high level of instability and uncertainty.

All this does not mean that the term 'terrorism' will cease to be used. In fact, like the term 'imperialism', it will continue to be widely used, but its power and resonance is likely to diminish, as its coherence has done. This is by no means to argue that the age of terrorism has been without consequence. Many of the phenomena that were en-compassed under the term are likely to be a continued source of concern. Similarly, many of the measures that were adopted to combat particular forms of terrorism are likely to remain in place. In particular, it can confidently be predicted that passengers and their baggage will continue to be subject to security checks at airports. It also seems probable that continued efforts will be made to strengthen co-operation among states so as to make it more difficult for small groups to take advantage of gaps between different jurisdictions. In fact, the prospects for the successful outlawing of particular forms of international terrorism, such as hijacking, are good. The other side of that coin is that states perceived as sponsoring groups engaged in covert violence across international boundaries will continue to be isolated.

The intensification of global economic interdependence provides ideal conditions for the operation across state boundaries of small groups engaged in covert violence. The ease of air travel has increased the mobility of those engaged in violence as well as aiding the estab-lishment of transnational networks ready to support such violence. This process is set to continue. Indeed, with globalization contributing to a decline in the legitimacy of territorial democracy,[9] there is every reason to expect an expansion of the numbers of such networks. However, the disparate ideological sources of these networks are likely to continue to be a barrier to the construction of an anti-terrorist ideology. For example, significant as the role of Islamic fundamental-ism may prove to be as one of the inspirations for small group covert violence, it seems very unlikely that it will prove to be so dominant as to permit the construction of an ideology around resistance to its objectives. In any event, the multitude of challenges that exist to the stability of the international political system makes it unlikely that the world will remain preoccupied with the covert violence of small groups, even if it is a common occurrence. Further, it would be wrong to discount the impact of international co-operation in this area and its capacity to limit the form such violence takes.

Origins of the age of terrorism

However, the most persuasive basis for suggesting that the capacity of terrorism to hold society in thrall may be limited in future is to be found in consideration of why its impact on the West was so great in the late 1960s. In this context, there is a need to distinguish between the differing experiences of various societies. In particular, the American experience was somewhat different from that of Western

European societies. The 1960s were a turbulent period in the United States. That was not the case in Western Europe prior to the events of May 1968. But in both North America and Western Europe, it was an era of affluence following a long period of continuous economic growth. Material contentment was underpinned by full employment. At the same time, fear of nuclear war had waned. It was not surprising therefore that the period was infused with a spirit of optimism. It was also an era of hedonism, encapsulated in the British phrase 'the swinging sixties'. The onset of the age of terrorism in the form of hijackings, kidnapping, and bombings represented a considerable jolt to the assumptions of the times, challenging the prevailing belief in the innate goodness of human nature.

What compounded the impact was the fusing together of a number of different strands of political violence in the construction of the notion of terrorism: the varieties of terrorisms discussed in Chapter 4. In particular, the rhetoric of anti-imperialism gave the different strands of violence the appearance of a unity of purpose. That magnified the impact of each. In fact, the appearance was deceptive, as the different trajectories followed by violence in Latin America, by Middle Eastern violence, by violence on the fringe of Western society, and by ethnic conflict, such as that in Northern Ireland, were to show. With the passage of time, there has been a growing appreciation that the various strands – and their later additions – had divergent sources. Consequently, analysis increasingly reflected the recognition that while in some cases terrorist violence was an element in a much larger conflict, in others it was a fringe phenomenon. The literature on terrorism has struggled to establish points in common among the various terrorisms, but with only limited success. That has helped those who have wished to appropriate the powerful emotive force of the term and apply it to forms of violence which they wish to condemn, to do just that. These extensions and attempted extensions of the term have made the boundaries of the concept even vaguer.

Neither conspiracy theories, such as that developed by Claire Sterling, nor the portrayal of terrorism as a special, pathological form of political violence has provided a persuasive basis for the development of an overarching analysis of the concept. Thus, in practice, the analysis of particular campaigns of terrorism or political violence has for the most part been more productive than the attempts at generalization about terrorism *per se*. That is reflected in the fact that many of the better works in the field of the study of terrorism consist of collections in which the individual contributions analyse different situations with little reference to each other.[10]

Indeed, it is far from clear that the use of the term 'terrorism' adds much to the analysis these collections contain. Often there is little difference between analyses of, for example, the Northern Ireland conflict by writers who use the term and those who eschew its use. This is particularly true of the analysis of political violence within the state, where the function of the term 'terrorism' is often little more than a label of disapproval. This is not to decry such a limitation, since the attempt to use the term to reach conclusions about how those using the violence view the utility of their actions is often wrong-headed. Not surprisingly, those engaged in political violence tend to have a rather different perspective on their purposes and motivations than do those committed to the suppression of the violence as terrorism. Recognition of this reality does not require an acceptance of the view of the world held by those engaged in violence, though it does require that it be given a place in any serious explanation of their actions. A common weakness in the literature on terrorism remains the attempt to derive motives from the consequences of the actions analysed.

However, the term 'terrorism' would not have the resonance it does, nor would the notion of an age of terrorism have the force that it does, if it were simply a label of disapproval. That is clearest in an international context. With good reason, episodes with an international dimension tend to dominate chronologies of terrorism. Of these, the single event to be most closely identified with the dawn of the age of terrorism was the hijacking of an El Al airliner by the Popular Front for Liberation of Palestine (PFLP) in July 1968. It was far from being the first hijacking of a plane. These went back practically to the start of commercial aviation. It was not even the first time that international travellers were taken hostage to advertise a political cause. In January 1961, a group of opponents of the Salazar dictatorship seized a Portuguese luxury liner cruising in the Caribbean. They sailed the ship to Recife, in Brazil where they surrendered to the authorities.[11] The limited impact of the seizure of the ship, *Santa Maria*, despite the perpetrators' hopes of attracting world-wide publicity to their cause, stands in marked contrast to that of the first PFLP hijacking.

What the PFLP was able to exploit was the arrival of a global audience, made possible by the revolution in communications. In fact, international terrorism can be seen as one of the first fruits of globalization. Violence spilling across state boundaries was not a new phenomenon, nor had travellers been immune to violence carried out by small groups in the past. The holding of hostages also has a long history. The new element was that with the arrival of mass travel, a large part of the new global audience could envisage themselves as the victims of a hijacking drama. Thus, citizens of stable liberal-democracies enjoying a large measure of security suddenly saw themselves as potential targets of political violence. The concept of terrorism gave expression to their sense of shock and outrage at this transformation. That is to say, the age of terrorism originated in the Western public's discovery of its vulnerability to political violence emanating from other societies. Once made, the discovery cannot be unmade. That explains the difficulty of identifying an end to the age of terrorism, even though the shock of discovery has begun to wear off and the actual dangers from the various sources of violence that have fallen under the banner of terrorism have begun to be put into perspective.

Dangers of absolutism

The absence of a sense of proportion to the West's reaction to the onset of the age of terrorism has prompted comparison with other periods when public opinion has been in the grip of a great fear. R. J. Vincent has drawn parallels between the reaction of the guardians of order to terrorism and their reaction in previous periods to communism, liberal nationalism, and Jacobinism.[12] The alarmist nature of the response to terrorism was somewhat akin to the fear of domestic communism that arose in the United States in the late 1940s and early 1950s. But whereas McCarthyism's enemies were largely imaginary, at the root of the moral panic over terrorism in the late 1960s and early 1970s was the emergence of small groups engaged in clandestine violence across national boundaries. What caused especial outrage was not simply the violence itself, which had many precedents, but claims of responsibility for the violence made by the small groups, usually with the justification of fighting imperialism. The application of the term 'terrorism' was intended to deny such a contention any legitimacy. However, from the beginning, this involved glossing over important political differences among the small groups engaged in clandestine violence as well as in the context in which they operated. This problem was compounded by the fact that the absolutism of the term did not lend itself to the drawing of distinctions.

The absolutist judgement contained in the terms 'terrorism' and 'terrorist' provides a justifiable reason for unease about their use. In his book on Lebanon, *Pity the Nation*, Robert Fisk entitled his chapter on the massacre of Palestinians at Sabra and Chatila in September 1982, 'Terrorists'.[13] The title arose out of Fisk's conviction that the very word 'terrorists' 'had helped to bring about this atrocity', and he headed the chapter with a statement in justification of the massacre by a Phalangist participant in the killings: 'Pregnant women will give birth to terrorists; the children when they grow up will be terrorists.'[14] Fisk's account shows how, in the imagination of the Israeli soldiers and their Christian militia allies, the notions of terrorists, terrorist suspects, and terrorist population merged together. He describes how Israeli soldiers at the entrance to Chatila, even though they themselves had become enveloped in the stench of the massacre inside the camp, continued to take cover from phantom terrorists, so gripped were they by the notion that demons, rather than poverty-stricken and helpless refugees, who were now mostly dead, inhabited the camp.[15]

The peace process in the Middle East holds out the hope of political accommodation that will end the cycles of violence which have poisoned relations among its different communities. In time, the stereotype of a terrorist as a Palestinian hijacker threatening the lives of air-travellers may fade, to be replaced by new images, such as the Latin American drug baron or the anti-abortionist activist prepared to kill in the cause of protecting the unborn. Even if analysts continue to apply the term 'terrorism' to Palestinian hijackings, the application will tend to lose much of its sting once the threat of such hijackings is seen to be a thing of the past. Some writers insist on describing as terrorist the French resistance to Nazi occupation because of the methods used,[16] but the connotations of such a judgement, whether warranted or not, are quite different from the application of the term to contemporary violence. In particular, words about the past cannot now affect the behaviour of the protagonists. By contrast, those used to describe contemporary violence may do so, especially when an immensely powerful term such as terrorism is used. Its absolutism may be a hindrance to a political settlement. To understand that is not to condone outrages.

Afterword

When I was working on an earlier draft of this book, I had a personal experience of the subject of my analysis. I was at home in Belfast composing the Northern Ireland chapter. Republican and Loyalist paramilitary publications were strewn about my study when I finally went to bed after 2 a.m. At about 4.30 a.m. (on Thursday, 5 September 1991) members of a Loyalist assassination squad came to my house. They broke down my front door with sledgehammers. However, I only awoke after they came into my bedroom and switched on the light. I am short-sighted and my first impression was of a group of men in uniform. I muttered my name and then heard one of the group say 'That's the man.' At that point I realized that guns were being pointed at me. I cowered behind a pillow as shots were fired. Fortunately, I was hit by only one bullet. It went into my side and out of my back, but missed all my vital organs. My wife, who witnessed the whole scene, screamed, and my would-be assassins ran off to a waiting car.

My wife ran after them. I followed as far as the hall-way, at which point I phoned for the police and an ambulance. Then I collapsed on a sofa in the dining room. An ambulance arrived soon afterwards. I was revived with oxygen and taken to hospital, where I underwent a simple operation. Initially, I was in a general ward with other patients. However, after the Ulster Freedom Fighters (UFF), a name used by assassination squads associated with the largest Loyalist paramilitary organization, the Ulster Defence Association (UDA), issued a statement claiming responsibility for the shooting, I was moved to a ward of my own, where I was protected by police bodyguards. The UFF statement claimed that I was an intelligence officer of the Provisional Irish Republican Army (IRA), that I had been involved in importing arms from the Middle East, that my current job was to liaise with European cells of the IRA, and that my activities were known to Mossad, MI5, and Interpol. The statement also explained that the members of the UFF assassination squad had failed in their mission to kill me because two of their guns had jammed. Since I survived, little of the UFF statement could be published by the media because it was clearly libellous. My centrist views on the Northern Ireland conflict were well known in Belfast, though apparently not to the new and young leadership of the UDA. The UFF statement naturally alarmed me since it raised the obvious possibility, even probability, of further attempts on my life. I was rescued from this nightmare by an enterprising journalist, Alan Murray. From Special Branch and Loyalist paramilitary sources he pieced together what had happened to me. His account appeared in two Sunday papers, just three days after the shooting.

From his Special Branch source, he learnt that the description given in the UFF statement fitted a person well known to the security forces. Indeed, it closely matched information in this individual's file. What puzzled the Special Branch was why the Loyalists had mistakenly identified me as this individual. From his Loyalist paramilitary source, Murray learnt that the Loyalists had been approached by an outsider to Northern Ireland, who had shown them an intelligence file containing the information in the UFF statement and with my name and address on it. Further, the outsider had taken the Loyalists to my house, no doubt to obviate the need for any further inquiries by the Loyalists. Murray deduced from all this that I had been set up by someone outside Northern Ireland with access to intelligence information. He argued that my South African background, my continuing research on violence in South Africa, and recent visits to South Africa pointed to a South African connection. Within a week of Murray's reports, I was told through third parties that the paramilitary organization which had shot me wished to reassure me that there would be no further attempt on my life by the UFF. However, I was also told that the organization did not intend to issue a public apology, although it accepted that a mistake had been made.

Indirect confirmation of the South African connection to my shooting came the following year. On 15 July 1992, *The Independent* published a remarkable story of the arrest of two agents of South African Military Intelligence. They had been arrested in the company of members of a Loyalist paramilitary organization outside the London flat of Captain Dirk Coetzee. Coetzee had fled South Africa after revealing details of the operations of police assassination squads of which he had been a member. A previous attempt had been made on his life in Zambia. After being questioned by the British police, the two South African agents were deported, while the Loyalist paramilitants were sent back to Northern Ireland. *The Independent* explicitly linked this case to my shooting. The South African government was embarrassed by the April episode, and as a result of pressure from the British government, one of the agents was sacked from Military Intelligence. He was blamed by the South African authorities for engaging in an unauthorized mission. However, their claim that the proper mission of the two agents had been to investigate links between the African National Congress and the IRA was scarcely credible.

More credible was the explanation that the government was not in full command of its own security forces. This was in fact to be demonstrated time and again during South Africa's transition to democracy. It was encapsulated by the concept of a Third Force, a term used to describe elements within the security forces who engaged in violent activities intended to destabilize the transition. The existence of such a grouping highlights a weakness of both the concept of a terrorist state and that of state-sponsored terrorism. Both involve the implicit assumption of unity of purpose among the different actors, government, state, and clandestine group. The nature of covert operations creates many other possibilities.

How or why I fell foul of some person or group in South Africa to the extent that I became a target for assassination I do not know. Perhaps my writing about South Africa's supply of arms to Loyalist paramilitary organizations gave offence, or a brief investigation I carried out into extreme right-wing violence in South Africa may have been the cause. There were a number of other possibilities. From my experience of Northern Ireland I know how utterly trivial the reason someone becomes a target can be. In general, campaigns of violence are rarely conducted with precision, whatever their ultimate purpose.

The changes in South Africa make any repetition of what happened to me unlikely. The present government is committed both to un-covering the truth about the past and to reconciliation. It remains to be seen whether in practice it can honour both commitments. But in any event I think it is unlikely that much more about my particular case will come to light. That is often the case in respect of violent events, particularly those involving clandestine groups. Indeed, un-certainty about what actually happened is one reason why the interpretation of violent events remains so contentious.

Notes

1. Introduction: barriers to understanding terrorism

1. Rachel Ehrenfeld, *Narcoterrorism*, Basic Books, New York 1990; Alexander George (ed.), *Western State Terrorism*, Polity Press, Cambridge 1991; Phyllis Johnson and David Martin, *Apartheid Terrorism: The Destabilization Report*, James Currey, London 1989 (for the Commonwealth Secretariat); Clodagh Corcoran, *Pornography: The New Terrorism*, Attic Press, Dublin 1990.

2. As, for example, in 'Michael Winner's true crimes', British Broadcasting Corporation (BBC) Television 1, 4 August 1991.

3. On 'Larry King Live', Cable Network News (CNN), 11 September 1990.

4. Claudia Card, 'Rape as a terrorist institution', in R. G. Frey and Christopher W. Morris (eds), *Violence, Terrorism, and Justice*, Cambridge University Press, Cambridge 1991, pp. 296–319.

5. *Financial Times* (London), 10 May 1989.

6. 'Headline News', CNN, 31 October 1990. Use of the term 'economic terrorism' seems to be catching. In August 1992 the South African government characterized as economic terrorism a stayaway from work organized by the African National Congress. See *The Independent* (London), 4 August 1992.

7. Simon de Bruxelles, 'Terrorists on Four Legs', *The Observer*, 4 June 1989.

8. Brian Jenkins, *International Terrorism: A New Mode of Conflict*, Crescent Publications, Los Angeles 1975, pp. 1–2.

9. See, for example, J. Bowyer Bell, *A Time of Terror*, Basic Books, New York 1978, and Walter Laqueur, *The Age of Terrorism*, Little, Brown and Company, Boston 1987.

10. *Ten Years of Terrorism*, Royal United Services Institute for Defence Studies, London 1979, p. 172.

11. See the section on the Middle East in Lester A. Sobel, *Political Terrorism: Volume 1*, Clio Press, Oxford 1975, pp. 9–81. Compiled from reports printed by *Facts on File* in its weekly coverage of world events, the section brings out the contemporary application of the term 'terrorism' to political violence by Palestinians after the 1967 war. The reports chart the displacement of the terms 'guerrilla' and 'commando' by 'terrorist'.

12. Norman W. Provizer, 'Defining Terrorism', in Martin Slann and Bernard Schechterman (eds), *Multidimensional Terrorism*, Lynne Rienner Publishers, Boulder, Colorado 1987, p. 3.

13. *Oxford English Dictionary: Volume XVII*, Clarendon Press, Oxford 1989, p. 821.

14. Zeev Ivianski, '"The Blow at the Centre": the concept and its history', in

Ariel Merari (ed.), *On Terrorism and Combating Terrorism*, University Publications of America, Frederick, Maryland 1985, pp. 53–62.

15. For a critical discussion of the popular association of anarchism with heinous acts of violence, see David Miller, *Anarchism*, Dent, London 1984, pp. 109–16. See the account in Walter Laqueur, *Terrorism*, Sphere Books, London 1980, pp. 67–72.

16. The text of the first of these conventions is reproduced in Robert A. Friedlander, *Terrorism: Documents of International and Local Control – Volume 1*, Oceana Publications, Dobbs Ferry, New York 1979, pp. 253–8.

17. Charles Townshend, *Britain's Civil Wars: counterinsurgency in the twentieth century*, Faber and Faber, London 1986, p. 157.

18. 'There is no real disagreement about defining "terrorism". The term refers to the threat or use of violence, generally for political ends, directed at non-combatant civilians.' Noam Chomsky, 'International terrorism: what is the remedy?', in Raana Gauhar (ed.), *Third World Affairs 1988*, Third World Foundation for Social and Economic Studies, London 1988, p. 2.

19. See John Horgan, 'Violence subsided before reports reached Dublin', *Irish Times*, 10 November 1988. This article reviewed contemporary accounts of *Kristallnacht*. It quotes the *Irish Independent*'s characterization of *Kristallnacht* as 'an orgy of anti-Jewish terrorism on an unparalleled scale'.

20. *Oxford English Dictionary: Volume XVII*, p. 821.

21. See, for example, David Johnston, *Lockerbie: The Real Story*, Bloomsbury, London 1989, p. 211.

22. 'Terrorism is aimed at the people watching, not at the actual victims', Brian Jenkins, 'International Terrorism: The Other World War', in Charles W. Kegley, Jr (ed.), *International Terrorism: Characteristics, Causes, Controls*, St Martin's Press, New York 1990, p. 34.

23. For example, Edward F. Mickolus, *Transnational Terrorism: A Chronology of Events 1968–1979*, Greenwood Press, Westport, Connecticut 1980, p. xxviii, estimated the number of deaths from transnational terrorism between 1968 and 1977 at 1,695. More recent estimates of deaths through international terrorism given in the United States Department of State annual publication, *Patterns of Global Terrorism*, are as follows (in the case of conflict, taking the updated figure): 1992: 93; 1991: 102; 1990: 200; 1989: 407; 1988: 638; 1987: 633. These figures have been compiled on the basis of both contestable and changing assumptions about what is appropriate to include, so they should not be regarded as in any sense definitive, but as impressionistic and reflective of the political perspectives of their authors. See, for example, note 31 below.

24. For example, Laqueur, *Terrorism*, pp. 258–9, estimated the 'human toll of terrorism, domestic and international' between 1966 and 1976 as being 'between 6,000 and 8,000'.

25. Quoted by Chomsky in Gauhar (ed.), *Third World Affairs*, p. 5.

26. Alex P. Schmid argued that the absence of domestic terrorism in the 1980s in the Netherlands was partly a matter of definition. 'The Dutch authorities go to great lengths not to label politically motivated violent activists "terrorists" out of a (probably correct) apprehension that it could become a self-fulfilling prophecy'. Alex P. Schmid, 'Politically-motivated Violent Activists in the Netherlands in the 1980s', in Juliet Lodge (ed.), *The Threat of Terrorism*, Wheatsheaf, Brighton 1988, p. 145.

27. For example, the *New York Times* (27 June 1989) described it as 'an apparent sabotage attempt'.

28. Her statement was critically dissected by Joe Rogaly, 'What is a terrorist?', *Financial Times*, 12 November 1987, and in 'Commonwealth Conference: Maggie Mucks Things Up', *Front File: Southern Africa Brief* (London), November 1987. Also referred to in *South Africa Foundation Review* (Johannesburg), April 1989. See also David Martin and Phyllis Johnson, *The Struggle for Zimbabwe: The Chimurenga War*, Ravan Press, Johannesburg 1981, p. 312. They record Thatcher's characterization of the Patriotic Front (an alliance of the two main African nationalist movements) to the Commonwealth Secretary-General as 'terrorists ... just like the IRA'.

29. *Patterns of Global Terrorism: 1987*, United States Department of State, Washington, DC, 1988, pp. 41 and 65.

30. The liberal South African Institute of Race Relations in calling for an end to the language of vilification included the term 'terrorists' in that category. *Race Relations News* (Johannesburg), July/August 1991. An earlier example of the attitude of the South African press is quoted in *Oxford English Dictionary: Volume XVII*, p. 821: 'The Minister cannot expect journalists to do violence to the English language ... by describing guerrilla warfare as terrorism at all times and in all circumstances', *Cape Times*, 27 October 1972.

31. Menachem Shalev, 'US reaction "astonishes" Israel', *Jerusalem Post* (international edition), week ending 15 July 1989. On the issue of the United States government's characterization of Palestinian violence, see also *Patterns of Global Terrorism: 1991*, United States Department of State, Washington, DC 1992, p. 83: 'In past years, serious violence by Palestinians against other Palestinians in the Occupied Territories was included in the data base of worldwide international terrorist incidents because Palestinians are considered stateless people. This resulted in such incidents being treated differently from intraethnic violence in other parts of the world. In 1989, as a result of further review of the nature of intra-Palestinian violence, such violence stopped being included in the US Government's statistical data base on international terrorism.'

32. *Patterns of Global Terrorism: 1987*, pp. 27–8.

33. See, for example, Raymond D. Duvall and Michael Stohl, 'Governance by Terror', in Michael Stohl (ed.), *The Politics of Terrorism* (3rd edition), Marcel Dekker, New York 1988, pp. 234–40.

34 See, for example, Grant Wardlaw, 'State Response to International Terrorism: Some Cautionary Comments', in Robert O. Slater and Michael Stohl (eds), *Current Perspectives on International Terrorism*, Macmillan, London 1988, p. 225.

35. *Guardian* (London), 22 November 1974.

36. *House of Commons Debates*, vol. 882, col. 35, 25 November 1974.

37. On this episode as a turning point in attitudes in England, see Brian Gibson, *The Birmingham Bombs*, Rose, Chichester 1976, pp. 116–18. (In common with others at the time Gibson wrongly assumed that those convicted for the Birmingham bombs had received a fair trial.)

2. Distinguishing terrorism from other forms of violence

1. Alex P. Schmid (and Albert J. Jongman), *Political Terrorism: A New Guide to Actors, Authors, Concepts, Data Bases, Theories and Literature*, North-Holland Publishing Company, Amsterdam 1988.

2. Ibid., p. 28.

3. Gerald Priestland, *The Future of Violence*, Hamish Hamilton, London 1974, p. 11.

4. Antony Arblaster, 'What is Violence?', in Ralph Miliband and John Saville (eds), *The Socialist Register: 1975*, The Merlin Press, London 1975, p. 235.

5. See the discussion in Frank Wright, *Northern Ireland: A Comparative Analysis*, Gill and Macmillan, Dublin 1987, pp. 20–7.

6. Section 14(1) of the Prevention of Terrorism (Temporary Provisions) Act, 1984, quoted in Clive Walker, *The Prevention of Terrorism in British Law*, Manchester University Press, Manchester 1986, p. 4.

7. Ibid.

8. Quoted in *Political Imprisonment in South Africa*, Amnesty International, London 1978, p. 21.

9. See Wright, *Northern Ireland*, pp. 11–20.

10. The classic study of this is Rosemary Harris, *Prejudice and Tolerance in Ulster*, Manchester University Press, Manchester 1972.

11. See, for example, Bernard Schechterman, 'Irrational terrorism', in Martin Slann and Bernard Schechterman (eds), *Multidimensional Terrorism*, Lynne Rienner Publishers, Boulder, Colorado 1987, pp. 19–30.

12. Hannah Arendt, *Crises of the Republic*, Penguin, Harmondsworth 1973, p. 140.

13. Ibid., p. 141.

14. See the description of *The War of the Roses* in Robin May, *A Companion to the Theatre: The Anglo-American Stage from 1920*, Lutterworth Press, Guildford 1973, p. 76. On the acclaim for the *Henry VI* trilogy, see *Sunday Times* (London), 10 July 1977.

15. Simon Schama, *Citizens: A Chronicle of the French Revolution*, Viking, London 1989.

16. 'Robespierre, the "Incorruptible", allowed to join the party', *Irish Times*, 16 July 1989.

17. 30,000 died in the 1798 uprising in Ireland. Ruth Dudley Edwards, *An Atlas of Irish History*, Methuen, London 1981, p. 71.

18. A quarter of a million died in the Vendée. *Irish Times*, 16 July 1989.

19. Thus the *OED*'s first definition of terrorism is 'government by intimidation as directed and carried out by the party in power in France during the Revolution of 1789–94'. *Oxford English Dictionary: Volume XVII*, Clarendon Press, Oxford 1989, p.820.

20. Ibid., p. 821.

21. See the entry on the guillotine in *The New Encyclopaedia Britannica: Volume 5*, 15th edition, Encyclopaedia Britannica, Chicago 1992, pp. 552–3.

22. See Benny Morris, *1948 and After: Israel and the Palestinians*, Clarendon Press, Oxford 1990, pp. 28–9. In contrast to criticism of one's own side for revealing unpleasant truths, honesty may be valued in an opponent as exposing his or her intentions. See the editorial, 'Honesty among terrorists', *Jerusalem Post* (Jerusalem), 1 July 1991, favourably comparing George Habash's 'honesty' with Yasser Arafat's 'mask'.

23. *The Good Old IRA: Tan War Operations*, Sinn Fein, Dublin 1985.

24. See the discussion on '"Revisionist" historiography: Nationalist attitudes towards Northern Ireland', in John Whyte, *Interpreting Northern Ireland*, Clarendon Press, Oxford 1990, pp. 130–3.

25. Schmid (and Jongman), *Political Terrorism*, p. 8.

26. See, for example, *New York Times*, 16 February 1989.

27. See, for example, Richard Gillespie, 'The Urban Guerrilla in Latin America', in Noel O'Sullivan (ed.), *Terrorism, Ideology and Revolution: The Origins of Modern Political Violence*, Wheatsheaf, Brighton 1986, p. 173, which describes Sendero Luminoso as the insurgent movement which 'indisputably practises terrorism'.

28. Christopher Dobson and Ronald Payne, *The Never-Ending War: Terrorism in the 80's*, Facts on File, New York 1989, pp. 307–53.

3. The poverty of general explanations

1. See, for example, the survey that Schmid carried out among writers on terrorism, which showed that they had a highly negative opinion of the state of theory in the field. Alex P. Schmid (and Albert J. Jongman), *Political Terrorism: A New Guide to Actors, Authors, Concepts, Data Bases, Theories and Literature*, North-Holland Publishing Company, Amsterdam 1988, pp. 61–2.

2. Claire Sterling, *The Terror Network: The Secret War of International Terrorism*, Holt, Rinehart and Winston, New York 1981.

3. Ibid., pp. 286–93.

4. See, for example, Noam Chomsky and Edward S. Herman, *The Washington Connection and Third World Fascism*, Spokesman, Nottingham 1979, and Ernst Henry, *Stop Terrorism!*, Novosti Press Agency, Moscow 1982.

5. Paul Wilkinson, *Political Terrorism*, Macmillan, London 1974, p. 17.

6. See, for example, Paul Wilkinson, 'Social Scientific Theory and Civil Violence', in Yonah Alexander, David Carlton, and Paul Wilkinson (eds), *Terrorism: Theory and Practice*, Westview Press, Boulder, Colorado 1979, pp. 68–9, and Paul Johnson, 'The Seven Deadly Sins of Terrorism', in Charles W. Kegley, Jr (ed.), *International Terrorism: Characteristics, Causes, Controls*, St Martin's Press, New York 1990, pp. 63–8.

7. Martha Crenshaw, 'The Causes of Terrorism', *Comparative Politics*, April 1981, p. 381.

8. Ibid.

9. Ibid.

10. Ibid., p. 382.

11. See, for example, J. Bowyer Bell, 'Explaining International Terrorism: The Elusive Quest', in Kegley (ed.), *International Terrorism*, pp. 178–84.

12. Sterling, *The Terror Network*, pp. 14–15.

13. For Crozier's theory see Brian Crozier, *South-East Asia in Turmoil*, Penguin, Harmondsworth 1965. However, more recent accounts of the post-war period in this region have emphasized the role of nationalism and the failure of Western policy to take into account the rivalries between different communist parties. See, for example, Stanley Karnow, *Vietnam: A History*, Viking Penguin, New York 1991, pp. 55–7.

14. See, for example: Stefan Aust, *The Baader-Meinhof Group*, The Bodley Head, London 1987; Leonard Weinberg and William Lee Eubank, *The Rise and Fall of Italian Terrorism*, Westview Press, Boulder, Colorado 1987, especially pp. 6–9 where the authors criticize the Soviet-conspiracy view; Robert P. Clark, *The Basque Insurgents: ETA, 1952–1980*, University of Wisconsin Press, Madison, Wisconsin 1984; and Alfred McClung Lee, *Terrorism in Northern Ireland*, General Hall, Inc., New York 1983, especially p. 159.

15. See, for example, the denunciation of the Official leadership as 'a totalitarian dictatorship of the Left' in the Provisionals' paper *An Phoblacht* (Dublin), February 1970.

16. See, for example, Benjamin Beit-Hallahmi, *The Israeli Connection: Whom Israel Arms and Why*, I.B.Tauris, London 1987.

17. The issue of terrorism is not addressed at all in Peter Duignan and Alvin Rabushka, *The United States in the 1980s*, Hoover Institution Press, Stanford 1980, despite the book's conservative orientation, and it receives only fleeting reference in Charles W. Kegley, Jr and Eugene R. Wittkopf, *American Foreign Policy: System and Process*, St Martin's Press, New York 1987, notwithstanding Kegley's own writings on the subject of international terrorism.

18. See, for example, Sterling, *The Terror Network*, p. 286, where she quotes a German official in the Office for the Defence of the Constitution.

19. On allegations of financial help to Western terrorist organizations from the Communist Party of the Soviet Union, see *The Times* (London), 26 May 1992.

20. See, for example, Chalmers Johnson, *Revolutionary Change*, Longman, London 1983, p. 167.

21. Hans Josef Horchem, 'Terrorism 2000', *Euro-Terrorisme: Information Sheet 11*, Institut Européen pour la Paix and la Sécurité, Brussels 1993. Horchem's article, which was published in a German magazine in 1992, sees reaction to Islamic terrorism as a factor in the rise of the extreme right in France.

22. See, for example, the attitude survey on law and order in Northern Ireland quoted in Adrian Guelke, *Northern Ireland: The International Perspective*, Gill and Macmillan, Dublin 1988, p. 25.

23. For an extreme version of this viewpoint, see Jean-François Revel, 'Democracy versus Terrorism', in Benjamin Netanyahu (ed.), *Terrorism: How the West can win*, Weidenfeld and Nicolson, London 1986, pp. 196–8.

24. Sterling, *The Terror Network*, p. 7.

25. Charles Townshend, *Political Violence in Ireland: Government and Resistance since 1848*, Clarendon Press, Oxford 1983, p. 2.

26. Walter Laqueur, *Terrorism*, Sphere Books, London 1978, p. 229: 'free-floating aggression has been a frequent phenomenon in Irish history'.

27. Lawrence Freedman, 'Terrorism and strategy', in Lawrence Freedman, Christopher Hill, Adam Roberts, R. J. Vincent, Paul Wilkinson and Philip Windsor, *Terrorism and International Order*, Routledge and Kegan Paul, London 1986, pp. 57–60.

28. 'It is a comfort to know that the common wisdom has accepted the fact that, however defined, terrorism (nonstate variant) *kills relatively few people (but has a great impact)* ...', J. Bowyer Bell (*A Time of Terror*), quoted in Schmid (and Jongman), *Political Terrorism*, p. 69.

29. Hannah Arendt, *Origins of Totalitarianism* (3rd edition), George Allen and Unwin, London 1967.

30. Crenshaw, 'The Causes of Terrorism', p. 394, and Schmid (and Jongman), *Political Terrorism*, pp. 93–7.

31. Schmid (and Jongman), *Political Terrorism*, p. 95.

32. John Walton, *Reluctant Rebels: Comparative Studies of Revolution and Underdevelopment*, Columbia University Press, New York 1984.

33. Richard E. Rubenstein, *Alchemists of Revolution: Terrorism in the Modern World*, I.B.Tauris, London 1987.

34. Ibid., pp. 12 and 14.

35. J. M. Cameron, 'On Violence', *New York Review of Books*, 2 July 1970.

36. Christopher Dobson and Ronald Payne, *The Never-Ending War: Terrorism in the 80's*, Facts on File, New York 1989, p. 308.

37. *Terrorism: A Staff Study prepared by the Committee on Internal Security for the US House of Representatives*, US Government Printing House, Washington, DC 1974, p. 166.

38. Hijackings have occurred episodically throughout the history of commercial air transport, the first in 1930. The number of incidents has increased over the years, but in no way matches the exponential growth in air traffic measured in passenger-miles. Thus, the global total for 1930 was just under 170 million passenger-miles (R. E. G. Davies, *A History of the World's Airlines*, Oxford University Press, London 1964, p. 537). By 1990, the passenger-miles flown in the United States *alone* had risen to over 400,000 million (*1992 Britannica: Book of the Year*, Encyclopaedia Britannica, Chicago 1992, p. 817). Andy Pollak, 'Heroes' welcome for early hijackers', *Irish Times* (Dublin), 14 April 1988, gives a figure of 347 hijackings world-wide between 1931 and 1981.

39. See, for example, Ted Robert Gurr, 'Some Characteristics of Political Terrorism in the 1960s', in Michael Stohl (ed.), *The Politics of Terrorism* (3rd edition), Marcel Dekker, New York 1988, pp. 31–58.

40. See, for example, Richard Shannon, *The Crisis of Imperialism: 1865–1915*, Paladin, St Albans 1976.

4. Varieties of terrorisms

1. See, for example, *Ten Years of Terrorism*, Royal United Services Institute for Defence Studies, London 1979. This links the onset of terrorism to May 1968. See also Brian Jenkins, 'The Future Course of International Terrorism', in Anat Kurz (ed.), *Contemporary Trends in World Terrorism*, Mansell Publishing Limited, London 1987, pp. 150–1: 'international terrorism as we know it today had its origins in the political circumstances that prevailed at the end of the 1960s'. Jenkins mentions specifically Palestinian reaction to the 1967 war; reaction to the failure of rural guerrilla warfare in Latin America; and protests prompted by the war in Vietnam.

2. See, for example, Geula Cohen, *Women of Violence: Memoirs of a Young Terrorist, 1943–1948*, Hart-Davis, London 1966.

3. The classic study is that by Benny Morris, *The Birth of the Palestinian refugee problem 1947–1949*, Cambridge University Press, Cambridge 1987.

4. Sameer Y. Abraham, 'The Development and Transformation of the Palestinian National Movement', in Naseer Aruri (ed.), *Occupation: Israel over Palestine*, Zed Books, London 1984, p. 392.

5. Ibid., pp. 400–25.

6. Maxime Rodinson, *Israel and the Arabs*, Penguin, Harmondsworth 1982, p. 215.

7. Lester A. Sobel, *Political Terrorism: Volume 1*, Clio Press, Oxford 1975, pp. 26–8.

8. Ibid., pp. 50–3.

9. Ibid., p. 20.

10. The handbook is reproduced as a chapter in Carlos Marighela, *For the Liberation of Brazil*, Penguin, Harmondsworth 1971, pp. 61–97. For the influence

of Marighela on the Red Army Faction in West Germany, see, for example, Conor Gearty, *Terror*, Faber and Faber, London 1991, p. 134.

11. Sobel, *Political Terrorism: Volume 1*, pp. 138–9.

12. See the section on Latin America in Sobel, *Political Terrorism: Volume 1*, pp. 82–166.

13. Peter Flynn, *Brazil: A Political Analysis*, Ernest Benn, London 1978, p. 412.

14. Ibid., pp. 443–51.

15. See, for example, David Rock, 'The Survival and Restoration of Peronism', in David Rock (ed.), *Argentina in the Twentieth Century*, Duckworth, London 1975, pp. 211–14.

16. Robert Cox, 'Total Terrorism: Argentina, 1969 to 1979', in Martha Crenshaw (ed.), *Terrorism, Legitimacy, and Power: The Consequences of Political Violence*, Wesleyan University Press, Middletown, Connecticut 1983, p. 131.

17. From a press conference by Montoneros, quoted in *Keesing's Contemporary Archives* (Longman, London), 14–20 October 1974, p. 26763.

18. This is the estimate given by Cox in Crenshaw (ed.), *Terrorism, Legitimacy, and Power*, p. 128.

19. George A. Lopez, 'Terrorism in Latin America', in Michael Stohl (ed.), *The Politics of Terrorism* (3rd edition), Marcel Dekker, New York 1988, p. 514.

20. Walter Laqueur, *Terrorism*, Sphere Books, London 1980, p. 33.

21. Marighela, *For the Liberation*, pp. 79–80.

22. Ibid., p. 95.

23. Most strongly in *Ten Years of Terrorism*.

24. Most active by far in attacking Americans was the West German Red Army Faction. For example, in May 1972 it bombed the headquarters complex of the Fifth US Army Corps in Frankfurt, killing one officer. The Italian Red Brigades kidnapped an American officer, General James Lee Dozier, in December 1981, while the Japanese United Red Army attacked the US consulate in Kuala Lumpur, Malaysia, in August 1975, seizing 52 hostages, including the US consul.

25. Leonard Weinberg, 'The Violent Life: Left- and Right-Wing Terrorism in Italy', in Peter H. Merkl (ed.), *Political Violence and Terror: Motifs and Motivations*, University of California Press, Berkeley 1986, pp. 147–9

26. Sobel, *Political Terrorism: Volume 1*, p. 225.

27. Ibid., p. 226.

28. *Patterns of Global Terrorism: 1987*, United States Department of State, Washington, DC 1988, p. 63.

29. The NPD failed to get the 5 per cent of the vote it required to secure representation in the Bundestag.

30. Peter H. Merkl, 'Rollerball or Neo-Nazi Violence?', in Merkl (ed.), *Political Violence and Terror*, p. 236.

31. Ibid., p. 245.

32. Alison Jamieson, 'The Italian Experience', in H. H. Tucker (ed.), *Combating the Terrorists: Democratic Responses to Political Violence*, Facts on File, New York 1988, p. 114.

33. Weinberg in Merkl (ed.), *Political Violence and Terror*, pp. 148–9.

34. Jamieson in Tucker (ed.), *Combating the Terrorists*, p. 117.

35. See, for example, Hugh O'Shaughnessy, 'Gladio: Europe's best kept secret', *Observer*, 7 June 1992.

36. Jamieson in Tucker (ed.), *Combating the Terrorists*, p. 114.
37. Weinberg in Merkl (ed.), *Political Violence and Terror*, p. 149.
38. Ibid., p. 150.
39. Jeffrey Ian Ross and Ted Robert Gurr, 'Why Terrorism Subsides: A Comparative Study of Canada and the United States', *Comparative Politics*, July 1989, p. 412.
40. Ibid.
41. Lester A. Sobel, *Political Terrorism: Volume 2 – 1974–78*, Clio Press, Oxford 1978, p. 200.
42. Edward Moxon-Browne, 'Terrorism and the Spanish State: The Violent Bid for Basque Autonomy', in Tucker (ed.), *Combating the Terrorists*, p. 157.
43. Robert P. Clark, 'Patterns of ETA violence: 1968–80', in Merkl (ed.), *Political Violence and Terror*, p. 134.
44. For a full discussion of the elections, see Edward Moxon-Browne, 'Regionalism in Spain: The Basque Elections of 1990', *Regional Politics and Policy*, Summer 1991, pp. 191–6.
45. Jamieson in Tucker (ed.), *Combating the Terrorists*, p. 115.
46. Anthony Alcock, 'Terrorism in South Tyrol', in Peter Janke (ed.), *Terrorism and Democracy*, Macmillan, Basingstoke 1992, p. 25.
47. See Raymond D. Duvall and Michael Stohl, 'Governance by Terror', in Stohl (ed.), *The Politics of Terrorism*, pp. 234–40. See also Noam Chomsky, 'International Terrorism: Image and Reality', in Alexander George (ed.), *Western State Terrorism*, Polity Press, Cambridge 1991, especially pp. 25–7. Chomsky contrasts the 'wholesale' terrorism of states with the 'retail' terrorism of small groups.
48. See, for example, *New York Times* (New York), 25 October 1989, summarizing an Amnesty International report that tens of thousands of people were illegally killed by government agents in at least 24 countries during the course of 1988.

5. The legitimization of terrorism

1. See, for example, Alan R. Ball, *Modern Politics and Government*, Macmillan, London 1983, pp. 30–1.
2. See the description in *Keesing's Contemporary Archives* (Longman, London), 27 July 1979, p. 29744.
3. *Keesing's Contemporary Archives*, April 1986, p. 34302.
4. *Keesing's Contemporary Archives* (Keesing's Publications, Bristol), 20–27 July 1968, described the Gaullist demonstration on 30 May 1968 as 'the greatest demonstration to be held in Paris since the start of the emergency' (p. 22818).
5. For a detailed comparison of the two cases, see Frank Wright, *Northern Ireland: A Comparative Analysis*, Gill and Macmillan, Dublin 1987, pp. 164–216.
6. On the failure of the general strike called by the opposition in Panama, see *The Times* (London), 18 May 1989.
7. On the students' struggle to mobilize peasant support, see *The Times*, 14 June 1989.
8. B. N. Pandey, *South and South-East Asia, 1945–1979: Problems and Policies*, Macmillan, London 1980, p. 18.
9. Examples are the Irish National Liberation Army (INLA) in Northern Ireland; Front de la Libération Nationale de la Corse (FLNC – Corsican National

Liberation Front) in Corsica; and Fuerzas Armadas de Liberacion Nacional (FALN – Armed Forces of National Liberation), seeking independence for Puerto Rico.

10. The classic study is Martha Crenshaw Hutchinson, *Revolutionary Terrorism: The FLN in Algeria, 1954–1962*, Hoover Institution Press, Stanford 1978.

11. Thus there is no section on Vietnam in the two-volume compilation on political terrorism around the world by Lester A. Sobel, drawn from contemporary reports for *Facts on File*.

12. See, for example, Robin Smyth, 'Rebels control the roads in France's Ulster', *Observer* (London), 2 December 1984.

13. See *Keesing's Record of World Events* (Longman, London), May 1989, p. 36702, and June 1989, p. 36734.

14. David Martin and Phyllis Johnson, *The Struggle for Zimbabwe: The Chimurenga War*, Ravan Press, Johannesburg 1981, p. 309.

15. See Robert Taber, *The War of the Flea: A Study of Guerrilla Warfare Theory and Practice*, Paladin, St Albans 1970, pp. 123–5.

16. According to official figures up to the end of 1956, 95 Europeans had been killed (including military and civilians). In the same period over 13,000 Africans had been killed. Carl G. Rosberg, Jr, and John Nottingham, *The Myth of "Mau Mau": Nationalism in Kenya*, East Africa Publishing House, Nairobi 1966, p. 303.

17. See Keith Kyle, *Cyprus*, Minority Rights Group, London 1984, p. 6.

18. See the description in Fred Halliday, *Arabia without Sultans*, Penguin, Harmondsworth 1974, pp. 199–203.

19. See, for example, the description of Kenyatta's trial in Rosberg and Nottingham, *The Myth of "Mau Mau"*, pp. 281–5. On Makarios's deportation to the Seychelles in 1956 over links to EOKA terrorism, see Anonymous, Christopher Hitchens and Peter Loizos, *Cyprus*, Minority Rights Group, London 1978, p. 6.

20. General Assembly Resolution 2625 (XXV), 24 October 1970. 25 UNGAOR, Supp. 26 (A/8026).

21. See Phil Gunson, Andrew Thompson, and Greg Chamberlain, *The Dictionary of Contemporary Politics of South America*, Routledge, London 1989, p. 127.

22. See Anthony Brewer, *Marxist Theories of Imperialism: A Critical Survey*, Routledge and Kegan Paul, London 1980.

23. Thus, while commonly described as an anarchist student group, the Angry Brigade did not have a place within British anarchism of the period. See Peter Marshall, *Demanding the Impossible: A History of Anarchism*, Fontana Press, London 1993, pp. 492–3.

24. Quoted in the *Irish Times* (Dublin), 4 August 1990.

6. On the fringe: political violence in stable democracies

1. See Stefan Aust, *The Baader-Meinhof Group*, The Bodley Head, London 1987, pp. 344–5.

2. Quoted in Aust, *The Baader-Meinhof Group*, p. 502.

3. *Financial Times* (London), 6 December 1989.

4. See David Marsh and David Goodhart, 'Murder of an idea', *Financial Times* (London), 3 April 1991.

5. Quoted in Tony Paterson, 'Red Army Faction raises white flag and political row', *The European* (London), 23–26 April 1992.

6. Aust, *The Baader-Meinhof Group*, p. 552.

7. Quoted in Aust, *The Baader-Meinhof Group*, p. 154.

8. Klaus Wasmund, 'The Political Socialization of West German Terrorists', in Peter H. Merkl (ed.), *Political Violence and Terror: Motifs and Motivations*, University of California Press, Berkeley 1986, p. 198.

9. 'Astrid Proll on Ulrike Meinhof', *The Independent Magazine* (London), 19 August 1989.

10. Quoted in Aust, *The Baader-Meinhof Group*, p. 336.

11. Wasmund in Merkl (ed.), *Political Violence and Terror*, pp. 214–20.

12. Quoted in Aust, *The Baader-Meinhof Group*, p. 257.

13. Quoted in Gunther Wagenlehner, 'Motivation for Political Terrorism in Germany', in Marius H. Livingston (ed.), *International Terrorism in the Contemporary World*, Greenwood Press, Westport, Connecticut 1978, pp. 196–7.

14. Aust, *The Baader-Meinhof Group*, p. 154.

15. For example, Walter Laqueur, while explaining the West's rejection of Soviet propaganda against West Germany, described Germany as 'in the eyes of many ... still on probation'. Walter Laqueur, *Europe since Hitler*, Penguin, Harmondsworth 1972, p. 408. Henry Kissinger, *The White House Years*, Weidenfeld and Nicolson and Michael Joseph, London 1979, p. 97, describes the Federal Republic as 'like an imposing tree, with shallow roots, vulnerable to sudden gusts of wind'.

16. See Leonard Maltin (ed.), *Movie and Video Guide 1992*, Signet, New York 1991, p. 982.

17. Wagenlehner in Livingston (ed.), *International Terrorism in the Contemporary World*, pp. 196–7.

18. Proll, 'Astrid Proll on Ulrike Meinhof'.

19. *Keesing's Contemporary Archives* (Keesing's Publications, Bristol), 21–28 September 1968, pp. 22930–1.

20. Meinhof, quoted in Aust, *The Baader-Meinhof Group*, p. 259.

21. Richard E. Rubenstein, *Alchemists of Revolution: Terrorism in the Modern World*, I.B.Tauris, London 1987, p. 12.

22. For a brief description of this unusual group, which regarded West German society as diseased, see Peter Janke, *Guerrilla and Terrorist Organisations: A World Directory and Bibliography*, Harvester Press, Brighton 1983, p. 22.

23. This point is particularly well made by Maxwell Taylor, *The Terrorist*, Brassey's, London 1988, pp. 145–7.

24. See Kissinger, *The White House Years*, pp. 96–100.

25. See, for example, the discussion of the historical roots of West German terrorism in Raymond R. Corrado and Rebecca Evans, 'Ethnic and Ideological Terrorism in Western Europe', in Michael Stohl (ed.), *The Politics of Terrorism* (3rd edition), Marcel Dekker, New York 1988, pp. 410–21.

26. Jeffrey Ian Ross and Ted Robert Gurr, 'Why Terrorism Subsides: A Comparative Study of Canada and the United States', *Comparative Politics*, July 1989, p. 415.

27. Lester A. Sobel, *Political Terrorism: Volume 1*, Clio Press, Oxford 1975, p. 188.

28. Ross and Gurr, 'Why Terrorism Subsides', pp. 419–20.

29. See, for example, Peter Millar with Ronald Payne and Tony Paterson, 'Stasi secret files linked to IRA arrests', *The European* (London), 22–24 June 1990.

30. Eva Kolinsky, 'Terrorism in West Germany', in Juliet Lodge (ed.), *The Threat of Terrorism*, Wheatsheaf, Brighton 1988, pp. 61–2.

31. Alison Jamieson, 'The Italian Experience', in H. H. Tucker (ed.), *Combating the Terrorists: Democratic Responses to Political Violence*, Facts on File, New York 1988, p. 127.

7. Bomb culture: the case of Northern Ireland

1. For example, Northern Ireland receives extensive treatment in such well-known texts as Walter Laqueur, *The Age of Terrorism*, Little, Brown and Company, Boston 1987, and in Paul Wilkinson, *Terrorism and the Liberal State* (2nd edition), Macmillan, London 1986.
2. A few examples are Martha Crenshaw (ed.), *Terrorism, Legitimacy, and Power: The Consequences of Political Violence*, Wesleyan University Press, Middletown, Connecticut 1983 (with two chapters); Juliet Lodge (ed.), *Terrorism: A Challenge to the State*, Martin Robertson, Oxford 1981; H. H. Tucker (ed.), *Combating the Terrorists: Democratic Responses to Political Violence*, Facts on File, New York 1988.
3. John Whyte, *Interpreting Northern Ireland*, Clarendon Press, Oxford 1990, pp. 297–308.
4. Andrew Boyd, *Holy War in Belfast*, Pretani Press, Belfast 1987, p. 9.
5. J. Bowyer Bell, *The Secret Army: The IRA 1916–1979*, The Academy Press, Dublin 1979, pp. 362–6.
6. *An Phoblacht* (Dublin), March 1970
7. Frank Burton, *The Politics of Legitimacy*, Routledge and Kegan Paul, London 1978, p. 82.
8. J. Bowyer Bell, *The Secret Army*, p. 366.
9. J. Bowyer Bell, *The Irish Troubles: A Generation of Violence 1967–1992*, St Martin's Press, New York 1993, pp. 170–1.
10. For basic details of the film, see Leslie Halliwell, *Halliwell's Film Guide* (6th edition), Guild Publishing, London 1987, p. 543.
11. W. D. Flackes and Sydney Elliott, *Northern Ireland: A Political Directory 1968–88*, Blackstaff Press, Belfast 1989, p. 415.
12. Michael Farrell, *Northern Ireland: The Orange State*, Pluto Press, London 1980, p. 287.
13. Quoted in *Fortnight* (Belfast), 13 April 1972.
14. *Republican News* (Belfast), 2 January 1972.
15. See, for example, *The Ulster Defence Regiment: The Loyalist Militia*, Sinn Fein, Dublin n.d. (circa 1990).
16. *UDA* (Belfast), vol. 1, no. 2, 19 October 1971.
17. Quoted in Martin Dillon and Denis Lehane, *Political Murder in Northern Ireland*, Penguin, Harmondsworth 1973, p. 282.
18. Sarah Nelson, *Ulster's Uncertain Defenders: Protestant Political, Paramilitary and Community Groups and the Northern Ireland Conflict*, Appletree Press, Belfast 1984, p. 104.
19. *Ulster* (Belfast), September 1976.
20. These figures are the calculations of Michael McKeown, *Two Seven Six Three*, Murlough Press, Lucan 1989, pp. 41–3.
21. Quoted in Tim Pat Coogan, *The I.R.A.*, Fontana, London 1980, p. 579.
22. Patrick Bishop and Eamonn Mallie, *The Provisional IRA*, Heinemann, London 1987, p. 256.

23. Two-thirds of killings by the security forces in the period 1969–1984 occurred before 1976. See David Roche, 'Patterns of Violence in Northern Ireland in 1984', *Fortnight*, 29 April–12 May 1985, which provides a detailed breakdown of the agencies responsible for killings based on the data collected by the Irish Information Partnership.

24. *Beyond the Religious Divide*, New Ulster Political Research Group, Belfast 1979.

25. Analysed further in Adrian Guelke, 'Loyalist and Republican Perceptions of the Northern Ireland Conflict: The UDA and the Provisional IRA', in Peter H. Merkl (ed.), *Political Violence and Terror: Motifs and Motivations*, University of California Press, Berkeley 1986, pp. 107–11.

26. Quoted in Bishop and Mallie, *The Provisional IRA*, p. 264.

27. Frank Wright, 'The Ulster Spectrum', in David Carlton and Carlo Schaerf (eds), *Contemporary Terror*, Macmillan, London 1981, p. 207.

28. From the text of the communiqué, quoted in the *Irish Times* (Dublin), 9 December 1980.

29. See, for example, Phillip Knightley, 'Is Britain Losing the Propaganda War?', *Sunday Times* (London), 31 May 1981.

30. *Iris* (Dublin), November 1982, p. 3.

31. For a full account of the agreement, see Tom Hadden and Kevin Boyle, *The Anglo-Irish Agreement: Commentary, Text and Official Review*, Sweet and Maxwell, London 1989.

32. Andy Tyrie interview with *Marxism Today* (London), December 1981.

33. Quoted in *Ulster*, April 1982.

34. See *Ulster*, July/August 1986.

35. *Fortnight* (no. 231), 16 December 1985–26 January 1986.

36. *Common Sense: Northern Ireland – An Agreed Process*, Ulster Political Research Group, Belfast 1987.

37. Quoted in *Fortnight* (no. 254), September 1987.

38. Reproduced in *An Phoblacht*, 7 May 1987.

39. See *The Sinn Fein/SDLP Talks*, Sinn Fein, Dublin 1989.

40. For further details of the Libyan connection, see Adrian Guelke, 'British Policy and International Dimensions of the Northern Ireland Conflict', *Regional Politics and Policy*, Summer 1991, pp. 152–4.

41. The spirit of the coverage given to the talks was captured by the cover of *Fortnight* (no. 295), May 1991: '10 weeks to end 20 years of stalemate'.

42. For the antagonism towards the Unionists, see the leader by Robin Wilson, 'The world looks on in disbelief', *Fortnight* (no. 297), July/August 1991.

43. *Irish Times*, 1 and 2 January 1992.

44. Details of the shipment are given in Ed Moloney, 'UDA-army agent in South African arms deal', *Sunday Tribune* (Dublin), 12 January 1992.

45. *An Phoblacht*, 28 June 1990.

46. Mark Brennock, 'Soul-searching Sinn Fein accepts a number of, hitherto ignored, realities', *The Irish Times*, 23 June 1992.

47. *Towards a lasting peace in Ireland*, Sinn Fein, Belfast 1992.

48. Robin Morton, 'Brooke: the first 100 days – Talks with Sinn Fein are not ruled out in the long term', *Belfast Telegraph* (Belfast), 3 November 1989.

49. *Belfast Telegraph*, 31 August 1994.

50. Thus, for Rose's 1968 survey 1,287 out of 1,291 interviewed accepted the

label of either Protestant or Catholic. Richard Rose, *Governing without Consensus*, Faber and Faber, London 1971, p. 248.

51. See survey evidence provided in the Table, 'Religious Affiliation and Political Party Identification', in Adrian Guelke and Frank Wright, 'On a "British Withdrawal" from Northern Ireland', in Peter Stringer and Gillian Robinson (eds), *Social Attitudes in Northern Ireland: The Second Report 1991–1992*, Blackstaff Press, Belfast 1992, p. 44.

8. Violence, inequality, and the Third World

1. The case for a close link is cogently argued in Ted Honderich, *Violence for Equality: Inquiries in Political Philosophy*, Penguin, Harmondsworth 1980.

2. Paul Kennedy, *The Rise and Fall of the Great Powers: Economic Change and Military Conflict from 1500 to 2000*, Fontana Press, London 1989, p. 190.

3. World Bank, *World Development Report 1994*, Oxford University Press, Oxford 1994, pp. 162–3.

4. Ibid., p. 163.

5. Ibid., p. 162.

6. Ibid., p. 221.

7. Carole Cooper, Jennifer Schindler, Colleen McCaul, Robin Hamilton, Mary Beale, Alison Clemans, Lou-Marie Kruger, Isabelle Delvare, and John Gary Moonsamy, *Race Relations Survey 1988/89*, South African Institute of Race Relations, Johannesburg 1989, p. 423.

8. See the figures in World Bank, *World Bank Development Report 1993*, Oxford University Press, Oxford 1993, p. 274.

9. Thus, the target the Chinese leadership has set for annual economic growth in the period 1991–2000 is lower than the annual growth rate the country actually achieved in 1986–1990. See *Keesing's Record of World Events* (Longman, London), March 1991, p. 38097, and April 1991, p. 38145.

10. Seymour Martin Lipset, *Political Man*, Heinemann, London 1983, pp. 33–4.

11. Ibid., p. 471.

12. Che Guevara, *Guerrilla Warfare*, Penguin, Harmondsworth 1969, p. 14.

13. See, for example, 'Democracy and the Chinese', *The Times* (London), 27 December 1986.

14. World Bank, *World Development Report 1994*, pp. 220–1.

15. Quoted in Lipset, *Political Man*, p. 49.

16. Bruce M. Russett, 'Inequality and Instability: The Relation of Land Tenure to Politics', *World Politics*, April 1964, p. 449.

17. Ibid., pp. 452–4.

18. See the debate among Manus I. Middlarsky, Edward N. Muller, Mitchell A. Seligson, and Hung-der Fu in 'Land Inequality and Political Violence', *American Political Science Review*, June 1989, pp. 577–95.

19. See, for example, Edward N. Muller and Michell A. Seligson, 'Inequality and Insurgency', *American Political Science Review*, June 1987, pp. 425–51.

20. Johan Galtung, 'A Structural Theory of Imperialism', *Journal of Peace Research*, vol. 8, 1971, p. 81.

21. Ibid., p. 91.

22. The most obvious example was El Salvador during the 1980s.

23. The absence of a claim of responsibility may also simply reflect the fact that

in the context of extensive conflict an act of violence speaks for itself and does not require explanation, whoever committed the act.

24. See, for example, Robert H. Jackson and Carl G. Rosberg, 'Why Africa's weak states persist', *World Politics*, October 1982, pp. 16–24.

25. Richard Gillespie, 'The Urban Guerrilla in Latin America', in Noel O'Sullivan (ed.), *Terrorism, Ideology, and Revolution: The Origins of Modern Political Violence*, Wheatsheaf, Brighton 1986, p. 173.

26. Ibid., pp. 152–71.

27. See, for example, Noam Chomsky, *The Culture of Terrorism*, South End Press, Boston, Massachusetts 1988, especially pp. 39–61.

28. Sean Gervasi and Sybil Wong, 'The Reagan Doctrine and the Destabilization of Southern Africa', in Alexander George (ed.), *Western State Terrorism*, Polity Press, Cambridge 1991, p. 218.

29. See John A. Marcum, *The Angolan Revolution: Volume 2*, MIT Press, Cambridge, Massachusetts 1978, pp. 195 and 429.

30. See *Southscan: A Bulletin of Southern African Affairs* (London), 13 October 1989.

31. Both are included in the long 'Directory of Terrorist Organizations', in Alex P. Schmid (and Albert J. Jongman), *Political Terrorism: A New Guide to Actors, Authors, Concepts, Data Bases, Theories and Literature*, North-Holland Publishing Company, Amsterdam 1988, pp. 620 and 655–6. They are also included in Jay M. Shafritz, E. F. Gibbons, Jr, and Gregory E. J. Scott, *Almanac of Modern Terrorism*, Facts on File, New York 1991, pp. 71 and 234. The authors refer to the 1988 classification of the ANC as a terrorist organization by the US Department of Defence. Christopher Dobson and Ronald Payne, *The Never-Ending War: Terrorism in the 80's*, Facts on File, New York 1989, p. 305, include the ANC in their list.

32. Ray S. Cline and Yonah Alexander, *Terrorism as State-sponsored Covert Warfare: What the Free World must do to protect itself*, Hero Books, Fairfax, Virginia 1986, pp. 92 and 97.

33. See, for example, the description of SWAPO's campaign of guerrilla warfare in Donald L. Sparks and December Green, *Namibia: The Nation after Independence*, Westview Press, Boulder, Colorado 1992, pp. 30–2.

34. 'The winner was no surprise' commented *Newsweek* (New York), 27 November 1989.

35. See note 30 to Chapter 1.

36. *Patterns of Global Terrorism: 1988*, United States Department of State, Washington, DC 1989, pp. 55 and 82.

37. *Patterns of Global Terrorism: 1989*, United States Department of State, Washington, DC 1990, p. 85

38. See, for example, Declan Kiberd, 'When terrorism ceases to be "terrorism"', *Irish Times*, 21 June 1988, explaining why he put the term in inverted commas. See also Christopher Hitchens, *Prepared for the Worst*, Hill and Wang, New York 1988, pp. 297–304 (chapter entitled: 'Wanton Acts of Usage').

39. 'Burundi's tribal regime says calm restored', *The Irish Times*, 23 August 1988.

40. Charles W. Kegley, Jr (ed.), *International Terrorism: Characteristics, Causes, Controls*, St Martin's Press, New York 1990, p. 1.

41. Ibid., p. 3.

THE AGE OF TERRORISM

9. The international dimensions of terrorism

1. An example is the bomb attack by the Red Army Faction in August 1985 in which two Americans were killed, one of whom was a soldier. In United States law, terrorism is defined as 'premeditated, politically motivated violence perpetrated against noncombatant targets by subnational or clandestine agents'. In this context 'noncombatant' includes 'military personnel who at the time of the incident are unarmed and/or not on duty'. It also includes attacks on 'armed military personnel when a state of military hostilities does not exist at the site, such as bombings against US bases in Europe, the Philippines, or elsewhere'. *Patterns of Global Terrorism: 1992*, United States Department of State, Washington, DC 1993, p. v.

2. The kidnapping and subsequent murder of the president of Fiat in Argentina in 1972 is included in the chronology of Christopher Dobson and Ronald Payne, *The Never-Ending War: Terrorism in the 80's*, Facts on File, New York 1989, p. 313.

3. An example is the case of Dulcie September. See Jacques Pauw, *In the Heart of the Whore: The Story of Apartheid's Death Squads*, Southern Book Publishers, Halfway House 1991, pp. 207–8.

4. Paul Wilkinson, 'Trends in international terrorism and the American response', in Lawrence Freedman, Christopher Hill, Adam Roberts, R. J. Vincent, Paul Wilkinson and Philip Windsor, *Terrorism and International Order*, Routledge and Kegan Paul, London 1986, pp. 49 and 39.

5. The classic study of this norm is R. J. Vincent, *Non-Intervention and International Order*, Princeton University Press, Princeton, New Jersey 1974.

6. See, for example, Richard Little, 'Revisiting intervention: a summary of recent developments', *Review of International Studies*, January 1987, pp. 49–60, and Stephen John Stedman, 'The New Interventionists', *Foreign Affairs*, America and the World 1992/93, pp. 1–16.

7. See, for example, the debate between James N. Rosenau ('International Studies in a Transnational World') and F. S. Northedge ('Transnationalism: The American Illusion'), *Millennium*, Spring 1976, pp. 1–27.

8. *Patterns of Global Terrorism: 1988*, United States Department of State, Washington, DC 1989, p. 8.

9. *Patterns of Global Terrorism: 1990*, United States Department of State, Washington, DC 1991, p. 26.

10. The legislation is described in *Patterns of Global Terrorism: 1988*, pp. iv–v.

11. *Patterns of Global Terrorism: 1990*, p. 35.

12. See note 1 above.

13. *Patterns of Global Terrorism: 1989*, United States Department of State, Washington, DC 1990, p. 43.

14. *Patterns of Global Terrorism: 1990*, p. 34.

15. *Patterns of Global Terrorism: 1988*, p. 43.

16. Ibid., p. 42.

17. *Patterns of Global Terrorism: 1991*, United States Department of State, Washington, DC 1992, p. 24.

18. *Patterns of Global Terrorism: 1988*, p. 38.

19. See, for example, Fred Halliday, *The Making of the Second Cold War*, Verso, London 1983.

20. Quoted in Conor Gearty, *Terror*, Faber and Faber, London 1991, p. 95.

21. See, for example, Ray S. Cline and Yonah Alexander, *Terrorism: The Soviet*

Connection, Crane Russak, New York 1984, and Uri Ra'anan, Robert L. Pfaltzgraff, Jr, Richard H. Shultz, Ernst Halperin, and Igor Lukes (eds), *Hydra of Carnage: International Linkages of Terrorism*, Lexington Books, Lexington, Massachusetts 1986.

22. Chalmers Johnson, *Revolutionary Change* (2nd edition), Longman, London 1983, p. 167.

23. Quoted in Charles W. Kegley, Jr (ed.), *International Terrorism: Characteristics, Causes, Controls*, St Martin's Press, New York 1990, p. 17

24. Following Hindawi's conviction, Britain broke off diplomatic relations with Syria. They were resumed in the context of the crisis caused by Iraq's invasion of Kuwait in November 1990. See *The Times* (London), 29 November 1990.

25. Quoted in Adam Roberts, 'Terrorism and international order', in Freedman *et al.*, *Terrorism and International Order*, p. 8.

26. Ibid., p. 19.

27. Ibid.

28. See, for example, Amos Perlmutter, 'Begin's Rhetoric and Sharon's Tactics', *Foreign Affairs*, Fall 1982, pp. 67–83.

29. Noam Chomsky, 'International Terrorism: Image and Reality', in Alexander George (ed.), *Western State Terrorism*, Polity Press, Cambridge 1991, p. 26.

30. Robert Fisk, *Pity the Nation: Lebanon at War*, Andre Deutsch, London 1990, p. 581.

31. See, for example, Farzad Bazoft, 'Arms deal won freedom', *Observer*, 8 May 1988.

32. Lester A. Sobel, *Political Terrorism: Volume 1*, Clio Press, Oxford 1975, p. 282.

33. See, for example, J. M. Roberts, *The Hutchinson History of the World*, Hutchinson, London 1976, p. 684.

34. J. V. Davidson-Houston, *The Pirates of the Nanchang*, Cassell, London 1961.

35. Ibid., p. 48.

36. Ibid., p. 130.

37. Michael Jansen, 'Western hostage saga finally closes', *Irish Times*, 18 June 1992.

38. Robert C. Ritchie, *Captain Kidd and the War against the Pirates*, Harvard University Press, Cambridge, Massachusetts 1986, p. vi.

39. Ibid., pp. 153–4.

40. See, for example, Noam Chomsky and Edward S. Herman, *The Washington Connection and Third World Fascism*, Spokesman, Nottingham 1979.

41. Thus, according to *Patterns of Global Terrorism: 1992*, p. 1, the total number of deaths caused by international terrorism in 1992 was 93 (compared to 102 in 1991).

42. See, for example, Ronald Payne, Tony Paterson and Robert Melcher, 'Terror grows as Wall falls', *The European* (London), 8–10 June 1990.

10. Stopping terrorism

1. Robert A. Friedlander, *Terror–Violence: Aspects of Social Control*, Oceana Publications, Dobbs Ferry, New York 1983, p. 74.

2. Quoted in Michael Farrell, *Sheltering the Fugitive?: The Extradition of Irish Political Offenders*, Mercier Press, Cork 1985, p. 9.

3. See Friedlander, *Terror–Violence*, p. 78.

4. For the text of the first of the two conventions, see Robert A. Friedlander, *Terrorism: Documents of International and Local Control – Volume 1*, Oceana Publications, Dobbs Ferry, New York 1979, pp. 253–8.

5. Friedlander, *Terrorism: Documents – Volume 1*, pp. 283–9, reproduces a 1972 proposal for an international court. In a plenary address on 'The United Nations, Europe, and the New World Order' given to the *Inaugural Pan-European Conference on International Relations* at Heidelberg between 16 and 20 September 1992, Professor Ernst-Otto Czempiel of Johann Wolfgang Goethe University in Frankfurt suggested that an international criminal court should be used to try international drug-dealers and terrorists.

6. The draft code is reproduced in Friedlander, *Terrorism: Documents – Volume 1*, pp. 314–17.

7. The texts of the Hague and Montreal Conventions are reproduced in Robert A. Friedlander, *Terrorism: Documents of International and Local Control – Volume 2*, Oceana Publications, Dobbs Ferry, New York 1979, pp. 101–12. For the 1991 Convention, see *Patterns of Global Terrorism: 1991*, United States Department of State, Washington, DC 1992, p. 26.

8. For the text of the 1979 International Convention against the Taking of Hostages, see United Nations General Assembly Resolutions, *Official Records*, 34th Session, 1980, supplement no. 48, pp. 245–7.

9. See Friedlander, *Terrorism: Documents – Volume 1*, pp. 487–92.

10. Ibid., pp. 493–4.

11. See Seymour Maxwell Finger, 'The United Nations and International Terrorism', in Charles W. Kegley, Jr (ed.), *International Terrorism: Characteristics, Causes, Controls*, St Martin's Press, New York 1990, pp. 259–60.

12. The text of the European Convention is reproduced in Noemi Gal-Or, *International Co-operation to Suppress Terrorism*, Croom Helm, London 1985, pp. 370–7.

13. Ibid., pp. 277–8.

14. Ibid., pp. 283–4.

15. According to section 14(1) of the Prevention of Terrorism (Temporary Provisions) Act, 1984, '"terrorism" means the use of violence for political ends and includes any use of violence for the purpose of putting the public or any section of the public in fear'. Quoted in Clive Walker, *The Prevention of Terrorism in British Law*, Manchester University Press, Manchester 1986, p. 4.

16. Quoted in Jack Holland, *The American Connection: U.S. Guns, Money and Influence in Northern Ireland*, Viking Penguin, New York 1987, p. 174.

17. Ibid., p. 175.

18. See Martin Dillon, *Killer in Clowntown: Joe Doherty, the IRA and the Special Relationship*, Hutchinson, London 1992, pp. 214–17.

19. *Protocols additional to the Geneva Conventions of 12 August 1949*, International Committee of the Red Cross, Geneva 1977, p. 90.

20. Ibid.

21. Hans-Peter Gasser, 'A measure of humanity in internal disturbances and tensions: proposal for a Code of Conduct', *International Review of the Red Cross*, January–February 1988, pp. 38–58.

22. Quoted in Paula Casey-Vine, 'Tackling the terrorists', *Fortnight* (Belfast), December 1991.

23. R. W. ('Tiny') Rowland, 'The UN has a duty to obey the law', *Observer* (London), 28 June 1992.

24. Mary Kaldor and Paul Anderson (eds), *Mad Dogs: The US Raids on Libya*, Pluto Press, London 1986, p. 1.

25. The document is *Lethal Terrorist Actions against Americans, 1973–1986*, United Stated Department of State, Bureau of Diplomatic Security, Washington, DC 1987. It is reproduced in full in Robert A. Friedlander, *Terrorism: Documents of International and Local Control – Volume 5*, Oceana Publications, Dobbs Ferry, New York 1990, pp. 199–250.

26. Ibid., p. 201.

27. *Patterns of Global Terrorism: 1987*, United States Department of State, Washington, DC 1988, p. 65.

28. For analysis along these lines, see Michael MacDonald, *Children of Wrath: Political Violence in Northern Ireland*, Polity Press, Cambridge 1986, and Donald Harman Akenson, *God's Peoples: Covenant and Land in South Africa, Israel, and Ulster*, Cornell University Press, Ithica, New York 1992.

29. See text at note 33 of Chapter 7. It is a sentiment that has been widely expressed. Thus, Friedlander, *Terror–Violence*, p. 109, proposes: 'Perhaps it is time to terrorize the terrorizers'.

30. The suppression of terrorism from below in Argentina is graphically described in Robert Cox, 'Total Terrorism: Argentina, 1969 to 1979', in Martha Crenshaw (ed.), *Terrorism, Legitimacy, and Power: The Consequences of Political Violence*, Wesleyan University Press, Middletown, Connecticut 1983, pp. 132–42. The way that terrorism from below was suppressed has left a legacy of bitterness in both Argentina and Uruguay. On the controversy over the Expiry Law in Uruguay, indemnifying the security forces against prosecution for human rights violations during military rule, see *Amnesty International Report 1989*, Amnesty International Publications, London 1989, pp. 153–4.

31. Hannah Arendt, *Crises of the Republic*, Penguin, Harmondsworth 1973, p. 140.

32. See, for example, Walter Laqueur, *Terrorism*, Sphere Books, London 1978, pp. 266–7.

33. Von Clausewitz, *On War*, Penguin, Harmondsworth 1968, p. 223.

34. Thomas Karis and Gwendolen M. Carter (eds), *From Protest to Challenge: A Documentary History of African Politics in South Africa 1882–1964*, Hoover Institution Press, Stanford, California 1977, p. 772.

35. Ibid., p. 778.

36. Ibid., p. 717.

37. See, for example, R. W. Johnson, *How long will South Africa survive?*, Macmillan, London 1977, p. 22.

38. Karis and Carter (eds), *From Protest to Challenge*, p. 780.

39. Howard Barrell, *MK: the ANC's armed struggle*, Penguin, Johannesburg 1990, p. 23.

40. Lester A. Sobel, *Political Terrorism: Volume 1*, Clio Press, Oxford 1975, p. 259.

41. Nelson Mandela, *Long Walk to Freedom*, Macdonald Purnell, Randburg 1994, p. 506.

42. Interview with Shimon Peres broadcast on *Sky News* (London), 12 December 1994.

216 THE AGE OF TERRORISM

43. Antonio Vercher, *Terrorism in Europe: An International Comparative Legal Analysis*, Clarendon Press, Oxford 1992, p. 276.

44. Jeffrey Ian Ross and Ted Robert Gurr, 'Why Terrorism Subsides: A Comparative Study of Canada and the United States', *Comparative Politics*, July 1989, p. 406.

45. Ibid., pp. 413–14.

46. Ibid., p. 418.

47. Ibid.

48. Miscalculation on the part of the leaders of states is commonly seen as a cause of war within the international political system. According to Professor Ernst-Otto Czempiel in his plenary address cited in note 5, it is one of the main threats to the New World Order.

11. Conclusion: the end of terrorism?

1. See Robert A. Friedlander, *Terror–Violence: Aspects of Social Control*, Oceana Publications, Dobbs Ferry, New York 1983, p. 202. See also the ground rules enunciated by Paul Wilkinson in Paul Wilkinson (ed.), *British Perspectives on Terrorism*, George Allen and Unwin, London 1981, pp. 163–5.

2. Most often singled out for criticism was President Jimmy Carter for his handling of the Iranian hostage crisis. See, for example, Eric Morris and Alan Hoe, *Terrorism: Threat and Response*, Macmillan, Basingstoke 1987, p. 40. Wilkinson contrasts Thatcher's 'courage and firmness in refusing to surrender to terrorist blackmail' with the hostage deals of 'successive French governments and the Reagan administration'. Paul Wilkinson, 'British Policy on Terrorism: An Assessment', in Juliet Lodge (ed.), *The Threat of Terrorism*, Wheatsheaf, Brighton 1988, p. 53.

3. For example, Chalmers Johnson argued that détente led the West to tolerate Soviet support for terrorism. Chalmers Johnson, *Revolutionary Change*, Longman, London 1983, pp. 166–7.

4. See, for example, Vladimir Bukovsky, 'The Curse of Complicity', in Benjamin Netanyahu (ed.), *International Terrorism: Challenge and Response*, The Jonathan Institute, Jerusalem 1981, pp. 350–8.

5. An example of the use of the concept to restrict the media was the passage of legislation by the Greek conservative government making it an offence for newspapers to publish statements made by terrorist organizations after specific incidents. It resulted in the (temporary) imprisonment of seven Greek newspaper editors in 1991. See Peter Thompson, 'Union moves frees jailed Greek editors', *Irish Times* (Dublin), 21 September 1991.

6. Wilkinson, quoted in Michael Stohl, 'Conclusion', in Michael Stohl (ed.), *Politics of Terrorism* (3rd edition), Marcel Dekker, New York 1988, pp. 583–4.

7. Henry Kissinger, *The White House Years*, Weidenfeld and Nicolson and Michael Joseph, London 1979, pp. 59–62.

8. See, for example, Michael Cox's description of the Cold War system in 'From Detente to the "New Cold War": The Crisis of the Cold War System', *Millennium* (Vol. 13, No. 3), Winter 1984, pp. 265–6.

9. See, for example, the discussion of this issue in William E. Connolly, 'Democracy and Territoriality', *Millennium* (Vol. 20, No. 3), Winter 1991, pp. 463–84.

10. Examples of books based round case studies of individual countries or particular violent organizations are Lodge (ed.), *The Threat of Terrorism*, and Peter

H. Merkl (ed.), *Political Violence and Terror: Motifs and Motivations*, University of California Press, Berkeley 1986.
11. See the account by George Martelli, 'Conflict in Portuguese Africa', in D. M. Abshire and M. A. Samuels (eds), *Portuguese Africa: a handbook*, Pall Mall Press, London 1969, pp. 406–7 and 430. The episode does not rate a mention in Neville Williams, *Chronology of the Modern World 1763–1965*, Penguin, Harmondsworth 1975, 1020 pp.
12. R. J. Vincent, 'Concluding observations', in Lawrence Freedman, Christopher Hill, Adam Roberts, R. J. Vincent, Paul Wilkinson and Philip Windsor, *Terrorism and International Order*, Routledge and Kegan Paul, London 1986, p. 106.
13. Robert Fisk, *Pity the Nation: Lebanon at War*, Andre Deutsch, London 1990, p. 359.
14. Ibid., pp. 366 and 359.
15. Ibid., p. 368.
16. For example, Martha Crenshaw, 'Introduction: Reflections on the Effects of Terrorism', in Martha Crenshaw (ed.), *Terrorism, Legitimacy, and Power: The Consequences of Political Violence*, Wesleyan University Press, Middletown, Connecticut 1983, p. 4.

Concise bibliography

The age of terrorism has spawned a vast literature. Listed below is a selection of some of the most significant, well known, or influential general works on the subject. With a relatively small number of exceptions, the books listed adopt a conventional view of terrorism. The exceptions include Chomsky and George, who use the concept to attack the practices of Western governments. From a more centrist position, Stohl also insists on applying the concept to state behaviour. Among those who broadly equate the phenomenon with clandestine violence by small groups, there is a vast range of perspectives, from the sophisticated (examples: Crenshaw, Gearty, Merkl, Rubenstein) to the crudely propagandistic and conspiratorial (examples: Alexander, Cline, Sterling). The theme of an age of terrorism runs through a number of the studies (examples: Bell, Laqueur). The ideological perspective of most of the writers in the field is strongly conservative (examples: Clutterbuck, Netanyahu, Wilkinson). This is often combined with a narrowly Western perspective on events (examples: Dobson and Payne, Morris and Hoe). But even writers with a more liberal perspective seem to find it difficult to see the world from the perspective of someone other than a member of a politically stable Western society (examples: Lodge, Schmid). Another common characteristic is the tendency to exaggerate the threat posed by the violence of small groups (examples: Kegley, Segaller).

Alexander, Yonah (ed.), *International Terrorism: Political and Legal Documents*, Martinus Nijhoff, Dordrecht, Netherlands 1992.

Alexander, Yonah, David Carlton, and Paul Wilkinson (eds), *Terrorism: Theory and Practice*, Westview Press, Boulder, Colorado 1979.

Bell, J. Bowyer, *A Time of Terror*, Basic Books, New York 1978.

Carlton, David, and Carlo Schaerf (eds), *Contemporary Terror*, Macmillan, London 1981.

Chomsky, Noam, *The Culture of Terrorism*, South End Press, Boston, Massachusetts 1988.

Cline, Ray S., and Yonah Alexander, *Terrorism as State-sponsored Covert Warfare: What the Free World must do to protect itself*, Hero Books, Fairfax, Virginia 1986.

Clutterbuck, Richard, *Terrorism and Guerrilla Warfare: forecasts and remedies*, Routledge, London 1990.

Crenshaw, Martha, 'The Causes of Terrorism', *Comparative Politics*, April 1981.

Crenshaw, Martha (ed.), *Terrorism, Legitimacy, and Power: The Consequences of Political Violence*, Wesleyan University Press, Middletown, Connecticut 1983.

Dobson, Christopher, and Ronald Payne, *The Never-Ending War: Terrorism in the 80's*, Facts on File, New York 1989.

Freedman, Lawrence, Christopher Hill, Adam Roberts, R. J. Vincent, Paul Wilkinson, and Philip Windsor, *Terrorism and International Order*, Routledge and Kegan Paul, London 1986.

Frey, R. G., and Christopher W. Morris (eds), *Violence, Terrorism, and Justice*, Cambridge University Press, Cambridge 1991.

Friedlander, Robert A., *Terrorism: Documents of International and Local Control – Volumes 1 to 6*, Oceana Publications, Dobbs Ferry, New York 1979–1992.

Gal-Or, Noemi, *International Co-operation to Suppress Terrorism*, Croom Helm, London 1985.

Gearty, Conor, *Terror*, Faber and Faber, London 1991.

George, Alexander (ed.), *Western State Terrorism*, Polity Press, Cambridge 1991.

Janke, Peter (ed.), *Terrorism and Democracy*, Macmillan, Basingstoke 1992.

Jenkins, Brian, *International Terrorism: A New Mode of Conflict*, Crescent Publications, Los Angeles 1975.

Kegley, Charles W. Jr (ed.), *International Terrorism: Characteristics, Causes, Controls*, St Martin's Press, New York 1990.

Kurz, Anat (ed.), *Contemporary Trends in World Terrorism*, Mansell Publishing Limited, London 1987.

Lakos, Amos, *International Terrorism: A Bibliography*, Westview Press, Boulder, Colorado 1986.

Laqueur, Walter, *The Age of Terrorism*, Little, Brown and Company, Boston 1987.

Livingston, Marius H. (ed.), *International Terrorism in the Contemporary World*, Greenwood Press, Westport, Connecticut 1978.

Lodge, Juliet (ed.), *The Threat of Terrorism*, Wheatsheaf, Brighton 1988.

Merari, Ariel (ed.), *On Terrorism and Combating Terrorism*, University Publications of America, Frederich, Maryland 1985.

Merkl, Peter H. (ed.), *Political Violence and Terror: Motifs and Motivations*, University of California Press, Berkeley 1986.

Mickolus, Edward F., *Transnational Terrorism: A Chronology of Events 1968-1979*, Greenwood Press, Westport, Connecticut 1980.

Morris, Eric, and Alan Hoe, *Terrorism: Threat and Response*, Macmillan, Basingstoke 1987.

Netanyahu, Benjamin (ed.), *Terrorism: How the West can win*, Weidenfeld and Nicolson, London 1986.

O'Sullivan, Noel (ed.), *Terrorism, Ideology and Revolution: The Origins of Modern Political Violence*, Wheatsheaf, Brighton 1986.

Ra'anan, Uri, Robert L. Pfaltzgraff, Jr, Richard H. Shultz, Ernst Halperin, and Igor Lukes (eds), *Hydra of Carnage: International Linkages of Terrorism*, Lexington Books, Lexington, Massachusetts 1986.

Ross, Jeffrey Ian, and Ted Robert Gurr, 'Why Terrorism Subsides: A Comparative Study of Canada and the United States', *Comparative Politics*, July 1989.

Rubenstein, Richard E., *Alchemists of Revolution: Terrorism in the Modern World*, I.B.Tauris, London 1987.

Schlagheck, Donna M., *International Terrorism: An Introduction to Concepts and Actors*, Lexington Books, Lexington, Massachusetts 1988.

Schmid, Alex P. (and Albert J. Jongman), *Political Terrorism: A New Guide to Actors, Authors, Concepts, Data Bases, Theories and Literature*, North-Holland Publishing Company, Amsterdam 1988.

Sederberg, Peter C., *Terrorist Myths: illusion, rhetoric, and reality*, Prentice Hall, Englewood Cliffs, New Jersey 1989.

Segaller, Stephen, *Invisible Armies: Terrorism into the 1990s*, Sphere, London 1987.

Slann, Martin, and Bernard Schechterman (eds), *Multidimensional Terrorism*, Lynne Rienner Publishers, Boulder, Colorado 1987.

Slater, Robert O., and Michael Stohl (eds), *Current Perspectives on International Terrorism*, Macmillan, London 1988.

Sobel, Lester A., *Political Terrorism: Volumes 1 and 2*, Clio Press, Oxford 1975–1978.

Sterling, Claire, *The Terror Network: The Secret War of International Terrorism*, Holt, Rinehart and Winston, New York 1981.

Stohl, Michael (ed.), *The Politics of Terrorism* (3rd edition), Marcel Dekker, New York 1988.

Taylor, Maxwell, *The Terrorist*, Brassey's, London 1988.

Ten Years of Terrorism, Royal United Services Institute for Defence Studies, London 1979.

Tucker, H. H. (ed.), *Combating the Terrorists: Democratic Responses to Political Violence*, Facts on File, New York 1988.

Vercher, Antonio, *Terrorism in Europe: An International Comparative Legal Analysis*, Clarendon Press, Oxford 1992.

Wardlaw, Grant, *Political Terrorism: Theory, tactics, and counter-measures*, Cambridge University Press, Cambridge 1982.

Wilkinson, Paul, *Terrorism and the Liberal State* (2nd edition), Macmillan, London 1986.

Index